To the End of the Earth

The Race to Solve Polar Exploration's

Tom Avery

Dominic,

Keep exploring!

Tom Avery

To the End of the Earth

Greatest Mystery

ATLANTIC BOOKS
LONDON

First published in the United States of America in 2009 by
St. Martin's Press, 175 Fifth Avenue, New York, N.Y. 10010.

First published in hardback in Great Britain in 2009 by
Atlantic Books, an imprint of Grove Atlantic Ltd.

1 3 5 7 9 8 6 4 2

A CIP catalogue record for this book is
available from the British Library.

ISBN: 978 1 84887 043 7

Printed in Great Britain by MPG Books Ltd, Bodmin, Cornwall

Atlantic Books
An imprint of Grove Atlantic Ltd
Ormond House
26–27 Boswell Street
London
WC1N 3JZ

www.atlantic-books.co.uk.

To Mary

Contents

Tom Avery's achievements have cemented his place as one of the foremost explorers in the world today and, as Patron of his record-breaking expeditions to the South Pole in 2002 and the North Pole in 2005, I am delighted to introduce this book documenting Tom's extraordinary journey in the footsteps of Robert Peary and Matthew Henson, *"To The End of The Earth"*.

The North Pole, on foot and with dogs, is as elusive and difficult a prize as it was in Peary and Henson's day. However, the Barclays Capital Ultimate North Expedition proved themselves more than equal to this challenge and succeeded not only in resolving the mystery of the discovery of the North Pole, but also in beating the original record through sheer determination and seemingly unquenchable good humour! For me, it was particularly special to be able to speak to Tom and his team by satellite telephone as they ended their epic journey and I can only say that, at the dawn of the 21st Century, it is refreshing to know that this country's tradition of producing refreshingly eccentric adventurers is very much alive…

Of course, as President of The Prince's Trust, I was hugely grateful to Tom for nominating The Trust as the chief beneficiary of the expedition. And what better example can you have for the young people my Trust is trying to help than Tom, who has achieved his dream battling against the odds?

To the End of the Earth tells the story of the extraordinary journey undertaken by Tom and his intrepid young team across a precious wilderness which is so severely threatened by climate change. It makes fascinating reading and is a tribute to the endurance, bravery and sheer willpower of the human spirit.

Acknowledgements

THERE ARE MANY WHO HAVE HELPED ME turn a collection of diary scribbles, website dispatches, photographs, memories, and general thoughts into this book. I shall forever be indebted to my brilliant, supportive, and incredibly patient editors, Marc Resnick and Sarah Norman, as well as my agents at William Morris, Mel Berger and Cathryn Summerhayes, whose unfailing encouragement and energy saw the book through to its completion. A heartfelt thank you also to my mother for proofreading countless drafts late into the night as deadlines approached.

Others to whom I will be eternally grateful include John Gilkes for producing the book's excellent map, Toby Mundy, Michael Lockyer, Professor Jeremy Bloxham, Doug Davies, Nick Smith, Jim Gill, and Dan Bennett. I trawled through hundreds of books and papers to help my research, but I'd like to give special mention to Fergus Fleming's *Ninety Degrees North* and Pierre Berton's *The Arctic Grail,* which really brought the spirit of the early polar pioneers to life and inspired me to follow in their footsteps.

Ever since the seeds of the expedition were sown, a growing list of individuals, equipment manufacturers, and organisations came on board. All of them played some part in helping us achieve our goal and for that we will forever be in their debt. The list is too long to include them all, but I would especially like to thank Peter Rostron and Paul Kraymer at Mountain Hardwear; Charlie Bell and Anna Adsetts at Champagne Mumm; Niki Perry, James Massey, and H Pinkham at TAG Heuer; Lord Coe, Barbara Cassani, Jackie Brock-Doyle, and Gizela Menezes at London 2012; Naomi Edler at The Prince's Trust; Jason Ash at Cadbury's; and Nicky Holford at Snow and Rock.

However, this expedition would never have even got off the ground had it not been for Barclays Capital, and the belief, enthusiasm, and unwavering support of Jerry del Missier, Bob Diamond, Mark Dearlove, Catherine Shields, and Claire Lewis. I could not be more thankful that they put so much faith in us and helped turn this dream into reality.

Many others gave up much of their time to make the expedition happen, and I would like to say a big thank you to Sir Ranulph Fiennes, Dax Moy, Martin Hartley, Marc de Jersey, Geraldine McGrory, Elizabeth Buchanan, Shane Winser, Geoffrey Hattersley-Smith, Louis Gerber, Geoff Somers, Will Steger, Sjur Modre, Paul Landry, Peter Stringfellow, Luke Kelly, and Oliver Shepard.

It was an enormous honour to have received the patronage of HRH The Prince of Wales and we are so grateful that His Royal Highness should have played such an active role in the expedition.

Further thanks go to Sarah and Eric McNair-Landry for all their assistance during the run-up to our departure and keeping us in good spirits when stress levels were high. Paul Crowley offered invaluable dog driving advice, Louis-Philip Pothier helped build the sleds, and Lynn Peplinski, Siu-ling Han, and Martine Dupont in Iqaluit ensured the dogs were kept in shape whilst Matty was away in Antarctica.

Our logistics team were the real unsung heroes of the expedition and integral to our success once we had left civilization. In particular I would like to thank Ozzie Kheraj at the South Camp Inn, Resolute Bay; Tim Moffat and Mickey Riley at Kenn Borek Air; Brian Porter at First Air;

and Wayne Davidson at Environment Canada. Tom and Tina Sjogron at Explorers Web were instrumental in making sure the expedition website ran smoothly, and were a voice of calm when a major communications equipment malfunction halfway to the Pole jeopardized the entire expedition.

I must also thank the many tens of thousands of well-wishers from around the world who followed the expedition online. We were bowled over by the sheer volume of emails and text messages that came flooding into expedition headquarters every day. Those messages gave us an enormous lift when times were hard.

My greatest sense of gratitude goes to my fellow teammates, Andrew, George, Hugh, Matty, and the dogs for their dedication, friendship, hard work, and sense of fun. What an adventure we have had.

My final thank-you goes to our long-suffering families and friends, especially Mary, Rowena, Annie, Amy, Wynne, Sarah, and Eric. You never left our sides.

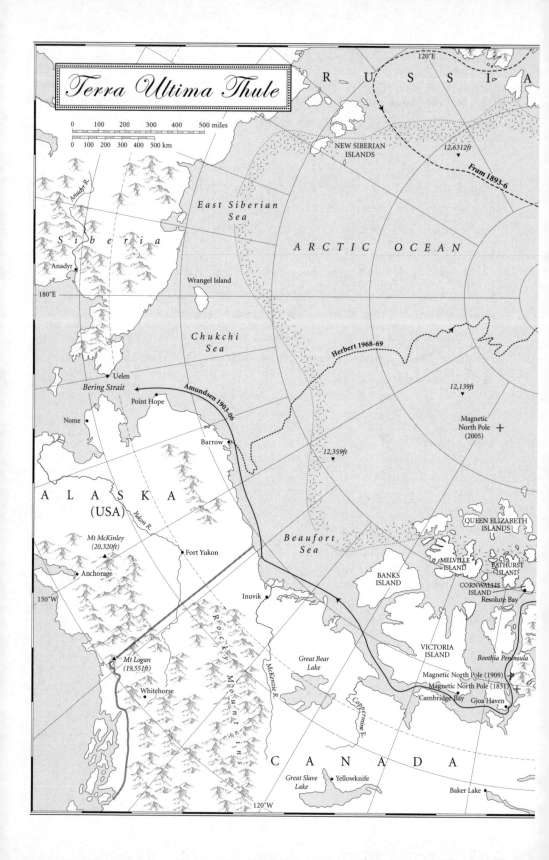

Terra Ultima Thule

0 100 200 300 400 500 miles

0 100 200 300 400 500 km

R   U   S   S   I   A

120°E

NEW SIBERIAN
ISLANDS

12,6312ft ▼

Fram 1893-6

*East Siberian
Sea*

A R C T I C   O C E A N

S i b e r i a

Anadyr

Anadyr R.

Wrangel Island

180°E

*Chukchi
Sea*

Herbert 1968-69

12,139ft ▼

Uelen

Bering Strait

Amundsen 1903-06

Magnetic
North Pole
(2005) +

Point Hope

Nome

Barrow

12,359ft ▼

A L A S K A
(USA)

Yukon R.

QUEEN ELIZABETH
ISLANDS

*Mt McKinley
(20,320ft)* ▲

Fort Yukon

*Beaufort
Sea*

MELVILLE
ISLAND

BATHURST
ISLAND

Anchorage

BANKS
ISLAND

CORNWALLIS
ISLAND

Resolute Bay

150°W

Inuvik

VICTORIA
ISLAND

Boothia Peninsula

R o c k y   M o u n t a i n s

*Great Bear
Lake*

McKenzie R.

Magnetic North Pole (1909) +

▲ *Mt Logan
(19,551ft)*

Magnetic North Pole (1831) +

Whitehorse

Coppermine R.

Cambridge Bay

Gjoa Haven

C A N A D A

*Great Slave
Lake*

Yellowknife

Baker Lake

120°W

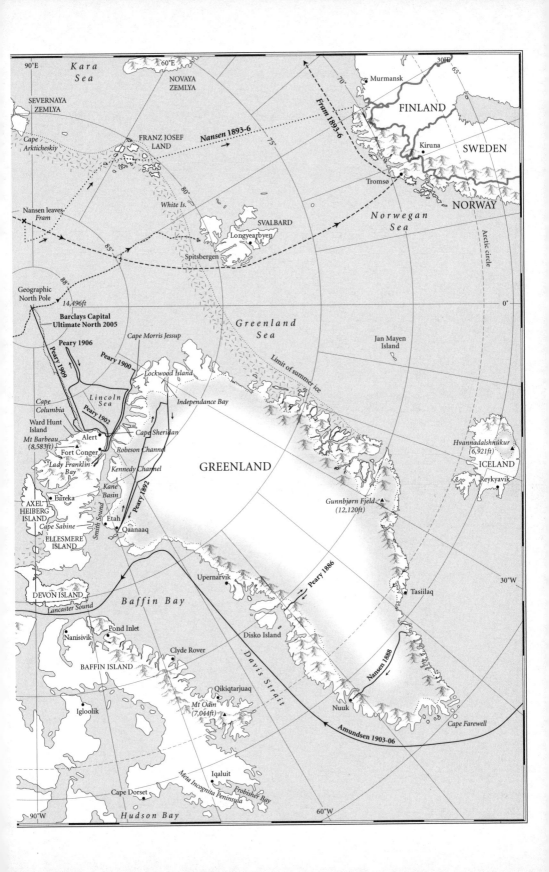

Prologue

THE BARRICADE OF GIANT ICE BOULDERS reared up ahead of us. More than forty feet high, the pressure ridge was the largest we had encountered in the seven grueling days since we had joined battle with the Arctic Ocean. The surface of the frozen sea had been set in motion by a combination of a ferocious wind and the tides of the full moon. Great pans of multiyear ice, weighing millions of tons apiece, were on the move, causing towering pressure ridges to erupt all around us as they smashed into one another. It was as if hell had frozen over.

As we approached, it became clear that the pressure ridge was still growing, an awesome and frightening sight. A rhythmical throbbing sound emanated from the bowels of the vast barrier, as if an army of blacksmiths was hammering away on some colossal cast-iron anvil. The noise was deafening. The dogs looked on anxiously, ears pricked and eyes wide open. Everyone's nerves were stretched to the limit. The tectonic forces deep within the pack caused the ice floe upon which we stood to vibrate with every beat.

When a massive slab of blue ice careered down the

flanks of the ridge and disintegrated by our feet, it was clear that we needed to get out of there as fast as possible. We had already scouted both sides of the ridge in the hope of finding a chink in its armor, but its defences seemed impregnable. The only way through was going to be over the top.

After what felt like an eternity of backbreaking lifting, shunting, and groaning, the rickety timber sled teetered precariously near the summit. A few yards ahead, our eight dogs leapt at their traces, barking uncontrollably as they tried desperately to get the 600-pound sled moving.

We used the axe to chop away a couple of impeding ice blocks before heaving our bodies against the handlebars of the sled. Still it refused to budge. We had been on the go for nine hours straight and our bodies, numbed by the cold, were more exhausted than was good for us. The reward for our day's efforts was little more than two miles of northerly progress. I wanted to call it quits, but the whole place was so pitted and unstable that it would have been impossible to find a safe place to camp. We had no alternative but to keep pushing on.

With a windchill in the minus sixties,★ the frostbite scars on my face from previous expeditions had started to reopen. It was so cold that we had to force ourselves to keep blinking to prevent eyes from freezing shut. We swung our arms around in giant windmills and ran on the spot to get the blood circulating again in our frozen extremities. Although I had been convinced all day that we were being followed by a polar bear, our vantage point on top of the ridge revealed nothing but a contorted mass of heaved-up ice in every direction.

The one blessing was that the ice was being compacted rather than pulled apart. Later, as the expedition wore on and the polar winter turned to spring, the twenty-four-hour sun would get to work on the fragile ice pack. Cracks in the ice, some many hundred yards wide, would open without warning, leading to soul-destroying detours or enforced layovers as we waited impatiently for the channels of black water to refreeze.

Due to the increasing temperatures, leads★★ would remain open for days,

★ Temperatures throughout the book are measured in degrees centigrade.
★★ The old whaling term for a lane of open water.

requiring ingenious crossing methods to be thought up so we wouldn't get cut off. Little did we know that in the closing stages of our marathon journey, team members and dogs alike would lose their footing and end up in the freezing waters of the Arctic Ocean.

As the ice pack began to disintegrate, so, too, would the blind optimism that had carried us so far. The common thread that held our diverse team together would be put under tremendous strain by a combination of the horrific conditions, sleep deprivation in the cramped and frosty confines of our tent, disagreements over strategy, diminishing food supplies, and deteriorating health. Our time on the frozen sea would take more out of us than any of us had ever dared imagine during two years of training and planning. By the time it was all over we would be physical and emotional wrecks.

For now, however, all we could think about was getting away from this frozen war zone. One final heave of the handlebars and the sled was free. It quickly began picking up speed, charging uncontrollably down the far side of the ridge as the dogs, terrified of being run over, ran for their lives. George, my sledging partner, and I collapsed to our knees, trying to catch our breath. I turned to him and, panting heavily, gasped, "What the hell are we doing up here?"

His iced-encrusted fur hood and frosted beard obscured much of his face, but from the animated look in his eyes, I could tell that he was relishing the challenge.

"Don't ask me, this was your bloody idea. But I think if the great man could see us now, he'd be cheering us on."

With that we scrambled to our feet and sped off in pursuit of the sled.

The man who George referred to was the real reason why we were there. He was a man whom we had never met but had come to know very well over the previous two years. He was a true giant of the Arctic, recognized wherever he went, a friend of the president of the United States, and America's first real celebrity. Even today, he is as much of a household name in his native country as the likes of Scott and Shackleton are in Great Britain. Few epitomized the extraordinary bravery of an era that has become known as the Heroic Age of Polar Exploration* more than this man. Although he had become our inspiration.

However, his expedition to the North Pole in 1909, his eighth and final Arctic mission, would spark the greatest controversy in the history of exploration. The man had an iron will to succeed but he also had his failings, which later would be scrutinized in minute detail by generations of polar scholars determined to discredit him. Nevertheless, our respect and admiration for him had grown by the day as we chased his shadow across the frozen Arctic Ocean. The name of this man was Commander Robert Edwin Peary.

THE ORIGINS OF OUR JOURNEY CAN BE TRACED BACK MORE THAN two years previously to a discussion over a cup of hot chocolate in a tent on the opposite side of the world on Christmas Eve 2002. Our team of four had spent more than six weeks manhauling and kite-skiing from the coast of Antarctica towards the South Pole. With nearly 600 miles under our belts, we were only a few days' march from our goal.

The conversation in the tent that evening turned, as it often did, to the great explorers of the past. After a lively debate, Paul Landry, the only non-British-based member of the team, opened up a Pandora's box when he asked who we thought was the first person to reach the North Pole.

"It was Sir Wally Herbert in nineteen sixty something, wasn't it?" I answered, not very confident of my knowledge of Arctic history.

"Any of you guys heard of Robert Peary?" came Paul's reply.

Our vacant expressions gave him his answer.

Paul continued. "Well, I believe Peary actually got there sixty years before Herbert, but if you look at the history books, particularly in your country, it's usually Herbert who's given credit for getting to the Pole first. Peary rarely even gets a mention anymore."

"Why not?" I asked.

---

*Generally regarded as lasting from Fridjtof Nansen's crossing of Greenland in 1888 to Shackleton's escape from Antarctica in 1916.

"People think Peary cheated. In recent years a number of historians, including Herbert, have tried to prove that Peary's thirty-seven-day journey to the Pole was impossibly fast. They believe that the only way he could have got to the Pole in the time he claimed was to exaggerate his speeds and fake his daily positions."

"What do you think?" I asked.

"I think he probably did it," replied Paul, "but I guess we'll never really know."

Many months later, I found myself reading about this Peary character in the hallowed library of the Royal Geographical Society in London. The controversy surrounding the discovery of the North Pole was far more explosive than I had ever imagined and still showed no sign of being resolved. The more I immersed myself in Peary's story, the more I warmed to him. He was quite simply the most fearless, single-minded, and driven man I had ever come across. There was also a softer side to Peary; he was a committed family man who cared deeply about the well-being of his team and had a genuine passion and respect for the polar regions. I could identify with a lot of what he stood for and increasingly felt duty-bound to try to tell his side of the story.

When it appeared that nobody had ever attempted to re-create Peary's disputed journey to the Pole, an idea slowly began to crystallize in my mind that would bring his great expedition to life. I would assemble a small team, equipped with Eskimo dogs and identical sleds to those used by Peary. Our mission would be to cover the 413 miles from Peary's base camp on the shore of the Arctic Ocean all the way to the North Pole itself. I felt it was time that somebody should champion this much maligned figure. Our expedition would provide the platform to make a balanced judgment on Peary's motives and the key decisions he made.

If we could defy the odds and match or better the thirty-seven days it supposedly took him to reach his goal, we would prove to the world that Peary could have easily reached the Pole in the time he claimed. The mystery of who discovered the North Pole then might be solved once and for all.

The scale of the challenge ahead was truly daunting, and it would consume the next two and a half years of my life. It was an impossible mission for me alone, and I was completely dependent on the enthusiasm and dedicated support of not only my fellow teammates, but also of countless others who played their part in turning our absurdly bold idea into reality.

So much was there to organise and prepare for, that the expedition itself was just the final act of an immense production. The opening words to Peary's book, *The North Pole,* read, "It may not be inapt to liken the attainment of the North Pole to the winning of a game of chess, in which all the various moves leading to a favourable conclusion had been planned in advance, long before the actual game began." Only when we finally reached the shore of the Arctic Ocean, would I be able fully to understand what he meant.

My dream was much more than an inventive excuse to go expeditioning with friends again in some far-flung corner of the planet. The Arctic Ocean is the ultimate testing ground for any budding adventurer, and now I would be able to find out just what I was capable of.

It wasn't only the challenge, however, that got my juices flowing. Because the frozen sea is in a constant state of flux, we would be seeing things in this bizarre but beautiful world of ice that nobody had seen before, or would ever see again. It would be the chance to achieve that rare thing in exploration, to do something new and completely original. By retracing Peary's footsteps, and travelling in the same style as he had done all those years ago, we were perfectly placed to set the record straight on the old explorer's accomplishments. We had the power to rewrite the history books.

1. The Man with Two Toes

AT 3:34 P.M. ON 28 DECEMBER 2002, WE ARRIVED at the South Pole, becoming the fastest and youngest team in history to complete the journey. The Pole had filled my dreams ever since I was a young boy, when my mother gave me a book about the adventures of Captain Robert Falcon Scott. I was immediately captivated by Scott's heroic story, and my imagination ran wild trying to picture this otherworldly place called Antarctica. From that moment I knew my life wouldn't be complete until I had stood on that hallowed patch of snow at the bottom of the world.

Now that I actually was standing there, beside the red-and-white barber's pole that marks the exact position of 90° south, I felt strangely unfulfilled. While I was overjoyed and proud to have realized my childhood dream, I wasn't sure what my dreams were anymore. I needed a fresh challenge to get my teeth into but I wasn't sure where to start looking for it.

On my return home I was gradually overcome by a feeling of lassitude, unsure of where my life was going. For weeks I drifted around London, jumping from one idea to another. Friends commented on how vacant I had become. The question on everybody's lips seemed to be, "So, what are you going to do next?"

Things got so desperate that I even considered dusting off my calculator and retaking my professional accountancy exams. Still, going back to my former life as an accountant, or in fact to any job that involved putting on a suit and tie and sitting behind a desk all day, now filled me with dread. London life, which I had thrived on before going to Antarctica, had suddenly become claustrophobic and boring. I had to escape.

In early 2003 I headed straight for the ski resort of Verbier in the Swiss Alps. I had worked there as a ski guide three years earlier, and it was the place I thought of as my second home. I figured that being up in the mountains, detached from the real world, skiing, climbing, and writing a book about our South Pole adventure would be the perfect way to sort out my head. Unsurprisingly, my decision didn't go down well with my parents, with Dad in particular growing increasingly worried about my total lack of a career plan.

One afternoon towards the end of the winter, I was enjoying a drink with some old climbing friends on the sun-drenched terrace of Chez Dany, a picture-postcard, chalet-style restaurant nestling in the woods above Verbier. A man approached me whom I recognized instantly from my first ski season as Mark Dearlove. Little did I know that the next ten minutes would change my life forever.

Mark and a few work colleagues had come out to Verbier in 2000 for a few days skiing. As well as guiding for them on the mountain, I had also had the job of collecting a bleary-eyed Mark and his team from the Farm nightclub in the early hours of the morning and driving them back to their chalet. I never managed much sleep during their visit but I did remember them as being an entertaining bunch, so it was great to catch up with Mark again. While chatting about my time in Antarctica, Mark told me that he had been in the office the day the news broke of our arrival at the South Pole.

"There are TV monitors all over the trading floor, which we always have tuned in to Sky News. When your face appeared on one of the bulletins, one of the team pointed to the screen and said, 'Bloody hell, it's Tom from Verbier! He's just become the youngest Brit to ski to the South Pole!' Soon everyone was on their feet cheering."

Then came the bombshell. "Anyway, seeing what a great reaction your success had on the team, I think it would be great if we could get Barclays Capital to consider sponsoring your next trip. Where are you off to next?"

I was speechless. I had no idea where I was off to next. Our journey to the South Pole had been the tenth major expedition that I had put together. I had begun my outdoor career as a mountaineer, leading expeditions to the Alps, Africa, the Andes, New Zealand, and a previously unexplored range of virgin peaks in Kyrgyzstan in Central Asia. The toughest and most challenging part of each of those expeditions hadn't been the extreme altitude, the precipitous rock faces, or the mountain storms. It was trying to secure the sponsorship. Convincing an organisation to pay for me and my friends to go gallivanting off to some far-flung corner of the globe was an exhausting, demoralizing, and hapless task.

Over the years I had written thousands of sponsorship letters, sent countless e-mails and faxes, and tried to arrange meetings with whichever company would listen to me. Some had tenuous connections with the cold (things got so desperate that even Fox's Glacier Mints got a letter); others did not. Most of my pleas for cash fell on deaf ears, and as a result, some of those early expeditions had to be aborted. Of the ones that I did miraculously find the money for, sponsorship was usually only forthcoming at the eleventh hour after much stress and a truckload of postage stamps.

The South Pole had been a massive undertaking. The physical effort of the journey, during which we each walked more than one and a half million paces, had taken a huge toll on me both physically and mentally. Nevertheless, that effort was nothing compared to the hard slog of raising the funds, so much so that I did not even know if I could ever face putting myself through the whole expedition process again. I hadn't lost my passion for adventure; in fact by spending a winter in the mountains it was now probably stronger than ever, but I just wasn't sure I had the energy anymore for the often fruitless quest for sponsors.

Suddenly, for the first time in my life as an adventurer, I had a potential sponsor (and in Barclays Capital a sponsor that wasn't short of a few quid) talking positively, and voluntarily, about funding my next venture. It was the sort of situation any expedition leader would give his right arm for. The only problem was, I had no expeditions in the pipeline. After an awkward silence, I mumbled, "Ummm, well, I'm ummm, thinking of maybe errr, going to the North Pole."

"Excellent news," replied Mark. "Unfortunately, I don't have much of a say in these things, but I'll set up a dinner with a couple of key guys at the bank. Then it will be up to you to tell them about your plans and convince them that your mission will succeed."

As I walked back to my apartment that evening I kept asking myself, "What on earth have you just got yourself into?" To this day I have no idea what prompted me to give Mark the answer I did. Maybe it was the third glass of Dôle Blanche doing the talking, but up until that moment the thought of going to the North Pole had only ever been a pipe dream. I could have just as easily said, "I'm going to be an accountant again in London," and my life would have continued down a very different path.

For many polar adventurers, it is almost a rite of passage that after a successful expedition to the South Pole, they should don the skis again and set off for the other pole. I had always wondered what it must be like at the North Pole, but I had never even toyed with the idea of one day mounting my own expedition up there. With the ski season almost over, my escapist existence in the mountains was drawing to an end, and I had resigned myself to a return to normality and a search for some form of employment. Quite suddenly those plans had been thrown out the window.

I knew very little about the North Pole, but what I did know filled me with sheer terror. Unlike the South Pole, which is located ten thousand feet above sea level in the heart of Antarctica, the fifth largest continent on the planet, the North Pole lies in the middle of the sea, the frozen

Arctic Ocean. It had defeated such legendary figures as Reinhold Messner and Sir Ranulph Fiennes, and those explorers who had been fortunate to escape the clutches of the North with their lives often came home with a few less fingers or toes than they started out with. No wonder, then, that the North Pole was often referred to as the "Horizontal Everest."

What seemed to make North Pole expeditions particularly grisly was that they traditionally took place during the bitterly cold winter months before the pack ice of the Arctic Ocean had started to break up. As if things weren't hard enough, there was precious little daylight, making pressure ridges and areas of open water all the more treacherous to negotiate. And then there were the polar bears. As far as I could make out, the Arctic was a sinister place where most days were a battle for survival. Messner, the greatest mountaineer of them all, described the frozen ocean as "ten times more difficult than Everest." It made our route to the South Pole seem like a simple nursery slope.

My stomach was so tied up in knots that following my conversation with Mark, I hardly slept a wink. Most of this could be put down to blind panic, but despite the obvious dangers, my natural wanderlust sparked into life. I was intrigued by the Arctic and wondered if I had what it took to survive up there. Yes, I was filled with fear and trepidation, but I was totally exhilarated, too. At last I had found a new dream to follow. There was no getting away from it, the North Pole was beckoning, and the sooner I started learning about what I was letting myself in for the better.

The romance of the Heroic Age of Polar Exploration has stirred my imagination ever since I can remember. I had been very conscious of the link between our journey to the South Pole in 2002 and the giants whose footsteps we followed. Our expedition had deliberately coincided with the centenary of the relatively unknown *Discovery* Expedition (Captain Scott and Sir Ernest Shackleton's joint attempt to reach the South Pole in 1902), and I had spent many hours lying awake in the tent at night trying to comprehend what they must have endured. Despite unimaginable hardship, inadequate equipment, and paltry provisions, they had battled on with astonishing courage, tenacity, a sense of humor, and a British stiff upper lip. Their spirit had been a source of great inspiration to me as we hauled our own sleds across Antarctica's frozen wastes.

Now that I had decided to go to the North Pole, I knew that it would help my mental preparation for the long journey ahead if I could build a similar connection with the heroes of the North. The only problem (as our tent-bound Christmas Eve 2002 chat with Paul had made glaringly obvious) was that I didn't know much about them. As a child I remember reading about Winnie the Pooh and Christopher Robin embarking on an "expotition" to the North Pole, but my knowledge of Arctic exploration didn't stretch much beyond that.

The reason for this could be that we Brits can be somewhat blinkered when it comes to our polar history. While our Antarctic explorers have become household names in Britain, few people have heard of the likes of Edward Parry, George Nares, and Wally Herbert, who in their day were at the forefront of Arctic exploration. On the other hand, Captain Scott's ill-fated expedition to the South Pole in 1912 has now almost become part of the national curriculum, and in boardrooms throughout the country, Shackleton's achievements are used as a shining example of successful corporate leadership. This anomaly has often struck me as a bit strange, especially when one thinks that the North Pole is almost on our doorstep while the South Pole is nearly ten thousand miles away on the bottom of the world.

Eager to find out more about the Arctic explorers of yesteryear, on my return from the Alps I visited the library at the Royal Geographical Society in London, the home of British exploration, to begin my research. I wanted to understand what had made these men tick and hoped that reading about their experiences would broaden my knowledge of the frozen Arctic Ocean. I also wanted to learn more about this extraordinary character called Robert Peary. Little did I know that from the moment I walked through the old timber doors of the RGS that day, my life would be totally consumed by this incredible man and his final expedition to the roof of the world.

People might wonder why it matters who the first person was to reach the North Pole. I believe it's one of the most momentous achievements in the history of the human race. We've inhabited the earth for two hundred thousand years, and there are now over six billion of us crowded onto this giant rock in the centre of the solar system. Yet we only managed to conquer our planet's true summit during the last century, and I believe the people who first reached that northernmost place should be celebrated for eternity.

As I trawled through the polar history books, I was almost dumb-founded by the early polar adventures and misadventures I read about. Some were extraordinarily brave, others downright suicidal, but over the course of many centuries, generations of explorers had helped unlock the door to the frozen Arctic. Pioneers like Leif Erikson, William Baffin, Fridjtof Nansen, and Umberto Cagni had been responsible for nudging humankind's limit of discovery ever northward so that by the time Peary made his first concerted bid to reach the top of the world in 1902, the final 206 miles of the map were all that remained untouched. Nevertheless, those were to prove the hardest, most fought-over miles of all, and it would be another seven years of superhuman effort before the ultimate prize could finally be claimed.

By the dawn of the twentieth century, the North Pole had defeated almost every industrialized nation. Attention then turned south, with the hope that Antarctica would prove a less fearsome adversary than the frozen North. The British were amongst the first on the scene, when the young torpedo lieutenant Robert Falcon Scott, commanding the *Discovery* Expedition of 1901–1904, made the first concerted bid to reach the South Pole. The Germans, Belgians, Norwegians, French, Japanese, and Australians all followed suit as the world turned its back on the Arctic and headed south. Yet one man still refused to give up on his dream of conquering the North Pole – Robert Edwin Peary.

ON A COLD OCTOBER DAY IN 1898, THE NORWEGIAN OTTO SVERDRUP was sitting in his tent on Ellesmere Island's east coast. Sverdrup was just starting out on a four-year expedition to map one hundred thousand square miles of uncharted islands and waterways in the Canadian High

Arctic. He was preparing his dinner when a tall, powerfully built, barrel-chested man dressed from head to toe in animal furs strolled into camp. Peary's exploits in the Arctic were already becoming legendary, and Sverdrup recognized him instantly from his chiselled jaw, steely gray eyes, weathered face, and gravity-defying walrus moustache.

"Are you Sverdrup?" Peary asked.

The affable Sverdrup greeted him warmly and invited him in for coffee.

Peary declined, saying, "My ship is frozen in. There is no way of getting through Robeson Channel. It has frozen fast."

What Peary failed to tell Sverdrup was that he was planning an assault on the North Pole the following spring and hoped to use the American explorer Adolphus Greely's old huts at Fort Conger as his base camp. But before Sverdrup had the chance to talk to him more, Peary turned around and left. A baffled Sverdrup later wrote that Peary had barely had the time to remove his mittens.

Sverdrup had no intention of going anywhere near the Pole, but so convinced was Peary that Sverdrup posed a threat to his own polar ambitions, that on returning to his ship he yelled, "Sverdrup may at this minute be planning to beat me to Fort Conger! . . . I can't let him do it! I'll get to Conger before Sverdrup if it kills me!" It very nearly did.

This bizarre encounter with Sverdrup was an eye-opening introduction for me to Peary's extraordinary character. Never before had I come across a polar explorer who seemed so fiercely determined in the pursuit of his goal as Robert Peary. Some of the words that Peary's biographers used to describe him included single-minded, creative, paranoid, resolute, competitive, ruthless, meticulously prepared, arrogant, brilliant, egocentric, fearless, and controversial.

As I slowly discovered, however, these qualities helped explain why he was able to push on where others had failed, and why he was able to return to the Arctic again and again in his never-ending quest for the North Pole, a quest that he hoped would one day propel him to immortality. During the debate about Peary's attainment of the Pole, notwithstanding whether the polar fraternity loathed him or admired him, they almost universally seemed to regard him as one of the most formidable polar explorers that ever lived.

"I Must Have Fame"

Born in 1856 in Cresson, Pennsylvania, to a family of humble merchants, Robert Peary was brought up alone by his mother after his father died when he was just two years old. As a child he spoke with a lisp, a source of much ridicule from his classmates, but he worked hard to overcome it and by adulthood he had managed to disguise it by speaking slowly and clearly. Only when he lost his temper would the lisp reveal itself again.

Despite being a keen sportsman, hunter, and sailor, Peary was always somewhat of a loner, although fiercely ambitious. In an early letter to his mother Peary wrote, "I feel myself overmastered by a resistless desire to do something. I do not wish to live and die without accomplishing anything or without being known beyond a narrow circle of friends. I wish to acquire a name which can be an open sesame to circles of culture and refinement anywhere, a name which shall make my Mother proud and which shall make me feel that I am peer to anyone I may meet."

It was fascinating to gain such a personal and revealing insight into the forces that drove Peary. I am often asked why I choose to take part in dangerous challenges, and part of me can identify with some of what Peary was saying. Like Peary, I've always been a dreamer, with an insatiable urge to do something different with my life. Ever since my childhood, Dad has always told me to "Carpe diem," literally "Seize the day," with the result that I have always had a single-minded determination to fulfil my destiny, whatever it might be.

I find that expeditions, whether they be sledging to a Pole, sailing across an ocean, climbing up or skiing down a mountain, allow me to escape from modern life's many constraints and give me a more balanced view of the world. They offer me a unique sense of freedom that I would never find sitting behind an office desk.

But while I, too, hoped that my parents would be proud of my expeditions, I have never viewed my travels as a means of becoming rich and famous. It's flattering to be recognized for one's achievements, but that is completely different from deliberately seeking fame. Our South Pole exploits in 2002 generated a great deal of press interest, something we had actively promoted to keep our sponsors satisfied, but I would be horrified if my friends thought that my fifteen minutes in the media spotlight had changed me. I'd be lying if I said I didn't feel a warm glow of pride the first time I saw my photo in the newspapers, but the reality is that the novelty wears off very quickly.

After graduating with top honours as a civil engineer from Bowdoin College in Maine, Peary joined the U.S. Navy and was soon posted to Central America. With a team of 150 men under his control, the twenty-seven-year-old Peary was given the task of conducting a detailed survey of the jungles and swamps of Nicaragua for a possible shipping canal to link the Atlantic and Pacific Oceans, a discovery he hoped would give him the fame he yearned for. Sadly, all Peary's hard work was to no avail as neighboring Panama eventually emerged as the preferred choice of route.

Following his return to the United States, Peary was in a Washington, D.C., bookstore where "I picked up a copy on the Inland Ice of Greenland. A chord, which as a boy, had vibrated intensely in me at the reading of Kane's wonderful book,★ was touched again. I read all I could on the subject . . . and felt that I must see for myself what the truth was of this great mysterious interior."

In 1886 Peary took a summer's leave from the Navy to attempt the first crossing of the Greenland ice cap, a trip he hoped would be a springboard for a future assault on the Pole. After twenty-six days he turned back, having made little more than a hundred nautical miles and climbed to an altitude of seven and a half thousand feet.

As he would demonstrate throughout his expedition career, Peary was a master of giving the press a story that sold newspapers. He portrayed his defeat as a resounding success by claiming that he had penetrated the ice cap "a greater distance than any white man previously." This boast was extremely tenuous. Although Peary had beaten the Swedish explorer Erik

★Elisha Kane was America's first Arctic hero.

Nordenskiöld's record by a few miles, two of the Swede's Sami companions (often referred to as Lapps) had actually gone farther than Peary, but because they weren't white men, Peary ignored their achievement.

"My last trip has brought my name before the world; my next will give me a standing in the world. I will next winter be one of the foremost in the highest circles in the capital, and make powerful friends with whom I can shape my future," he wrote home, adding, "Remember, mother, I *must* have fame, and I cannot reconcile myself to years of commonplace drudgery and a name late in life when I see an opportunity to gain it now and sip the delicious drafts while yet I have youth and strength to enjoy it to the utmost . . . I want my fame now."

I found Peary's words quite extraordinary, but his dream of fame had to wait when news arrived that the great Norwegian explorer Fridjtof Nansen had made the first successful Greenland traverse in 1888. Peary was infuriated, claiming that Nansen had in effect stolen his plan. The fact that Nansen had actually been preparing his expedition for six years seemed irrelevant.

Peary married his beautiful fiancée, Josephine, the following summer and immediately began preparations for a traverse of the unexplored and much wider northern half of Greenland. It was still not known how far north Greenland extended, and Peary believed that his expedition might reveal a land route extending all the way to the North Pole.

This time he prepared meticulously, the journals of all those Arctic explorers who had preceded him providing invaluable background reading. He concluded, "The old method of large parties and several ships has been run into the ground. The English, with true John Bull obstinacy, still stick to the old plan. The new plan of a small party depending largely on native assistance . . . deserves to be recorded as the American plan, and a successful expedition . . . will put us far ahead in the race."

Peary was already proving himself an inventive thinker, although his next idea was particularly original. He wrote, "If colonisation is to be a success in the polar regions, let white men take with them native wives, then from this union may spring a race combining the hardness of the mothers with the intelligence of the fathers. Such a race would surely reach the Pole if their fathers did not." This was no joke, either, as he was to father at least two half-Inuit children on subsequent expeditions to the Arctic.★

By June 1891 Peary had raised ten thousand dollars for the venture and set sail from New York with seven companions, one of whom was his wife, Jo. This was highly controversial but Peary, just like the Inuit, believed that women were vital for team morale on a long trip. No Western woman had ever travelled so far north. Although I never put the question to her, I know that if I had asked my girlfriend, Mary, whether she fancied spending a few months on the ice with me, I would have got a resounding "No thank you!"

Another key member of the team was Matthew Henson, the black American Peary had met by chance back in 1887 while shopping for a sunhat for his travels in Nicaragua and impulsively employed as his personal assistant for his Central American fieldwork. Standing at just five-feet-six, Henson was wiry, hard working, well read, and extremely bright, and the two would go on to forge one of the strongest partnerships in polar history. Over the course of more than two decades, Henson was Peary's most loyal travelling companion, Peary later commenting, "I cannot get along without him."

The journey did not get off to the best of starts when the ship's rudder, having glanced off an iceberg, swung violently and broke Peary's right leg. Peary contemplated returning home, but Frederick Cook, the young expedition doctor who would one day become his fiercest rival in the race for the North Pole, did an expert job of resetting the leg, and Peary went on to make a full recovery.

After overwintering on the west Greenland coast, Peary set off on his "White March" over the inland ice alongside the expert Norwegian skier Eivind Astrup and a team of dogs. Nine weeks of hard sledging later, the two men arrived at what Peary thought was the northernmost point of Greenland on 4 July 1892. Appropriately, he named it Independence Bay.

★In the 1970s, one of Peary's grandsons, the Greenlander Peter Peary, became the first person in history to complete two successful expeditions to the North Pole.

Peary had failed to find a land route to the Pole but he had proven that Greenland was an island – or so he thought. Although his mistake would not be uncovered for another twenty years, the vast mountainous land-mass that he could see in the distance (and named Peary Land) wasn't the separate island he believed it to be, but a seventy-five-mile-long peninsula jutting out from Greenland's north coast.

Nonetheless, the expedition was a spectacular success. Peary and Astrup had completed the longest (both in terms of distance – 1,100 miles, and time – eighty-five days), fastest, and most efficient sledging journey in Arctic history. It had also given Peary an invaluable lesson in the Inuit way of life. The men were protected from the cold by their warm, lightweight deerskin parkas, polar bear fur trousers, and waterproof sealskin boots.

Peary learned how to build igloos and drive a dog team. When he could, he lived off the land. He understood the value of laying caches of fresh meat during the hunting seasons so that scurvy would never cripple his teams. And by providing the Inuit with western inventions like knives, boats, needles, and metal tools, Peary was able to win their trust and respect, something the early explorers had failed to do. He called them "my Eskimos," sometimes even "my children." To them, he was simply "Pearyarksuah," literally "The Big Peary."

Find a Way or Make One

When Peary returned home, he at last received the fame he had so desperately craved. He was in every newspaper, was recognized in the street, and even his former rival Nansen joined the chorus of adulation, signing a congratulatory letter to Peary as "Your Admirer." Peary went on a grueling lecture tour across America, giving 165 speeches in 103 days.

Now that I had set my mind on going to the North Pole, I, too, had in effect become a professional explorer. With barely a penny to my name, I urgently needed to find a way of earning a living until the expedition got under way and so, like Peary, I, too, joined the corporate lecture circuit. As a schoolboy, I used to be terrified of public speaking, not helped by my voice, which didn't break until I was seventeen. With a few talks under my belt my confidence grew, however, and I now find it really energizing and humbling to speak in front of an audience about my expeditions. My props aren't a match for Peary's, though. He would transform his stage into an Inuit camp, with Henson joining Peary on stage, decked out in full Arctic furs. He also brought with him five dogs from his Greenland crossing that howled in unison at the climax of his speech. The whole performance must have brought the house down.

With appearance fees of up to two thousand dollars a show, Peary had saved enough to fund a third expedition, which sailed for Greenland in the summer of 1893. He was still employed by the Navy and again had to go through the tricky conversation of asking his superiors for more time off. However Peary was fast becoming an A-list celebrity, and much to the aggravation of his fellow naval officers, he now had influential friends in high places who could pull the strings necessary for him to secure another long leave of absence.

Astrup, Henson, and a heavily pregnant Jo joined him again, but not Cook, who resigned from his position as team doctor after his leader disallowed him from publishing a medical report about expedition life. Peary actually got on quite well with Cook in those early years, but Peary's unquenchable thirst for fame meant that he couldn't let anyone take even the thinnest ray of the limelight away from him.

Other than the birth of Marie, the Pearys' first child, the two-year expedition achieved little. Peary and Henson made the strange decision to repeat his 1892 traverse to Independence Bay, although this time they took a slightly different route. The whole trip would have dealt Peary's credibility as an explorer a major dent had he not brought three large meteorites from the Greenland coast home with him on his ship. One of the stones weighed a world-record thirty-four tons and they proved to be hugely popular attractions at the American Museum of Natural History in New York, where they remain today.

Peary's other Arctic treasures were on display for far less time. Of the six Inuit men and women from Greenland he brought back as a gift to the museum's curator, five of them succumbed to pneumonia within twelve months of being put on display, and died. The only survivor, a young boy called Minik, not only had to watch all his relatives die, but was then made to attend a fake funeral in which his father's body was removed from its coffin and replaced with a log. As Minik later discovered, the corpse had been stripped to the bone and the skeleton exhibited in a glass cabinet at the museum. GIVE ME MY FATHER'S BODY screamed the newspaper headlines. Although much of the Inuit scandal could not be directly attributed to Peary, it wasn't his finest hour, and the huge media interest in the story threatened to tarnish his reputation.

Nevertheless, Peary's achievements were now receiving worldwide recognition. The American Geographic Society awarded him a gold medal for establishing the insularity of Greenland, as did the Royal Geographical Society in London, which described him as "without exception, the greatest glacial traveller in the world." Still, Peary, now aged forty-two, was no nearer his goal of discovering the North Pole, and he wasn't getting any younger.

Abandoning Greenland's inland route, Peary decided to take a different approach, sailing all the way up Smith Sound towards the Arctic Ocean. He planned to establish a base as close to the northern coasts of Ellesmere Island or Greenland as his ship could sail, where he would lie in wait until the ice and weather conditions allowed him to "shoot forward to the Pole like a ball from a cannon."

After securing a bumper five-year leave of absence from the Navy, he then approached the railway tycoon Morris Jesup for financial help. Jesup would become one of Peary's most ardent supporters, establishing the Peary Arctic Club with a group of prominent businessmen whose chief role was to bankroll and support Peary's future ventures. Peary set sail on 4 July 1898, with the brilliant Newfoundland sea captain Bob Bartlett at the helm, another person whose life would become inexorably linked with Peary's over the next decade.

The only other expedition in the Arctic that year was Otto Sverdrup's, whose ship was anchored just twenty miles away near Cape Sabine. Although Sverdrup had consistently repeated that his expedition was limited to scientific research, Peary didn't trust him an inch and thought

he had secret designs on the North Pole – particularly as his fellow countryman Nansen had, in his view, poached his Greenland traverse plans ten
years earlier. Consequently, on that chilly October evening in 1898, Peary
felt it necessary to jump on his sled and pay Sverdrup a brief visit to
dissuade him from heading north.

So convinced was Peary that Sverdrup would "forestall" him and steal
his idea of using Greely's former headquarters at Fort Conger as his base,
that he set off in the dead of winter to beat him to it. Travelling in almost
total darkness, the 250-mile journey was unimaginably horrific. The temperature hovered around −50°C, the team was ravaged by blizzards, and they
nearly ran out of food. It was a miracle they all survived. The huts were
found just as Greely had left them in 1883, with equipment and provisions
strewn everywhere. Incredibly, much of the food was still edible.

As Peary sat down to remove his boots, three toes from each foot
snapped off at the joint. "My god, Lieutenant!" cried Henson, "Why didn't
you tell me your feet were frozen?"

"There's no time to pamper sick men on the trail," Peary replied matter-
of-factly, "Besides, a few toes aren't much to give to achieve the Pole."

The more I read about Peary, the more I realized just how unbelievably
resilient this man was. When compared to us modern-day polar travellers
with our synthetic fleeces, down sleeping bags, and boil-in-the-bag freeze-
dried meals, I had always thought that those men from the Heroic Age of
Polar Exploration were tough as old boots. For all that, Peary struck me as
being in a league of his own. Even though I've had my fair share of frostbite
injuries over the years, there's no doubt that if I ever found so much as a
single toe rattling around at the bottom of my boot, I would throw in the
towel immediately. Peary merely saw it as a minor inconvenience.

Further amputations were carried out, leaving Peary with just the little
toe of each foot, but aborting the expedition and heading home never
crossed his mind. On the walls of the hut he inscribed, *"Inveniam viam aut
faciam,"* literally, "Find a way or make one." For the rest of his exploration
life, he developed an effective shuffle, which was just as fast as a brisk walk.

Peary lay in his bunk for six weeks before being strapped to a sled and
taken back to the ship. He must have been in excruciating pain during the

eleven-day journey but never once complained. A few frostbitten toes weren't going to deter him, and he made plans to spend three more years in the Arctic. In a letter back home to Jo, Peary wrote, "Life is slipping away. That cannot come more forcibly to you than it has repeatedly to me in times of darkness and inaction the past year. More than once I have taken myself to task for my folly in leaving such a wife and baby (babies now) for this work. But there is something beyond me, something outside of me, that compels me to the work."

More sledging forays followed during the summer of 1899. Although he still found it painful to walk on his mangled feet, in 1900 Peary reached Greenland's most northerly point at 83°39N, which he named Cape Morris Jesup after his chief benefactor. As he and Matt Henson gazed out over the rough ice and open water of the Arctic Ocean for the first time, it must have dawned on them just how challenging those final 381 miles to the Pole were going to be.★

A couple of tentative outings onto the polar sea confirmed this, and they returned to Fort Conger, a journey of some 350 miles, in a rapid nineteen days. Something else that I was becoming increasingly aware of as I made my way through the history books wasn't just Peary's indestructibility, but also his ability to cover vast distances in double-quick time.

In the summer of 1901 Peary was visited by Frederick Cook, the doctor from his first successful Greenland expedition in 1892, who had been dispatched by the Peary Arctic Club to check up on their man still holed up in the Arctic after three years. After examining Peary, Cook told him that he was suffering from anemia and should eat raw liver to

★I should mention that all the mileages in this book are given in nautical miles, which have been the standard units of distance on the high seas and the polar regions for centuries. About eight hundred feet (or fifteen per cent) longer than the statute mile seen on road signs, the nautical mile measures one-sixtieth of a degree of latitude, the imaginary lines that wrap themselves round the earth from the Equator to the Poles in a series of horizontal parallel lines. The starting point for our South Pole expedition in 2002 was at a latitude of 80°01S, precisely 599 nautical miles as the crow flies from the Pole at 90° south. It still irks me that we didn't start the expedition a couple of miles farther north at, say, 79°59S. A journey of "over 600 miles" would sound even more impressive in the pub than one of 599 miles, and bring the extra satisfaction of starting in the "seventies." Oh well.

help his condition. When he saw the condition of his feet, Cook urged him to return home, saying, "You are through as a traveller on snow on foot. For without toes and a painful stub you can never wear snowshoes or ski." Peary ignored him. A relationship that had begun with much mutual admiration had now turned sour.

This little spat with Cook only motivated Peary to stay on for one more year and launch another bid for the Pole. By now he realized that the only way he was going to achieve his goal was to confront the Arctic Ocean head-on. In early March 1902, along with Henson and four Inuit, he stepped out onto the sea ice and headed north.

For sixteen days the exhausted party battled to lift their sleds over forty-foot pressure ridges and around fissures of open water. They used pickaxes to chop a route through the jumbled mass of ice blocks on a surface that drifted erratically with the currents. Then at 84°17N, barely eighty miles out to sea, they came to an impassable lead. Peary called it the Big Lead and compared its appearance to the Hudson River. Despite the fierce cold, it showed no signs of freezing over, and they had little choice but to turn back and begin the long journey home. It wouldn't be the last time that the Big Lead put an end to his plans.

A dejected Peary wrote in his diary, "The game is off. My dream of sixteen years is over. I have made a good fight but I cannot accomplish the impossible . . . I close the book and . . . accept the result calmly . . . The goal still remains for a better man than I." He was a beaten man.

A few months later came the news that the Italian, Umberto Cagni, had set a new farthest north record, just 206 miles shy of the Pole and a massive 137 miles beyond Peary's best effort in all these years of trying. But when Peary learned that Cagni had announced to the Italian press, "We have conquered! We have surpassed the greatest explorer of the century" (clearly not referring to Peary but the previous record holder, Fridjtof Nansen, who had reached 86°13N in 1895), he hit the roof.

To Peary it was a harsh blow to his ego that the polar community should acknowledge someone else as the greatest. Any plans to retire from polar life were quickly abandoned. According to Henson, his jaw tightened as he snarled, "Next time I'll smash that all to bits. Next time!"

Farthest North

It took Peary three years to find a new team, raise the funds, recharge his batteries, and prepare for what he hoped would be his final Arctic mission. Peary had now accomplished more than any explorer in Arctic history. He had been promoted from lieutenant to commander, elected president of the American Geographical Society, and picked up three more gold medals. Yet still he wasn't satisfied. He wanted the Pole more than anything else, in spite of the desperate appeals from his family not to go north again.

Peary's long-suffering wife, Jo, begged members of the Peary Arctic Club to "let me keep my old man at home." In a letter to her father, eleven-year-old Marie pleaded, "I know that you will do what pleases Mother and me and that is to stay with us at home. I have been looking at your pictures, it seems ten years and I am sick of looking at them. I want to see my father. I don't want people to think me an orphan."

Peary was the most meticulous of expedition planners. Learning from past mistakes, he realized that a radical new approach was needed. He ordered a powerful new ship to be built, which could smash its way through the ice-choked Smith Sound like an icebreaker. All those long, tiring sled journeys along the jagged coasts of Ellesmere Island and Greenland had exhausted so many of his parties before they had even reached the Arctic Ocean. If he was going to achieve his dream, Peary was convinced that he and his companions needed to be dropped off as close to the frozen polar sea as possible, fresh and ready for battle. The ship was named the *Roosevelt* after the U.S. president, one of Peary's most ardent supporters.

He also figured he would need much more manpower this time and so devised a completely new travel strategy. He called it the "Peary System." The party would be split into three – a pioneer division to break the trail and build igloos; support divisions following on twenty-four hours behind ferrying supplies to those in front, and a small, lightweight polar division (where Peary would be), conserving its energy at the rear. As the whole caravan moved northward and the mass of food and fuel supplies gradually diminished, the various divisions would be sent back to the ship one by one, until just the polar division was left for the final dash to the Pole.

It was a huge logistical undertaking. In addition to making the whole operation much more efficient and opening up lines of communication between the various divisions, the real benefit of the Peary System was that the loads were always relatively light, and therefore the dog teams could travel much faster than they had on Peary's previous attempts. The maximum weight of a fully laden sled was six hundred pounds – a much lighter load than they had carried in the past.

On the journey north, the *Roosevelt* stopped off at the Inuit community of Etah to pick up hundreds of dogs and twenty local families. During the winter, the men's role would be to build sleds, care for the dogs, and supply fresh meat from the large herds of musk ox and caribou that inhabit northern Ellesmere Island. The women, meanwhile, would be employed as seamstresses, making polar clothing for the sledging parties.

The *Roosevelt* arrived at her winter quarters in September 1905 near Cape Sheridan on Ellesmere Island. They were just 450 miles from the Pole, and Peary was ecstatic, declaring, "I do not believe there is another ship afloat that would have survived the ordeal."

The following spring, a huge train of twenty-eight men (twenty-one of whom were Inuit) and 120 dogs set off across the frozen ocean for the Pole. Henson was out in front with the pioneer division, Peary at the rear, with the various support divisions in between shuttling loads back and forth along the trail.

After a grueling three weeks of pressure ridges, fields of ice boulders, fissures, and broken floes, they met the Big Lead, which had stopped them in their tracks in 1902. It was over two miles across in places and stretched from east to west as far as they could see. An impatient Peary paced back and forth along the water's edge, coaxing the waters to refreeze. Eventually they did, but the frustrating week-long delay must have felt like an eternity.

Peary cursed his luck again when three days after crossing the newly frozen Big Lead, they were ravaged by a series of blizzards that delayed them for a further week. To make the situation worse, when he got out his instruments to measure his longitude, he found that he had drifted off course a staggering seventy miles to the east. The forces of wind and ocean current on the ice pack had been far more powerful than he had ever anticipated.

Pinned down in his igloo, Peary realized that all hope of reaching the Pole was gone. Still, the humiliation of returning to America empty-handed was too much to bear, so with the consolation prize of beating Umberto Cagni's farthest north record of 86°34N still there for the taking, he discarded all unnecessary baggage and made a sprint for it. Conditions improved the farther north they went, and on some days they were able to travel nearly thirty miles.

By 21 April they had reached 87°06N, just thirty-two miles north of Cagni's position, but enough to claim the record. He wrote, "When I looked at the drawn faces of my comrades, at the skeleton figures of my few remaining dogs, at my nearly empty sleds . . . I felt I had cut the margin as narrow as could reasonably be expected."

It was time to head home. Because the drifting ice pack had carried them so far east, Peary decided that the quickest and safest way back was to head southeastwards and make for the nearest land, the north coast of Greenland, where the abundant game would be able to feed them for the final march to Cape Sheridan.

The return journey was all going according to plan until they arrived at the Big Lead, and to their horror found that it had opened up again. Once more they were forced to wait for it to refreeze, but they were now into May. Spring was gradually turning to summer and the temperatures were becoming much milder. Provisions were running so low that they were forced to kill their dogs, cooking them over a fire made from their chopped-up sleds.

When one of the Inuit found an area of precarious newly formed ice, Peary knew that unless they tried to cross now, they would starve to death. His description of their half-mile crossing made terrifying reading. While proving to me once again how Peary just never gave up, it also gave a stark reminder of what the Arctic Ocean had in store for me. "Once started, we could not stop, we could not lift our snowshoes. It was a matter of constantly and smoothly gliding one past the other with utmost care and evenness of pressure, and from every man as he slid a snowshoe forwards, undulations went out in every direction through the thin film incrusting the black water. The sled was preceded and followed by a broad swell. It was the first and only time in my Arctic work that I felt doubtful as to the outcome, but when near the middle of the lead the toe of my rear kamik [boot] . . . broke through twice in succession I thought to myself, "this is the finish," and when a little while later there was a cry from someone in the line, the words sprang from me of themselves: "God help him, which one is it?" but I dared not take my eyes from the steady, even gliding of my snowshoes, and the fascination of the glossy swell."

The remaining one hundred miles to the Greenland coast were equally fraught, but incredibly, after sixty-four days on the Arctic Ocean, everyone made it back to the ship alive. By now the *Roosevelt* had been released from the ice at Cape Sheridan, but the long winter had left her badly damaged. When Peary saw his crippled ship, he pleaded to Bartlett, "We have got to get her back, Captain. We are going to come again next year."

The crew patched up the *Roosevelt* as best they could, but it would be another four months before she finally limped back into New York. Bartlett's remarkable seamanship in getting the stricken craft home, despite having no fuel or rudder and being pounded by almost constant gales as winter drew in, has been compared for its brilliance with Ernest Shackleton and Frank Worsley's escape from Antarctica in the *James Caird* in 1916.

The Pole at Last

I was now totally engrossed in Peary's incredible story. Shortly after his return from the Arctic, a lavish black-tie dinner was held at the National Geographic Society to commemorate Peary's new farthest north record. He was to be presented with yet another gold medal by Theodore Roosevelt. However, he wasn't the only special guest that night. Peary would be at the head table by the man he had fallen out with so acrimoniously, Dr. Frederick Cook.

Cook had just made the first successful ascent of Mount McKinley in

Alaska, North America's highest peak. His exploits in the North and a recent expedition to Antarctica with Roald Amundsen (the man who in 1911 would be the first to reach the South Pole) had led to Cook's election to president of the Explorers' Club in New York. His profile was rapidly catching up with Peary's.

Peary was forever paranoid that someone would "forestall" his polar dreams and that Cook, with his growing exploration credentials, was the man most likely to steal his glory. So in his impassioned acceptance speech, Peary made it very clear to Cook, the president, and the many millionaires and potential sponsors amongst the audience that the Pole was still very much his territory, and that despite his recent failure, he was going to have one final go.

Peary proclaimed, "To me the final and complete solution of the polar mystery . . . is the thing which should be done for the honour and credit of this country, the thing which it is intended that I should do and the thing that I must do. As regards the belief expressed by some, that the attainment of the North Pole possesses no value or interest, let me say that should an American first of all men place the Stars and Stripes at that coveted spot, there is not an American citizen who would not feel a little better and a little prouder of being an American; and just that added increment of pride and patriotism to millions would of itself be ten times the value of all the cost of attaining the Pole."

It was a barn-storming performance that had the entire banquet hall, including President Roosevelt, on their feet roaring their approval. Seeing Peary receive a standing ovation, lauded a hero by the geographical establishment for something he hadn't yet achieved, would have a profound effect on the equally ambitious Cook. Unbeknown to Peary, before the chorus of bravos had even begun to die down, Cook was hatching a secret plot to steal a march on his rival and beat him to the Pole.

Peary's plans to head north again in the summer of 1907 were in disarray. Not only had the damage to the *Roosevelt* not been repaired but he was also on the verge of bankruptcy. He had always put his speaking and literary earnings into his expeditions, and he had mortgaged the family home on Eagle Island in Maine up to the hilt. He had no choice but to delay his plans for another year. Peary was now approaching fifty-two and despite having phenomenal strength and fitness for a man of his age, he knew that time was fast catching up to him.

His fund-raising efforts were dealt a major blow with the death of his chief benefactor, Morris Jesup, but his whole world was torn apart in late 1907 when the news came that Cook had secretly sailed to the village of Etah and had, "hit upon a new route to the North Pole . . . by way of Ellesmere and northward over the Polar Sea. There will be game to the 82d degree, and there are natives and dogs for the task. So here is for the pole." Peary must have been fuming. In his eyes, Cook was openly stealing *his* route to the North Pole, *his* game, *his* Inuit dog drivers and *his* dogs, and if Cook were to conquer the Pole, ultimately *his* glory.

It must have felt like daylight robbery, but with Cook having the luxury of a twelve-month head start on him, there was nothing Peary could do about it but continue with his own plans. He may have been outraged that Cook was blatantly poaching his idea, but Peary didn't appear to take the threat posed by Cook that seriously. He had always viewed him as a bit of a lightweight and, knowing how much effort was required for every mile of progress on the Arctic Ocean, he didn't give him much of a chance.

The one benefit of Cook's announcement was that he had rekindled public interest in the Pole, making it easier for Peary to raise the funds for a fresh bid. Nevertheless, it was still a frantic race to find the money in time: "But the money still came hard", wrote Peary. "It was the subject of my every working thought; and even in sleep it would not let me rest, but followed with mocking and elusive dreams. It was a dogged, dull, desperate time, with the hopes of my whole life rising and falling by the day."

The way Peary had to fire off thousands of letters, knock on the doors of potential backers, and do whatever he could to talk his way into corporate boardrooms, reminded me of my own desperate struggles for sponsorship. Like Peary, over the years I have been turned away, laughed at, sworn at, sympathized with, and even offered jobs, but despite being continually knocked back I always believed that the money was out there somewhere and so I stuck with it. I just hoped that this time around, with

Barclays Capital now showing such an interest in my North Pole plans, I wouldn't have to go through the same soul-destroying hunt for financial support another time.

On 6 July 1908, the fully repaired and bankrolled *Roosevelt* cast off on a boiling hot afternoon from her berth at Recreation Pier in Manhattan, with thousands of well-wishers cheering her on. The crew was the most able that Peary had ever assembled: Professor Ross Marvin, the civil engineer who had been with him in 1906, George Borup, the enthusiastic young sports scholar from Yale, Donald MacMillan, a sports coach and like Peary a Bowdoin College graduate, Dr. John Goodsell, the expedition surgeon, and, of course, his two most trusted companions, Matt Henson and Captain Bob Bartlett.

The following morning the ship pulled into Oyster Bay on Long Island where President Roosevelt spent two hours inspecting every nook and cranny on the ship. "I believe in you, Peary," he boomed as he climbed back over the rail.

The main difference from his 1906 expedition was that this time he planned to make his first steps on the Arctic Ocean at Cape Columbia, some forty miles west of his previous jumping-off point. As before, he would save himself, his best dogs, best sleds, best supplies, best equipment, and best men for the final dash. This time, however, his polar dash would begin from a camp well north of the Big Lead, a mere 130 miles from the Pole.

On her way north the *Roosevelt* stopped off at Etah, where Peary learned that Cook had set off for the polar ice some six months earlier. Much to Peary's relief, Cook had apparently chosen a small Inuit team from a separate community up the coast, meaning all of Peary's men and women were still there. Inuit families and hundreds of dogs were crammed onboard, along with seventy tons of whale meat and the blubber of fifty walruses. Bartlett wrote, "To my dying day I shall never forget the frightful noise, the choking stench and the terrible confusion that reigned on board." Two weeks later they were at Cape Sheridan from where sledging parties immediately began transporting food and equipment the eighty miles to Cape Columbia.

On 27 February 1909, the entire expedition party of twenty-four men, nineteen sleds, and 133 dogs assembled in the freezing half-light at Cape Columbia, 413 miles from the Pole. Peary must have known that it was now or never.

With Bartlett out in front blazing the trail, the polar caravan headed north. One by one, the support parties began making their way back to the *Roosevelt*, Goodsell and MacMillan the first to head back on 14 March at 84°29N, Borup six days later at 85°23N, and Marvin on 26 March, having made it as far as 86°38N.

The remaining men continued north at a steady pace of twelve to fifteen miles a day until they reached 87°47N. All was going according to plan. They were just 133 miles from glory, and it was time for Bartlett and the final support division to return to the ship. The captain wrote in his journal, "I leave Commander Peary with five men, five sleds with full loads and forty picked dogs. At the same average as our last eight marches, [they] should reach the Pole in eight days."

In the early hours of 2 April, Peary, along with Henson and his best Inuit dog drivers, Ootah, Ooqueah, Seegloo and Egingwah, set off under clear skies on the final leg of their journey. After five long marches in perfect travel conditions, a triumphant Peary was satisfied that they were at the North Pole. "The Pole at last!!!" he wrote, "The prize of 3 centuries, my dream and ambition for 23 years. Mine at last."

On the afternoon of 7 April, the party scurried southward, deeply worried that the spring break-up of the Arctic ice could leave them stranded, as had nearly happened in 1906. The men covered the 133 miles back to the igloos from where Bartlett had been sent back in three huge marches. On 10 April, a shattered Peary scribbled in his diary, "From here to the Pole and back has been a glorious sprint, with a savage finish. Its results are due to hard work, little sleep, much experience, first class equipment and good fortune as regards weather and open water."

Just two weeks later, they were back on solid land at Cape Columbia. The Inuit shrieked with joy, Ootah telling Henson, "The devil is asleep or having trouble with his wife, or we should never have come back so easily."

That night, Peary could relax for the first time in months and wrote, "My life's work is accomplished. The thing which it was intended from the beginning that I should do, the thing which believed could be done, and that I could do, I have done. I have got the North Pole out of my system . . . I have won the last geographical prize . . . for the credit of the United States. This work is the finish, the cap and climax, of nearly four hundred years of effort, loss of life and expenditure of fortunes, by the civilized nations of the world, and it has been accomplished in a way that is thoroughly American. I am content."

The Gold Brick

During her voyage back to the United States, the *Roosevelt* dropped anchor in Etah to return the Inuit, their families, and the few surviving dogs home. There they learned that Frederick Cook had recently passed through with the alarming news that he had successfully reached the North Pole via Axel Heiberg Island on 21 April 1908. But they didn't seem overly concerned, Henson commenting, "To us up there at Etah, such a story was so ridiculous and absurd. We knew Dr. Cook and his abilities . . . and aside from his medical ability, we had no faith in him whatsoever. He was not even good for a day's work, and the idea of his making such an astounding claim as having reached the Pole was so ludicrous that, after our laugh, we dropped the matter altogether."

Their suspicions were confirmed when Henson (who was fluent in the local dialect, Inuktitut) questioned the two Inuit who had been with Cook during the fourteen months that he had been away. They told him that while they had covered hundreds of miles and had survived an appalling winter with next to no food and shelter, they had never been out of sight of land and went no farther north than Axel Heiberg Island. Cook had seemingly fabricated the vast majority of his journey.

Peary cabled the news of his attainment of the Pole on 6 September 1909, at Indian Harbor, the first town they came to on the Labrador coast. The message read, "Stars and Stripes nailed to the Pole. Peary." Unbeknown to Peary, just five days earlier, Cook had announced that he had reached the Pole a full year earlier. The bitter public relations battle had commenced.

Having caught a lift from Greenland on board a Danish cargo ship,

Cook was mobbed by huge crowds on his arrival in Copenhagen on 4 September. Most of Fleet Street had made the journey from London to interview him, and an opulent banquet was held in his honour at the Tivoli Palace.

It wasn't long, though, before doubts in the story began to surface. Philip Gibbs, a prominent journalist from London's *Daily Chronicle,* noted that "a strange defensive look" appeared on Cook's face when he asked if he could see his expedition diary. To Gibbs, Cook's mileages seemed far-fetched, his daily rations way too low, and the few observation measurements he provided suspiciously precise. "I left my notebooks behind in Etah," he replied. On further questioning, Cook snapped, "You believed Nansen and Amundsen and Sverdrup . . . Why don't you believe me?" The answer was simple – they had all been accompanied by reliable witnesses whereas Cook had not, and his story failed to stack up.

Gibbs didn't let the matter drop, and in a subsequent interview asked Cook again, "Surely you brought your journal with you? The essential papers?" Cook then asserted that he had given his diaries to the University of Copenhagen for authentication, a claim that was subsequently denied. Cook then changed his mind again, saying that the papers had in fact been sent to the United States, causing Gibbs to have some serious reservations about the authenticity of his claim.

Nevertheless, apart from his initial outburst, Cook remained courteous and unflappable whenever questioned, leading Gibbs to comment, "I must now say that this man Cook is the most remarkable, most amazing man I have ever met. I will say honestly that I am filled with a sense of profound admiration for him. If he is an impostor he is also a very brave man – a man with such iron nerve, such miraculous self-control, and such magnificent courage in playing his game, that he will count for ever amongst the great impostors of the world. That and not the discovery of the North Pole shall be his claim to immortality."

Gibbs was a lone voice amongst a chorus of adulation throughout the world, and by the time Cook returned to New York the crowds had reached fever pitch. When an enraged Peary learned of Cook's apparent hoax, he fired off a second telegram that read, "Do not trouble about Dr.

Cook's story or attempt to explain any discrepancies in his statements. The affair will settle itself. He has not been to the Pole on April 21st 1908, or at any other time. He has simply handed the public a gold brick."

I found it hard not to sympathize with Peary. Whether he had made it to the Pole or not, he had sacrificed more than any other explorer in his quest for glory. In addition to the physical toll the Arctic had taken on him during all these years, he had been away from his wife for almost half of their marriage, he had missed almost all of his daughter's childhood, and he had never met his youngest daughter, who had died aged just seven months. Then, at his moment of triumph, to have his prize stolen from under his nose, whether by fair means or foul, must have felt like a dagger to the heart.

With the *New York Times* championing Peary and the *New York Herald* backing Cook, things soon escalated into an acrimonious circulation war. Cook was far more media-savvy than Peary. By choosing to congratulate his nemesis and declare, "I am proud that a fellow American has reached the Pole. There is glory enough for us all," and "Two records are better than one," he was seen as the nice guy in the mounting controversy. Meanwhile, Peary's hostile condemnation of Cook's claims was seen by many as a sign of petulance at having been beaten to the Pole. As one commentator put it, "Cook was a liar and a gentleman, Peary was neither."

Despite the best efforts of the Peary Arctic Club to discredit Cook, a series of newspaper surveys found that the weight of public opinion was with the doctor. A poll of seventy-six thousand people by the *Pittsburgh Press* showed that an astonishing ninety-six per cent of its readers believed Cook had reached the Pole while only twenty-four per cent thought Peary had got there.

Peary's ego must have taken a serious knock as the American public, who had lauded his past achievements, now turned on him and his team. As Bartlett later wrote, "I feel as if I'd been through the French Revolution, or something just as rough and noisy and horrible. It was all very confused; there was a lot of anger in it, as well as poisonous bitterness and recrimination. It seemed to me bad enough to have had a scientific debate; but to have almost a public riot over the question of who reached the Pole was pretty low. The papers kept the pot boiling furiously. I guess they didn't have any good murders just then."

In mid-October Cook's credibility was dealt a severe blow, however, when Ed Barrill, who had climbed Mount McKinley with him in 1906, confessed that their summit photograph had in fact been taken on a much lower peak twenty miles away and they had never even set foot on McKinley at all.*

Events quickly began stacking up against Cook. The Explorers' Club (where he had once been president) canceled his membership, the National Geographical Society denounced his polar claims, the *New York Herald* withdrew its support, and when an investigation by the Scandinavian polar establishment in December led the front page of the *New York Times* to declare, COOK'S CLAIM TO THE DISCOVERY OF THE NORTH POLE REJECTED; OUTRAGED DENMARK CALLS HIM A DELIBERATE SWINDLER, his reputation was in ruins.

With Cook now out of the picture, and America desperate for a hero, Peary was effectively crowned the winner by default. However, his misfortune was that the public had come to expect the very worst from polar explorers. The cynicism that had grown during the final months of 1909 never really died down, and many viewed Peary's claims with deep suspicion.

Initially, Peary had been reluctant to submit his journals and diaries for verification by the experts for fear that if they got into the wrong hands they could help Cook forge his own data. Realizing that remaining tight-lipped was doing nothing to help his cause, Peary decided to hand over his proofs to a committee at the National Geographic Society in New York. They didn't take long to validate their contents, prompting the society's vice president to remark, "Everybody who knows Peary's reputation knows he would not lie." The cynics refused to go away, however, arguing that because most members of the committee were longstanding friends

---

*Cook's fraudulent claim would eventually be confirmed beyond doubt, after a comprehensive analysis of his McKinley journal, maps, and photographs in 2001 by Bradford Washburn, one of America's greatest mountaineers and a man who dedicated his life to photographing and surveying North America's highest peak.

and sponsors of Peary, they were simply looking after one of their own.

In early 1910 two independent experts from the U.S. Coast and Geodetic Survey analyzed Peary's navigational data in painstaking detail, concluding that he "probably passed within one and six-tenths geographic miles of the North Pole." The Royal Geographical Society in London was much more cautious, its committee members only ratifying his claim by eight votes to seven. Nevertheless, its navigation expert, Edward Reeves, did say that Peary's equipment was up to the task of making the necessary observations required to pinpoint his position, and that Peary "either took them and got close to the Pole or 'faked' them to defraud the public and is an impostor of the very worst type."

With the Pole now back in his possession and the fierce row dying down, Peary at last had what he wanted. He lectured throughout America and Europe; congratulatory messages poured in from leading polar figures like Amundsen, Nansen, and Cagni; the Senate passed a bill recognizing his discovery of the North Pole; he was promoted to rear admiral; textbooks now listed him as the first man to reach the Pole; and he was showered with yet more gold medals from almost every geographical society in the world. Most importantly for Peary, he was able to spend time away from the media spotlight to begin reacquainting himself with his young family at his beloved Eagle Island home in Maine, the place he called his "Promised Land."

Still, a small but influential group remained determined to bring him down. When the House of Representatives tried to pass a bill similar to the one passed by the Senate, a committee of vociferous congressmen, many of them Cook supporters, subjected Peary to a rigourous three-day inquiry in January 1911. The tone of the questioning was so intense and at times completely off the subject that Peary became irritable and occasionally lost his cool.

The bill was eventually passed by a large majority, but the Congressional hearings left an indelible scar. Jo Peary later wrote, "The personal grilling which my husband was obliged to undergo at the hands of Congress, while his scientific observations were examined and worked out, although it resulted in his complete vindication, hurt him more than all the hardships he had endured during his sixteen years in the Arctic regions and did more towards breaking down his iron constitution than anything experienced in his explorations."

But the battle was far from over, and Peary's hopes of a peaceful, dignified retirement failed to materialize. Cook resurfaced from time to time. His book, *My Attainment of the Pole*, irritated Peary but did nothing to restore his credibility. Cook also attempted to sue anyone (including Peary) who questioned his polar claims, but the courts ruled against him every time. Then, in 1916, one of Cook's supporters in Congress, Henry Helgesen, tried to strip Rear Admiral Peary of his rank because his "claims to the discoveries in the Arctic regions have been proven to rest on fiction and not on geographical facts." Much to Peary's relief, Helgesen died the following year and the bill was dropped.

Nevertheless, the strain of the last few years had taken its toll on Peary, and he died on 20 February 1920, after a long fight with pernicious anemia, ironically, the very condition which Cook had diagnosed him with in 1901. He was sixty-four. He had achieved the fame he had craved throughout his adult life, but had he discovered the North Pole? The answer would go with him to the grave.

Cook outlived his rival by twenty years, but his spectacular fall from grace continued. In 1923 he was fined fourteen thousand dollars and sentenced to fourteen years in jail for selling a plot of land in Texas that he had fraudulently claimed to be oil-bearing. Shortly before his death in 1940 he recorded a tape for posterity. His final words were, "I have been humiliated and seriously hurt. But that doesn't matter anymore. I'm getting old, and what does matter to me is that I want you to believe that I told the truth. I state emphatically that I, Frederick A. Cook, discovered the North Pole." In a cruel twist, shortly after his death the land that he sold in Texas went on to produce millions of barrels of oil.

A Mystery Unsolved

The controversy at the top of the world still rumbles on today. At the time of his death Peary was accepted by most as the discoverer of the Pole, but the waters are now far more muddied. A detailed investigation of Peary's navigation data and daily mileages by the American astronomer Denis Rawlins in 1973 accused him of cheating. His book, *Peary at the North Pole: Fact or Fiction?*, was the first in the long history of the North Pole debate to quash the claims of both Cook and Peary. Rawlins's findings caused a shift in public perception and led to the *Encyclopedia Britannica* changing its entry on Peary from the "discoverer of the North Pole" to the man "usually credited" with discovering the Pole.

The screening on American television of a documentary called *The Race to the Pole* in 1984, which suggested that Cook had been deprived of his rightful claim by a vindictive Peary, so infuriated the Peary family that they were persuaded by the National Geographic Society, the custodians of the Peary archives, to publish his personal journal from his final expedition. It was the first time that anyone outside his closest circle had seen this most private of documents. "I do not care to let it out of my possession," Peary had once remarked, "It never has been." The journal had remained locked away throughout the intense period of investigation, and it was hoped that detailed analysis of its contents would settle the matter once and for all.

The British explorer Sir Wally Herbert, who had made the first surface crossing of the Arctic Ocean in 1968–1969, was given the task of analyzing all the material. Herbert's was a name I was familiar with before I began my Arctic research. He had personally surveyed and mapped over forty-five thousand square miles of virgin Antarctic territory and spent two years living with the Inuit in northern Greenland.

Many regard Herbert as Britain's greatest modern-day explorer. During his epic 407-day journey with dog teams from Alaska to Spitsbergen, Herbert and his three companions passed through the North Pole on 6 April 1969, exactly sixty years to the day after Peary. Incredibly, nobody had been to the North Pole on foot throughout all those intervening years, which explains why Herbert is sometimes listed as the first man to the Pole.

Herbert spent three painstaking years collecting evidence that Peary's supporters hoped would prove that his 1909 expedition was successful.

The outcome was not what they had expected. Herbert poured cold water on Peary's claims in his 1988 book, *The Noose of Laurels,* arguing that because of Peary's sensational travel speeds it would have been impossible for him to have reached the Pole in the time he claimed. He wrote that Peary's sprint-finish to the Pole, during which he supposedly covered twenty-six miles a day over the expedition's final five days, was unbelievably fast. To Herbert's astonishment, Peary's return speeds were even quicker. Herbert wrote, "No explorer, before or since, has claimed to have covered these sorts of distances across the polar pack ice over the same number of consecutive days."

Unlike Captain Scott's South Pole diary, which was clearly written for a public audience, Peary's was more a collection of private thoughts and observations. Some of his jottings revealed more about his inner world and craving for fame than anything since those early letters to his mother. "Faced with marble or granite," read one such memo about his plans for the mausoleum he hoped would be built on his death. "Statue with flag on top, lighted room at base for 2 sarcophagi? Bronze figures Eskimos, Dog, Bear, Walrus etc, etc or bronze tablets of flag on Pole & suitable inscription."

Herbert found no evidence that Peary took longitude readings during his journey to the Pole, making it more difficult for him to calculate how far east or west the unpredictable forces of wind and ocean current had carried him off course. Although he diplomatically skirted around the issue of whether he thought Peary was deliberately trying to deceive the world by faking his readings, or whether Peary genuinely believed that he had reached the Pole, Hebert estimated that Peary had missed his goal by sixty miles.

Inconsistencies in Peary's journal, a lack of credible witnesses in the polar party to verify his position, and Peary's strange behavior at the end of his journey only compounded Herbert's doubts. He also dismissed Cook's polar claims out of hand. Being the only Peary/Cook biographer to have travelled across the polar pack himself, Herbert's arguments carried much more clout than those of previous polar historians, and in most quarters *The Noose of Laurels* has now become accepted as the definitive analysis of Peary's final expedition. Given Herbert's phenome, exploration credentials, it was hard to disagree with him.

In 1989 the National Geographic Society undertook a comprehensive study of all the data and rebuffed Herbert's claims, but its own verdict could not be said to have been totally impartial because of the organisation's close relationship to the Peary family. A further study of all the material by the American historian Russell Bryce in 1997 also came to the same conclusion as Rawlins that Peary's claims were a total fabrication. I was finding these endless tit-for-tat exchanges by the pro- and anti-Peary camps more and more confusing. I was no closer to finding out the truth.

As my Arctic research drew to a close, I felt let down. The romance of the race to the South Pole was the thing that had first gripped me about Captain Scott's tale when I was a young boy. The history books show that he was narrowly beaten by Amundsen, but his tragic death, recorded so poetically in his diary, seemed to really capture the spirit of polar exploration. There have been other gallant tales throughout exploration history that have caught the public's imagination – Stanley's rescue of Livingstone in Central Africa in 1871, Mallory and Irvine's daring bid to climb Everest in 1924, and Armstrong's first steps on the moon in 1969.

In contrast to the way I felt after reading all these tales of extraordinary bravery, the centuries-old quest for the North Pole had such an unedifying, almost farcical ending. Part of my frustration lay with Cook, whose seemingly bogus claims sparked the whole debate in the first place, but I also felt let down by Peary for not taking the simple measures to prove to us whether or not he and his five companions had succeeded in reaching the Pole.

Nevertheless, there was no getting away from the fact that Peary and all those explorers before him had brought the Arctic Ocean to life for me. Their tales of the simple struggle of man against the elements had struck a chord with me, and I was now itching to see this awesome landscape of drama with my own eyes. A strange aspiration burned inside me to put myself through the same suffering they had endured. I wanted to find out if I had what it took to survive up there.

The unsolved mysteries of the North had also totally gripped me. Just who was the true conqueror of the North Pole? Part of me wanted to believe it was my fellow countryman, Wally Herbert. Throughout exploration history, Britain has repeatedly been beaten to the great geographical prizes on the map like the South Pole, the Northwest Passage, and the summit of Everest, often after doing all the hard work, and it would give us something to cheer about if our man won this time. But having now learned about this larger-than-life character called Robert Peary and the superhuman efforts he had taken to conquer the Pole, I also felt that he, too, probably deserved the title. To be honest, I didn't really mind either way. I just wanted to know. However, no history book or Arctic biographer was going to give me the answer. The millions of words that had already been written on the subject had all proven inconclusive.

I figured that the question would continue to be asked until somebody tried to replicate Peary's final journey across the frozen pack, travelling from northern Ellesmere Island to the North Pole with dog teams and wooden sleds to try to find out if his extraordinary travel speeds and unorthodox navigation techniques were as far-fetched as his detractors had alleged. Slowly it was beginning to dawn on me that as I wasn't aware of anyone who was planning such an adventure, that somebody might as well be me.

2. Arctic Monkeys

MY PLAN WAS BEGINNING TO TAKE SHAPE. Every waking moment was spent either preparing for the expedition or thinking about it. Even my dreams were becoming filled with images of pressure ridges and snowstorms. Using dog teams and replicas of wooden sleds, I had decided to retrace the footsteps of Robert Peary to the North Pole. Peary had claimed to have reached the Pole just thirty-seven days after setting off from the Canadian coast, but nobody had ever come close to beating him for the best part of a century.

The fastest time since 1909 was forty-two days by a Swedish team pulling their own sleds in 2000, but most expeditions typically took sixty or seventy days to reach the Pole. My aim was to do what nobody had done before and better Peary's time. I only had to deal with the small matter of putting my team together, convincing Barclays Capital to part with a large chunk of their marketing budget, and learning how to drive a dog team.

What had really stuck in my mind during my Arctic research was that the place seemed to be far more hostile than Antarctica. On our way to the South Pole in 2002, the dangers were confined to bottomless crevasses and violent blizzards, but there were no shifting ice floes or polar bears to worry about. We were also blessed with twenty-four hour daylight, we never had to negotiate open water or towering pressure ridges, and the temperatures, while cold, were far more tolerable than the mind-boggling minus-forties that appeared to be the norm in the Arctic.

The prospects of success were bleak: Over eighty per cent of recent North Pole attempts ended in failure. Even though over three thousand people have now reached the summit of Everest, fewer than 150 people have ever completed the journey from the shores of the Arctic Ocean to the North Pole since the days of Peary and Cook. Hundreds more have tried and failed, and some had never even made it home. As I studied the statistics, I began to wonder if I was biting off more than I could chew. It was going to be a huge challenge just to get to the Pole, let alone to try to compete with Peary's time.

The most sobering thought was just how many accomplished explorers had actually died up there. Back in Antarctica, it's hard to believe that Captain Scott was actually the last person to perish on a South Pole expedition, way back in 1912. Tragically, fatalities in the frozen North are far more common, with thin ice, polar bears, and the cold all claiming the lives of Arctic explorers in recent years. If we were going to succeed, and most importantly be safe, we had to be far better organised, fitter, and mentally prepared than our somewhat cavalier approach we had adopted for the South Pole.

The first call I made was to the Canadian, Paul Landry, who had been our guide in Antarctica. Paul is a warm, softly spoken, driven man with a wicked sense of humor, and we had got on extremely well during our seven-hundred-mile ski to the South Pole. With his long blond ponytail, weatherbeaten face, and squinty eyes, he looks as if he would be more at home in a Scandinavian rock band than on an ice cap. But looks can be deceiving and Paul is one of the best in the business.

Paul had made his home in Iqaluit on Baffin Island, high in the Canadian Arctic, which experiences some of the most hostile conditions on the planet. There he lived with his wife, Matty McNair, their two children, and a team of Eskimo dogs, running an outdoor adventure company called Northwinds, which specialized in polar training courses.

Having been to the South Pole twice and the North Pole three times, Paul had more poles to his name than anyone else in history. His most impressive expedition had been in 2000 when, along with his close friend and fellow Iqaluit resident, Paul Crowley, he reached the North Pole with aluminium dog sleds in just forty-three days. Matty's track record was equally impressive, having led the first-ever women's expedition to the North Pole in 1997 and having skied to the South Pole the same year we did.

Having served my polar apprenticeship under Paul in Antarctica, and with the best part of a decade of mountaineering experience now under my belt, I felt confident enough in my own ability to give serious consideration to leading my own party to the North Pole. When it came to driving dogs, however, I, like Peary had once been, was a complete novice.

I therefore wanted Paul, with all his dog-sledging credentials and intimate knowledge of Peary history, to be my co-leader. As it had been his words in Antarctica that had originally sparked the whole idea in my mind, it seemed only right. Paul said he would be thrilled to join me, and much to my relief he thought my plans, while very ambitious, were by no means impossible. He also said he would be happy for us to use his dogs.

"Tom," he said to me on the phone, "you do realize this expedition is going to create quite a storm? There are many people out there, particularly in the U.K., who are so emotionally involved in the Peary debate that if we do succeed, some of them are going to be seriously pissed off. Prepare yourself for some fireworks!"

I always realized that there was going to be some controversy, but that was one of the appeals of this expedition. This trip had so much more to it than my previous ones because for once the focus wasn't so much on those of us taking part, but more on this formidable explorer from the past, Commander Robert Peary. The expedition was designed to get people talking about Peary again and to improve our understanding of the way he travelled. I hoped that by testing his travel speeds, the argument at the heart of the debate, we would be in a position to prove whether or not he could have reached the Pole in the time he claimed so that the century-old controversy of the North Pole might finally be put to rest. It was also this strong connection with history that I hoped just might convince Barclays Capital to become our title sponsor.

The expedition had to be authentic and resemble Peary's as closely as possible. By building exact replicas of Peary's sleds, from similar materials to those he had used and of the same dimensions and design, our arguments would carry more weight.

One of my aims was to test the performance, speed, and sturdiness of the Peary sled to find out if a small dog team was able to pull it for hundreds of miles across the frozen ocean in the time he claimed. Even though most modern North Pole attempts had started from Ward Hunt Island, my intention was to set off from Peary's departure point at Cape Columbia, thirty miles farther east along Ellesmere Island's coast.

To make an objective judgment on Peary's disputed navigation methods, I felt we should try to use ancient route-finding techniques whenever possible and navigate by the sun, shadow, wind, sastrugi,★ watch, and compass. We had used these methods throughout our South Pole expedition to plot a straight course across the featureless white desert.

Unlike Peary, however, we weren't experts when it came to celestial navigation and so would use the Global Positioning System (GPS), similar to the satellite navigation devices found in most modern cars. This we would turn on once every evening to establish our position in the way that Peary would have done with his sextant and astrological tables.

Some details, however, were much harder to replicate. Peary had set off with twenty-four men, 133 dogs and nineteen sleds, but there was no way a potential sponsor would ever consider putting up the enormous sum of money necessary to get such a large logistical operation off the ground. The Peary System of sending support divisions back at equal intervals along the route meant that the weight of his fully-laden sleds

★ Ridges of wind-blown snow up to eighty feet long and six feet high that align themselves in the direction of the prevailing wind.

never exceeded six hundred pounds. We had to do the same if we were going to stand any chance of getting there within thirty-seven days.

The only viable alternative was to arrange for a Twin Otter ski plane to lay caches of food and fuel at each of the locations from where Peary had sent his four support divisions back to the *Roosevelt*. Without the luxury of regular airdrops, most of the dog-sledging expeditions since Peary's day have taken two months to reach the Pole because they have relied on heavy-duty, lumbering sleds weighing well over a thousand pounds. To have four aerial resupplies would not be cheap, but I was hoping that our nimble, relatively lightweight sleds would give us that vital edge, just as they had done for Peary.

When I asked Paul how he would feel about building igloos along the route, he said it would take us years to gain the igloo-building skills of Peary's Inuit, and unless I felt like spending hours every evening toiling away with ice saws and snow blocks, we were better off sleeping in a tent.

We also discussed if it was worth wearing traditional Inuit furs, but as it was Peary's speeds we were testing, something our choice of clothing would have no bearing over, we came to the conclusion that we should wear modern garments, primarily because they were much easier to get hold of. The fact that most Inuit hunters today still choose to wear caribou parkas and polar bear trousers, even though their modern Gore-Tex and Goose-Down equivalents are now widely available in the Arctic, shows that in terms of warmth and practicality, there is actually very little difference between the two.

In terms of diet, Peary gave his men a food ration weighing 2¼ pounds per day, consisting mainly of pemmican,* chocolate, and cookies. Although we lived off the latest expedition foods in Antarctica, our food and calorie intake was very similar to Peary's, and so we decided to stick to the expedition diet we knew. I was more than happy with this decision because I would have found it very difficult to swap our assortment of

---

*A nutritious, fatty cake made by mixing pounded dried beef with beef fat, sugar, and raisins.

tasty freeze-dried evening meals and Sicilian salami sticks for some unappetizing turn-of-the-century grab. Some provisions, however, such as breakfast muesli, chocolate, biscuits, tea, coffee, and powdered milk, were unchanged from Peary's day.

I would have loved to have had the option of making the return journey back from the Pole, but the effects of climate change, in particular the earlier annual breakup of the pack ice, have already had such a devastating impact on the fragile frozen sea that such a trip is now far too dangerous. Despite several attempts, only one expedition by the brilliant Canadian-Russian duo Richard Weber and Misha Malakhov in 1995 has successfully completed a return trip to the Pole since the days of Cook and Peary.

Scientific studies and NASA satellite images have shown that the thin film of ice that floats on the surface of the Arctic Ocean has reduced from an average thickness of twelve feet in 1909 to less than eight feet today, increasing the likelihood of the ice pack breaking up earlier in the season. During the last century the ice pack's surface area has halved, wiping more than a million square miles of multiyear ice off the map forever. With more thin ice and open water than ever before, modern-day explorers have to be prepared for longer detours and more frequent delays than in the past. Dr. Fritz Koerner, one of the world's leading climatologists and a member of Wally Herbert's Trans-Arctic expedition in 1968–1969, recently said of today's Arctic Ocean, "I look on it as a different world."

Paul felt that we were therefore well within our right to use inflatable kayaks to get across these new areas of open water. Peary actually toyed with the idea of using Inuit-designed kayaks to cross the Big Lead back in 1909, but he had no experience of using them so decided against it, particularly as he was by then well into his fifties and not as fit and agile as he once had been.

In recent years, a number of North Pole expeditions have used either sleds that floated or sleds that doubled as canoes to combat the increased problem of open water. Even though the ice conditions today are completely different from what they were in 1909, I felt that using kayaks would still give us an unfair advantage and, more importantly, give ammunition to the anti-Peary camp that would no doubt accuse us of cutting corners. Using kayaks would weaken our argument significantly, and we decided that if we came to an impassable lead, like Peary, we would either have to wait for it to close or for the water to refreeze.

Conditions in the Arctic are changing so rapidly that many in the exploration world believe that within a couple of years the ice will be so precariously thin that it will no longer be possible even to make the one-way journey to the Pole, never mind the return leg. Even more alarmingly, NASA estimates that the Arctic Ocean will be entirely ice-free in summer as early as 2013.

The only option for polar explorers these days is to be picked up at the Pole and hope that there is a pan of solid multiyear ice large enough for a Twin Otter to land on. Nevertheless, re-creating Peary's journey from Cape Columbia to the Pole would still be one of the most significant expeditions of the last few years and go a long way to establishing the feasibility of Peary's claims.

The key to the Peary System was its efficiency. Much in the same way that Sherpa teams are sent out ahead to find the best route through Mount Everest's Khumbu Icefall, Peary's route-finding teams were given the job of blazing the trail for the main party to follow. Paul and I figured that a team of five would be the most efficient, with one person skiing a few hundred yards ahead of the main party to find the best route through the pressure ridges and around open water.

We would take two sleds, with two dog drivers travelling alongside each one, providing the extra manpower to manoeuvre the sleds over difficult pressure ridges. One of the photographs from Peary's expedition shows four men struggling to lift a sled over a monster of a pressure ridge. Provided our two sleds stuck close together, our system of one skier and four dog drivers would enable us to deal with similar obstacles in the same way, with up to four men on hand to do the lifting. And just as Peary had done, there would be eight dogs per sled.

The Polar Party

I had learned from both my experience in Antarctica and my various mountaineering expeditions that team selection was the single most important decision I would make as leader. Indeed, Peary's perception was, "A season in the Arctic is a great test of character. One may know a man better after six months with him beyond the Arctic Circle than after a lifetime of acquaintance in cities. There is a something – I know not what to call it – in frozen spaces, that brings a man face to face with himself and his companions; if he is a man, the man comes out; and, if he is a cur, the cur shows as quickly."

Paul felt it was worth having another experienced dog driver on the team and asked if I would be happy if Matty joined us. Matty had been leading a separate team at the same time as our South Pole expedition, and our paths had crossed on various occasions before, during, and after our time in Antarctica. I had initially been struck by just how small she was and reasoned that what she lacked in brawn, she must more than make up for in mental determination. I found her to be kind, softly spoken, and with a real passion for a wide range of outdoor pursuits from kayaking to climbing.

Matty grew up in Pennsylvania, but the American life had not been for her so she moved north of the border to work as an instructor for Outward Bound. It was there that she met Paul, and it wasn't long before she took up Canadian citizenship. Although Matty had never driven dogs on the Arctic Ocean, she still had thousands of dog-sledging miles under her belt, and I thought that her quiet single-mindedness would be the perfect foil to Paul's more outgoing personality.

Women have been very poorly represented in Arctic exploration. Jo, Peary's wife, was the first non-native woman to spend time in the frozen north and probably the first to overwinter north of the Arctic Circle. Never having been on an expedition with a member of the opposite sex before, I initially had reservations about having Matty on the team. With the remaining positions likely to be filled by men, she would clearly be the odd one out.

There was also the question of whether her slight frame would give us the power we needed to get the sleds through difficult terrain. On the other hand, skiing to the North Pole in 1997 had given Matty an intimate understanding of the treacherous icescape of the Arctic Ocean, making her the ideal person to fill the role of the route-finding skier out ahead of the main party.

I wanted to fill the other two positions with strong characters who I knew would be able to perform and stay positive when the pressure was really on. Over the years I've learned that a successful expedition isn't necessarily packed with world-class mountaineers or cross-country skiers. Sometimes I've deliberately chosen people with no relevant technical experience but who showed a positive outlook and a willingness to be part of a team. I find it vitally important to make all team members feel included in the planning as well as during the expedition itself. Skills such as repairing a stove, tying knots, and driving dogs can all be learned, but being a team player, committed to seeing a project through to the end, is something that cannot be taught, only harnessed.

Disagreements amongst individuals fester on a long expedition and can easily lose all proportion, particularly when there are lots of big egos about. Polar history is littered with tales of expeditions that have come to grief when seemingly minor issues, often as petty as who had the largest helping at dinner, explode into spectacular bust-ups. My experience has been that however tough things become, if people are able to laugh at their own inevitable misfortunes, and somehow retain a sense of humor, a strong sense of camaraderie and harmony will naturally develop.

The next person I asked was George Wells. George is the most positive person I know – a vital attribute for days confined in a storm-bound tent. We met at Bristol University and have been climbing partners for years. During all the years I've known him, I've never seen him lose his temper, even in the most stressful of situations, and I can trust him implicitly.

George had been part of my expeditions to the Andes in 1997 and Kyrgyzstan in 2000, and although he had no previous polar experience, he had proven himself as a strong climber and more than capable of looking after himself in the cold. We often joked that after all those cumulative months living in tents, we had probably spent more nights together than we had with our respective girlfriends. We had been through a lot together over the years, including the time when his brother Fergus was struck down with altitude sickness while we were climbing in the Alps, started frothing at the mouth, lost consciousness, and had to be airlifted off the mountain. It was a miracle that he didn't die.

George had not been a part of the South Pole expedition in 2002. Having just set up a property-development business in London, it would have been commercial suicide to take three months' leave. Two years later, with Hartog Hutton Developments now well established, George agreed to join the North Pole team with all his customary enthusiasm.

The person I most wanted to fill the fifth and final place was someone whom I had barely known a year. Andrew Gerber emigrated from South Africa to London when he was seventeen, although you would never know it from his cut-glass public school accent. He's one of the most competitive people I've ever met. I was introduced to Andrew through a mutual friend back in 2002 at a time when we were still a man short for the South Pole. He had never been on an expedition before but was an experienced rower, yachtsman, and skier, and when he told me that for years he had harbored dreams of going to the South Pole, I took a risk and asked if he would like to join the team.

It may seem strange to pick someone for such a major venture as a polar expedition without knowing much about them, but Andrew had something about him, and I just sensed that he would fit into the team perfectly. It proved to be an inspired decision. It didn't take him long to pick up the technical side of things, but what impressed me most during our time on the ice together was his physical strength, unlimited reserves of energy, and the fact that no matter how tough things got, he never once complained.

When I told him I wanted him to be part of my North Pole plans, he could barely contain his excitement. He had just started a new role as a management consultant for the estate agents Bradford and Bingley and felt that if he gave his new employers enough notice, they might be willing to give him ten weeks' extended leave to go to the North Pole. He and some university friends were also looking for a new housemate, and as I still hadn't found anywhere to live in London since returning from Verbier, we agreed to move in together. It wasn't long before our rented house in Battersea became the official expedition HQ.

February 2005 was set as the expedition start date, which would give us just over eighteen months to raise the funds, get into shape, put all the expedition logistics together, and for George, Andrew and me to become proficient at dogsledging. As the only way we were going to be able to do this was to team up with Paul and Matty in Baffin Island, three weeks were set aside in February 2004 for our first major training exercise. The chief expedition cost was going to be our four resupplies and ski plane pickup from the Pole. Once the flights to Canada, training trips, insurance, food, Paul and Matty's expenses, equipment, and other odds and ends had been factored in, the total budget came to two hundred thousand pounds, a frightening sum to have to raise.

Mark Dearlove delivered on the promise he made to me in Verbier and invited me to dinner at his London home in June 2003. It was a way of introducing me to some of his colleagues at Barclays Capital and to gauge the level of interest within the company. What I hadn't expected was that two of the men sitting at the dinner table, Bob Diamond and Jerry del Missier, would be the bank's president and vice president respectively and amongst the most influential men in the City of London, as well as Sir Richard Dearlove, Mark's uncle and the Director General of MI6.

During coffee, Mark rigged up his plasma TV screen so that I could show the dinner guests some slides from my recent South Pole expedition. Feeling very out of place amongst such distinguished company, I nervously stuttered my way through the presentation before answering some questions. "Tell Bob and Jerry where you're going next," said Mark excitedly. As I revealed my North Pole intentions, Mark interrupted me and said, "And I think the bank should sponsor him."

I felt almost embarrassed that Mark was touting the expedition so blatantly, but he was the best sponsorship agent I could ever have wished for. In most of my previous dealings with potential backers, I thought I was doing well if I managed to line up a meeting with a company's marketing department.

Of course, there was no guarantee that Barclays Capital would say yes, but just to be able to sit down face-to-face with the two principal decision makers at the bank was an incredible opportunity, and I knew that this was my best hope of ever getting the expedition off the ground.

Over the course of the summer, monthly meetings were set up at Barclays Capital's offices in Canary Wharf. Being Canadian, incredibly active, and an outdoor sports enthusiast himself, Jerry already had a passion for cold pursuits and chose to oversee the bank's potential involvement in the expedition himself. Jerry believed that were we to beat Peary's thirty-seven-day time to the North Pole, the expedition would generate significant press attention on both sides of the Atlantic.

Barclays Capital had recently opened an office in New York, and if our clothing, sleds, and tent were suitably branded with their logos, they would get fantastic exposure in their two key markets whenever photos appeared in newspapers and on television.

Unlike every other sponsorship deal I had been involved with, however, the target audience for the marketing campaign wasn't the man on the street but in fact the sponsor's staff. "If our employees can see that we're supporting something as exciting, out of the ordinary, and groundbreaking as your expedition," Jerry told me, "it would inspire and motivate them in more ways than any team-building exercise we could ever put them through."

If Barclays Capital did decide to finance the trip, Jerry wanted the staff to feel a part of the expedition right from the outset, almost as if they were going to the Pole themselves. We discussed the feasibility of using the latest satellite communications equipment to send daily e-mails to the entire eight-thousand-strong workforce. It was a novel approach to sponsorship, and certainly very different from the motives of Peary's backers who expected to have new geographical landmarks named after them. But I thought it was brilliant. Apart from anything else, I knew how much of an inspiration it would be to us to know that we would have all those thousands of bankers following our progress and willing us on.

In October I had a conference call with Barclays Capital's marketing department. The words I heard would shape my life for the next eighteen months, and my heart was beating like crazy. Whether the expedition became a reality or not boiled down to whether a handful of people sitting round a table, most of whom I had never met before, chose to vote yes or no. It was as simple as that. I took a deep breath, trying to remain calm. "Tom, I've got some good news for you. We've decided to sponsor the expedition. Many congratulations."

I couldn't believe my ears and asked them to repeat the news – slowly. It was so incredible to hear that my dream wasn't going to remain a dream, it was actually turning into the real thing. I didn't know whether to laugh or cry. Apparently while we'd been chewing our fingernails, not knowing whether they were going to back us or not, Barclays Capital had been crunching the numbers and found that by the time all their internal and external marketing costs had been factored in, the total budget had rocketed to almost five hundred thousand pounds. Yet it was a commitment they were willing to make.

I suddenly felt a huge burden of responsibility on my shoulders. By making this commitment, Barclays Capital were putting their faith in the expedition and in me. I couldn't let them down. The only way to repay them was by being totally focussed on reaching the North Pole safely, with my team intact and as close to Peary's time as we could get.

I could barely contain my excitement and wanted to tell everyone. For sponsorship to be guaranteed so far in advance was a real boost to the team and gave us a fantastic platform to prepare meticulously for the challenges ahead. Despite that, I was so paranoid of a rival expedition stealing our plans and heading to the Pole a year before us (my fears no doubt exacerbated by reading about the bitter Peary–Cook debate and my experience with the South Pole expedition when someone had tried to poach our sponsor) that I convinced the bank to delay announcing the Barclays Capital Ultimate North Expedition to the media for another twelve months.

The day after sponsorship was confirmed I was at a reception at Buckingham Palace to "celebrate the achievements of British pioneers." I had no idea what I had done to get on the guest list and felt very out of place as I rubbed shoulders with pop stars, Hollywood actors, and sporting celebrities. As I turned to leave I found myself face-to-face with the Queen. We shook hands and I bowed hesitantly.

"Good evening, Your Majesty," I said, unsure of what to say.

"Now tell me, what do you do . . . Mr. Avery?" she asked, peering at my name tag.

"I just go on long walks, climb mountains, that sort of thing. As long as there's snow around I'm very happy."

"And where do you intend to go to next?"

One too many glasses of the Royal Household's champagne must have passed my lips by that stage of the evening and I had quite forgotten that I was supposed to be keeping my plans top secret. "I'm planning to take dogs across the Arctic Ocean to the North Pole, Ma'am."

"You are quite mad," she replied. "That strikes me as being a totally ridiculous thing to want to do." With that, and a wry smile, she walked off.

Canine Induction

The sixteen Eskimo dogs★ we would be taking to the North Pole were the same breed as Peary had used on his expeditions. As I had turned the pages of Arctic history, I had learned that these amazing dogs, which are part of the husky family and can weigh in excess of 120 pounds, were the key to Peary's success – and so they would be for us. "It's all about the dogs," I kept telling myself. As Peary had put it, "They are sturdy, magnificent animals. There may be larger dogs than these, there may be handsomer dogs; but I doubt it. Other dogs may work as well or travel as fast and far when fully fed; but there is no dog in the world that can work so long in the lowest temperatures on practically nothing to eat."

The breed's origins can be traced back thousands of years. As the great

★Even though the word "Eskimo" has been largely been removed from almost all aspects of Canadian life, the Eskimo dog is still the Canadian Kennel Club's official name for the breed.

glaciers of the last ice age retreated from northern Europe and Russia, the inhabitants of the Central Asian steppes began migrating northward. These were primitive, spear-wielding hunters who followed the herds of woolly mammoths and reindeer that had moved north with the warming climate as the ice sheets disappeared.

An ethnic group called the Sami populated the tundra of northern Scandinavia and western Siberia, while the more adventurous Eskimo people crossed the Bering Strait into North America, some making it as far east as Greenland. It's worth mentioning that the name Eskimo originates from the ancient word for "eater of raw meat." Understandably, many find the name highly derogatory, and today the Eskimo are known as the Inuit, literally "the people."

Anthropologists now believe that unlike the ancestors of the Red Indians, Aztecs and Incas of North and South America who had crossed the Bering Strait at least ten thousand years ago at a time when Russia and Alaska were still connected by a land bridge, the Inuit arrived by boat as recently as 2,000 BC. By this time, vast forests had sprung up throughout northern Canada. This natural barrier effectively cut the Inuit off from the rest of the continent, forcing them to adapt to the harsh environment of the Arctic.

These resourceful people adapted to their new environment thanks to a variety of ingenious inventions including the kayak, made by stretching animal hides over a simple driftwood frame the Inuit could navigate the region's numerous waterways. These fast-moving, highly manoeuverable hunting machines enabled them to pursue much larger prey such as walrus and even whales using flint-tipped harpoons.

The Inuit were nomadic, living in easily assembled animal-hide tents in the summer and snow-block igloos in the winter. They wore sealskin boots, caribou jackets called parkas, and polar bear trousers to protect them from the intense cold. So accustomed did they become to life in the Arctic that centuries later, Western explorers would eventually learn that the only way to survive in the Far North was to embrace the Inuit way of life and hunt the local wildlife, live in snow-block igloos, wear animal furs, and travel with sleds pulled by Eskimo dogs.

Although the Eskimo dog's appearance closely resembles that of the North American wolf and there are frequent reports of interbreeding, they're not as closely related as one might think. There's no doubt, though, that they still have one foot in the wild, and their ability to locate seal breathing holes in the ice along with their extraordinary powers of navigation in the worst polar storm made the Eskimo dog the perfect hunting partner. They were bred to pull heavy loads in the most extreme conditions, and dogs that didn't pull their weight were left by the wayside. The result of centuries of natural selection was a breed of incredibly powerful and iron-willed canine athletes with a total devotion to their human masters.

The pioneer of modern dog sledging is generally recognized as the Englishman Edward Parry, who used Eskimo dog teams during his search for the Northwest Passage in the early 1820s. But with many subsequent expeditions choosing instead to manhaul their sleds, it was not until Peary developed his Peary System that the true value of these dogs to Arctic exploration was fully realized. He wrote, "It is an absolute certainty that it [the North Pole] would still be undiscovered but for the Eskimo dog to furnish traction power for our sleds . . . enabling us to carry supplies where nothing else could carry them." Peary's words were mirrored by the Norwegian Roald Amundsen who used Eskimo dogs to discover the South Pole in 1911. "Dogs first, and dogs all the time!" he exclaimed.

Eskimo dog teams were used by scientific bases in Antarctica for much of the twentieth century to transport men and equipment across the continent. They often proved more reliable than mechanized transport, particularly over rough terrain, and although a small number of seals had to be killed to provide food for the dogs, their environmental impact was considered far less detrimental than that caused by heavy machinery. In addition to being much more practical than snow mobiles, dogs were a great source of companionship for the men in the bases, particularly during the long dark winters.

Everything changed in 1994, however, when the dozen or so governments responsible for the scientific operations in Antarctica signed a treaty banning the introduction and use of all nonindigenous animals on the frozen continent. The official line was that the debilitating disease, canine distemper, might be spread from dogs to seals.

This drastic decision made by men in suits thousands of miles away caused uproar amongst the scientific community, as there hadn't been a single recorded incident of canine distemper being transferred to the seal population in more than a century of close interaction on the continent. The result is that the only way to reach the South Pole on foot today is by pulling your own sled. In contrast, as the North Pole lies in international waters, there are no such restrictions to worry about on the Arctic Ocean.

A catastrophic distemper epidemic in the early 1960s wiped out the vast majority of the twenty thousand Eskimo dogs living in northern Canada, spelling disaster for the many thousands of Inuit still living off the land. The Canadian government decided the time was right to relocate the Inuit into Western-style communities with quality housing, electricity, and running water. As the traditional Inuit way of life died out, there was no longer any need for dogs.

Sadly, there are barely three hundred of these loyal, playful, phenomenally powerful animals alive today, most of which are used for recreation in Paul and Matty's hometown of Iqaluit, just two hundred miles south of the Arctic Circle. Waiting for us there when we arrived in Baffin Island in February 2004 to begin our dog-sledging induction were sixteen fit and healthy Eskimo dogs, ready to make fools of George, Andrew, and me.

BY THE TIME THE PLANE FINALLY TOUCHED DOWN IN IQALUIT, IT felt as if we had arrived at the last place on earth. There was literally nothing to see for the entire duration of the three-hour flight from Canada's capital, Ottawa, apart from trees, frozen lakes, and snow, and for the final two hours, just snow. The politest way to describe Iqaluit's brightly coloured buildings would be functional, and from the air the place looked like a giant toy town, in sharp contrast to the monochrome Arctic landscape.

The airport terminal had no covered walkway to shield passengers from the elements, and as we scurried across the tarmac in temperatures of −25°C George turned to me and shouted through the biting wind, "How could anyone live up here?" And, this was apparently mild for the time of year.

Iqaluit (literally "Place of Fish") is the main settlement on Baffin Island, located at the western end of the 150-mile-long Frobisher Bay, first explored by Martin Frobisher during an early search for the Northwest Passage.

Ever since Columbus had tried to reach the lucrative markets of Asia by sailing from east to west around the globe (he failed when America got in the way), Britain had searched for a passage that would lead to the Spice Islands without having to make the time-consuming and often treacherous journey around southern Africa's Cape of Good Hope or Cape Horn at the bottom of South America. This mythical channel, which many believed lay to the north of the Americas, was the Holy Grail of shipping routes, and the Admiralty in London believed that the discovery of the Northwest Passage would secure Great Britain's position as the world's seafaring superpower.

Early attempts in Tudor times by the likes of John Cabot, Sir Martin Frobisher, and Henry Hudson barely made any inroads. Then, in 1616, William Baffin (after whom Baffin Island is named) followed the west coast of Greenland farther north than anyone before him, discovering Lancaster Sound, Smith Sound, and the ice-choked inlets of southern Ellesmere Island. Unbeknown to him, these two deep, navigable sounds would later become the gateways to the Northwest Passage and the North Pole respectively. It was a masterful piece of seamanship, far ahead of its time, but Baffin's voyage was to be the last British success story in the Arctic for the best part of two hundred years as ship after ship disappeared without a trace.

Not until the end of the Napoleonic Wars was interest in the Northwest Passage rekindled. A victorious Royal Navy was now flexing its muscles again and willing to pour resources into further exploration of the Far North. Apart from anything else, with Europe now at peace and Napoleon behind bars, the Admiralty had to find something for its officers and ships to do. Prize money was even up for grabs, with the government offering a reward of twenty thousand pounds (over a million pounds in today's money) to the first person to reach the Pacific via the Northwest Passage. A further one thousand pounds was offered for the first successful crossing of each degree of latitude north of 80°N.

In the first half of the nineteenth century a number of British ships ventured deep into the Northwest Passage, most of these voyages being organised by the Second Secretary of the Admiralty Sir John Barrow. Throughout the 1800s, hundreds of ships penetrated the farthest corners of the Arctic. Many of the early polar explorers, lured by the romance of exploration and the promise of fame and fortune on their return, did little more than leave their names (and in many cases their bones) on the map.

This was an age of incredible bravery and often pure lunacy, when explorers were judged as much by their geographical achievements as by the way they got themselves out of sticky situations. Nevertheless, these journeys were to prove crucial in unraveling the mysteries of the Arctic so that one day future generations could claim the prizes of the Northwest Passage and the North Pole.

One of the most significant early Northwest Passage missions was Edward Parry's onboard the *Helca* in 1819, which covered more than half the distance between Greenland and the Bering Strait.

Overland expeditions through northern Canada were also launched, John Franklin leading a particularly gruesome trek along the Coppermine River in 1820 during which he lost eleven of his twenty men as the team slowly starved to death. His ramshackle team was so hungry that they were forced to eat lichen and even their leather boots. There was also a murder amongst the party and rumors of cannibalism. The sheer horror of the journey, and the fact that Franklin somehow survived made him the most famous man in England, the press nicknaming him "the man who ate his boots."

THE MAJORITY OF IQALUIT'S EIGHT THOUSAND RESIDENTS ARE Inuit, relocated after the distemper outbreak. The town has a real frontier feel to it. Iqaluit is the capital of Nunavut, Canada's largest and newest territory, covering eight hundred thousand square miles of Arctic tundra. Everyone in Iqaluit drives large trucks, and the street signs are displayed in both English and the hieroglyphic-like symbols of the local dialect, Inuktitut.

Paul and Matty's house, and our base for our first few nights, was down by the shore, and like all the local architecture, it was built on wooden stilts to protect it from the permafrost. The view from their sitting room down the length of bay and to the craggy hills beyond was quite spectacular. The adventure playground that stretched all the way to the far horizon was their back garden, and it was easy to appreciate why they had chosen this utterly unique place to be their home.

The waters of Frobisher Bay are frozen solid for eight months of the year, and it was precisely for this reason that we had chosen to go there. Thanks to one of the largest tidal variations in the world, the sea ice along the coast is a chaotic mass of constantly shifting ice blocks, making it the perfect training ground for driving dogs over the notorious pressure ridges of the Arctic Ocean.

The terrain and the bitterly cold temperatures would be the closest we could get to simulating the conditions at the roof of the world without actually having to go up there. Our plan was to spend a couple of days learning the basics before setting out with Paul, Matty, and the dogs on a two-week, 250-mile mini-expedition across the sea ice of Frobisher Bay and up over the snow-covered hills of the Meta Incognita Peninsula.

Squadrons of noisy black ravens circled overhead as we made our way down to the shore. The dogs were arranged in two lines, chained to an oil drum on the frozen bay, not far from some rusting shipping containers and an overturned fishing boat. As we approached, they howled and jumped around uncontrollably, one thick-set dog (who I later learned was called Ootah) frantically running around in circles and almost choking himself on his chain.

In all the mayhem, a second dog, Denali, slipped her collar and came sprinting over to greet us like lost friends. They were much bigger than I was expecting, similar in size to an Alsatian but with much broader shoulders. It was pretty disconcerting to think that these hysterical animals would be leading us across the Arctic Ocean to the North Pole and that our fate would be in their hands. We were all feeling slightly apprehensive.

The plan was to take the dogs on a lap around a small island in the bay to stretch their legs and give us a taste of what was to come. On the expedition itself we would be skiing alongside the sleds but for now, as they were empty, we would be sitting on them to act as ballast. The problem was that the sleds consisted of little more than a sheet of plywood nailed to some planks, and there was absolutely nothing to hold on to.

By the time we got the dogs harnessed up, they were so overexcited and desperate to get going that they appeared almost deranged. Amundsen confirmed their eagerness to pull when he wrote, "Strange as it may seem, I can assert that these animals love the harness. Although they must know that it means hard work, they all show signs of the greatest rapture at the sight of it."

There was a real sense of impending doom as we climbed onboard the rickety timber crafts. Paul and I were the first to go. As Paul jumped on the back, he cried out, "Pull the anchor!" At the very moment I yanked the heavy iron hook out of the snow we were propelled across the bay like a fighter jet taking off from an aircraft carrier. I clung on for dear life as we clattered into what seemed like every block of ice in the bay, totally out of control.

"Is it usually this hairy?" I shouted back to Paul. No reply. I turned around to see him rolling in the snow ten yards behind the sled.

"What the hell do I do now?!" I asked myself, alarmed that the one person on the sled who knew what he was doing had already been thrown overboard. It was like some sort of Arctic bucking bronco with the challenge to stay on for as long as possible. Up ahead, the dogs, who had stopped yapping as soon as we had blasted off, were going at full pelt and taking me out into the great white yonder.

"Wohhh!" I screamed, remembering the one bit of dog lingo that we had been taught so far. Ootah and a couple of dogs looked back at me, but this was not their master giving the orders and they just ignored me. I decided to flick the whip at them. My first strike was textbook, cracking right above their heads, but it only proceeded to make them run faster still. The second was not so effective and I ended up with coils of sealskin hide around my neck.

No sooner had I grabbed the anchor to try to slow us down than we slammed into yet another ice boulder and I was flung off. Thankfully, the anchor bit into the snow on its own accord and the sled came to a halt. Paul was laughing as we ran up to retrieve the team. "Welcome to the wild, crazy sport of dog sledging!" he said.

We weren't the only ones having problems, and a hundred yards back we could see Andrew and George struggling to right their capsized sled. Meanwhile, Matty, armed with a whip, was busy trying to break up a dogfight. I was beginning to understand what Peary meant when he said, "The art of guiding a team of lively Eskimo dogs by the voice and raw-hide whip . . . is something which requires long time and patience to master."

Eventually, we managed to get it together. Once the two sleds had left the confines of the town, the dogs got into a steady rhythm, and all was quiet as we floated across a thin layer of fresh snow out across the bay. It was such a joy to experience one of the purest forms of polar travel that can have changed little in the four thousand years since the Inuit populated this frigid world. I had never felt such peace and freedom in all my time in the great outdoors. For the dogs, it was as if they were answering their call to the wild. The only noises were the pattering of paws and the gentle whoosh of the sled runners as the sleds carved through the powder like off-piste skiers.

Paul and Matty told us to encourage the dogs as much as possible with commands like, "Hup, hup, hup," "Hike, hike, hike," and "Come on then, Ernie, get up there, thataboy, hup hup hup." Not only was it important to keep the animals motivated but the dogs were getting used to our voices. Those three weeks were as much about us getting to know the dogs as they were about the dogs getting to know us. Only by spending time together would we be able to earn their trust and respect, without which we would have no hope of ever getting close to the North Pole.

That evening, George, Andrew, and I headed off to the local watering hole, the Navigator Inn, to get out of Paul and Matty's hair for a few hours and pat ourselves on the back for getting through our first day of driving dogs more or less unscathed. We could console ourselves that we weren't the first novice dog-sledders to have had a rough initiation to the sport. Fridtjof Nansen, one of the greatest explorers of them all, was dragged unceremoniously across the ice on his dogsledging debut as his hapless instructor looked on. Nansen wrote, "I tugged, swore, and tried everything I could think of, but all to no purpose." When he tried to exert his authority with a whip, the dogs "jumped to both sides and only tore on the faster."

We were enjoying a quiet drink at the bar when we overheard a conversation that sent shivers down our spines. Four locals were discussing a harrowing polar bear attack that had taken place only four months earlier. Apparently, a local caribou hunter called Kootoo Shaw had been mauled by a young adult male bear as he lay asleep in his tent on the far side of Frobisher Bay. After taking an idle swat at his tent, the bear then proceeded to jump up and down on its hapless victim, clawing at his back and tearing at his scalp. On hearing Shaw's screams, his hunting companion in the neighboring tent woke up and was able to shoot the bear dead before it could inflict the fatal wound. Incredibly, Shaw survived but his body was peppered with deep lacerations and puncture wounds. More than three hundred stitches were needed to reattach his scalp.

The three of us were very aware of the threat posed by polar bears, but to hear such a graphic tale brought home just how dangerous these animals could be. The most worrying aspect of it was that the attack took place on the uninhabited Meta Incognita Peninsula – the place we were heading for on our training expedition. At the bar Andrew picked up some leaflets entitled *Safety in Polar Bear Country*. A mother and her two cubs had been seen rummaging around in the town's rubbish dump the week before, and the Parks Canada Agency clearly felt they should warn Iqaluit's residents what to do if they came face-to-face with a hungry bear.

The leaflets made good bedtime reading – they offered some helpful suggestions on what to do if we came across an agitated polar bear. "Act nonthreatening," it read, "Avoid direct eye contact. Stay in a group." The words "do not run" appeared four times on the leaflet. One of the most alarming recommendations was that if a bear happened to charge, you should, "stand your ground and be prepared to fight." Rocks, chunks of ice, and skis were recommended as potential weapons.

As soon as we left Paul and Matty's house we were effectively entering the bear's realm. They may be the top predator in the Arctic food chain, but their natural prey, the seal, is not that abundant in the Far North, meaning polar adventurers are a potential meal for a hungry bear. We would of course be taking a rifle out on the ice with us, but it would only be used as a last resort.

While a part of me wanted to see this beautiful creature in its natural habitat, I was also filled with complete terror at the thought of being attacked by a nine-foot-tall, thousand-pound bear with claws the size of kitchen knives.

We set off for the Meta Incognita Peninsula with food and fuel for two weeks. It took us a full day to cross the frozen waters of Frobisher Bay as we stuck close to the shore to practice travelling through the rough tidal ice. With the sleds now fully loaded, we skied alongside the sleds as there was no room to sit down.

On the far side of the bay was a wooden hut, which would be our accommodation for Night 1. From then on we would be in tents. The problem was that the hut could only sleep four and, as there were five of us, it meant someone sleeping outside. George volunteered to take the tent and I offered to keep him company. The horrors that befell Kootoo Shaw were still fresh in my memory, so before we turned in for the night I asked Paul what we should do if a bear came into camp. "Oh, you'll be fine. And besides, if there's a bear in the area the dogs will start doing this deep, throaty growl noise and we'll all know about it. Sleep well!" We were far from convinced.

A few hours later I was tucked up in my sleeping bag fast asleep when George started shaking me. His voice was trembling as he whispered, "Tom, I want you to be very still and very quiet, but there's something outside."

"Very funny," I replied, "I can't hear a thing. Go back to sleep."

Two minutes later he shook me again. "Did you hear that?"

"Hear what?"

"There's a fucking bear right outside the tent," he said, in a very slow, high-pitched whisper.

This time I could definitely hear footsteps. We both sat bolt upright in our sleeping bags and listened, bodies tense and hearts racing. Our ears strained for every sound. Not a word was spoken and we didn't move for a full twenty minutes. All the while, the intermittent crunching of snow continued, sometimes moving off into the distance, only to return closer again. Any second now I was expecting a big, white, hairy paw to pierce the tent wall. When the dogs started their throaty growl thing we knew we were in serious trouble.

"Oh my god," I said.

"Where's the gun?" asked George.

"Up in the hut."

"Shit. What do we do now?"

Feeling even more at a disadvantage dressed only in our thermal underwear, I whispered as quiet as a mouse, "We get dressed as quietly as we can. Next time the bear goes to the far side of the tent, we'll make a run for it. That leaflet told us to use whatever weapons we could get our hands on." The best we could muster was an inner ski boot and a thermos.

It took us a further twenty minutes to get dressed, clothes with zips being the most time-consuming and agonizing because of the noise they made. We psyched ourselves up and were about to go for it when the bear tripped over one of the guy lines, causing the freshly fallen snow on the tent to slide off the nylon roof in a great whoosh down to the ground. George and I just looked at each other in the gloom, trying not to breathe. When we heard it sniffing the walls I genuinely thought I was going to fill my trousers.

Moments later the bear ambled round to the rear of the tent. It was time to run the gauntlet to the hut, fifty yards up the hill. Ever so delicately, George began unzipping the tent door. He had only got it half open before the footsteps froze us to the spot yet again.

"You're not going to believe this," he whispered, peering out into the cold. "It's not a bear. It's bloody Denali. She must have got off the line again."

Still clutching our antibear weaponry, we hugged, laughed, and cried. We were just so happy to be alive and to have survived our first encounter with a would-be polar bear.

The following day we came face-to-face with our first open water. Polynias are bodies of water, surrounded by sea ice, which never freeze no matter how cold it gets. This particular polynia was no bigger than a football pitch but still fraught with danger. The ice beside it was incredibly thin, and we had to take great care that the sleds didn't break through. It was a loud wake-up call to the lanes of open water we could expect on the Arctic Ocean.

In the early nineteenth century, all sorts of theories were being put forward about the possible existence of a large, open sea at the North Pole. While it's easy to laugh at this fantasy today, the combination of months of continuous summer daylight in the high latitudes, and the fact that icebergs in the North Atlantic seemed to be driven south by a mysterious force, led many to believe in the Open Polar Sea concept.

One particularly imaginative American academic called John Cleve Symmes went so far as to say that the earth was in fact hollow and that explorers would discover craters hundreds of miles across at the Poles, which would open up into a vast inner universe, inhabited by an assortment of fairytale beings like gargoyles and griffins. Astonishingly, many people actually believed him.

Others suggested that there was a solitary pillar of basalt at the Pole, around which the earth rotated. Theories came and went, but the idea of an Open Polar Sea held firm. If only ships were able to penetrate the pack ice that bordered this hidden ocean, it was believed that they would be able to reach the bountiful riches of the Orient simply by sailing right over the top of the world.

Following his abortive search for the Northwest Passage, the indefatigable Edward Parry was given command of a British assault on the Pole in 1827. The expedition's Open Polar Sea strategy was bizarre in the extreme.

Starting out from Spitsbergen, teams of reindeer would drag two fifteen-hundred-pound rowboats, packed with provisions, across the ice to the shores of the Open Polar Sea with the men following on foot. Although the fairytale of Santa Claus driving a reindeer-drawn sled to the North Pole had yet to be conceived, it would be fun to imagine that the idea was dreamed up here.

Upon reaching open water, sails on the rowboats would then be hoisted and the winds would carry the men to the North Pole in style as they sang "Rule Britannia." So confident was Parry of success that he wrote, "Few enterprises are so easily practicable."

The reality was that the reindeer couldn't even get the boats moving, and the men had to resort to hauling the crafts themselves. Often their route to the north (as we, too, would find for ourselves) was blocked by pressure ridges. And when eventually they did find open water, typically it was barely wide enough for them to lower the boats into it and to pull them up again on the other side. It was backbreaking work; Parry wrote that they "were often under the necessity of crawling on all fours to make any progress at all."

Much to his alarm, Parry discovered that the ice across which they were travelling was actually drifting south at a rate of four miles a day, driven by a keen north wind. They were moving backwards quicker than they could advance, and when an ice floe they were crossing suddenly began to disintegrate, throwing several men into the frigid water, Parry was forced to admit defeat. Even though they had only travelled 172 miles in 35 days, they had ventured farther north than any men in history, and their new latitude record of 82°45N would stand for nearly half a century.

By the end of our time in Baffin Island we felt we were starting to master the ancient practice of driving dogs, but things hadn't started well. For the first few days our attempts to steer the dogs left by calling "haw" or right by calling "gee" fell on deaf ears. It didn't help that to begin with they only chose to listen to Paul and Matty. It was almost as if we weren't even there, and they walked all over us. George, Andrew, and I were treated with the same disdain that a supply teacher could expect from a classroom of unruly school children. The dogs were smart enough to realize that until we learned how to discipline them severely, they could get away with murder.

There's a strong hierarchy in a dog team, and one of the methods the dogs adopt to show their supremacy over one another is to pee on those animals they regard as being beneath them on the social ladder. I got a good indication of where I stood in the pecking order while I was feeding the dogs one morning and turned round to find Julius, possibly the lowest-ranked dog in the team, cocking his leg and soaking my trouser leg. Well, at least I knew I existed.

Gradually we won them over, and by the end of our mini-expedition the dogs seemed to treat us with the same respect they showed to Paul and Matty. George, Andrew, and I were now deemed experienced enough to run the dogs without supervision, and before returning to the U.K., we were sent back out into the cold to take three sleds and all sixteen dogs on an eighty-mile circuit across the land, over pressure ridges and through long stretches of rough ice on Frobisher Bay. The trip did wonders for our self-confidence and made us realize that we were more than capable of holding our own. Those three days also helped the dogs really get to know us. We bonded and developed a mutual respect and understanding for one another. We were becoming teammates.

The only noteworthy episode from our three-day foray around the bay happened on our way back to Iqaluit. We were within sight of the town and I foolishly turned my back on my dogs during a routine pit stop. Thinking that they would stay seated while we paused for a mug of hot soup, I then watched in horror as, without warning, they decided to sprint for home, the sled rattling along behind them.

I immediately set off in hot pursuit, skiing as fast as I could and yelling at them to stop. No response. I was fractionally slower than them, and after several desperate lunges at the sled's handlebars, I realized the only way I was going to bring the dogs to a halt was to ski out to one side. I was desperately hoping that by continually calling "gee" at the top of my voice, like me, the dogs would also turn right, and on seeing me skiing off to the side they would eventually make a complete loop and come running back towards me.

Much to my amazement, the plan actually worked, and a couple of minutes later I was reunited with my dogs. I didn't have an ounce of breath left in me to give the dogs a telling-off. They just looked at me facetiously as if to say, "What's the big fuss about?" I was just relieved that we didn't have to return to Iqaluit minus one dog team, but the experience taught me that once we set foot on the Arctic Ocean, never to take my eyes off the dogs.

The three of us returned to London from Baffin Island full of excitement. We were raring to go. Even in this short time we had all fallen under the spell of the Arctic. We had witnessed mesmerizing sunrises of reds, purples, and oranges that lingered for hours and reflected off the snow, bathing everything in a deep pink hue. The raw beauty of the landscape had had an almost hypnotic effect on us. The silence of the place was overpowering. It was easy to see why Peary had been drawn back there time and time again.

Ignoring the polar bear threat for once, we chose to sleep out in the open on our final night as there wasn't a breath of wind. From the warmth of our bivvy bags, we gazed to the heavens as the fabled Northern Lights began the most extraordinary celestial display. Not a word was spoken as curtains of green luminescence danced across the polar sky. It was almost like being in a trance and a privilege to witness.

Even so, one nagging doubt that had begun to take hold was how Paul and Matty were affecting the team dynamics. Paul had often been uncharacteristically quiet in the tent, and there seemed to be some kind of friction between the two of them. It never erupted into a row, but there was a lot of petty bickering and they weren't as close as I had expected this remarkable husband-and-wife team to be. We put it down to the fact that it was their first time on an expedition together in over ten years, and being extremely competitive individuals, they were both vying to be number one.

Countdown to Departure

One thing our time in Baffin Island had taught us was that we would need to get into serious shape before the expedition began in twelve months' time. We found that the temperatures, which often touched −30°C, were a drain on our energy reserves, and by the day's end we were physical wrecks. Not even Antarctica had been this cold, but as we would soon discover, they would seem almost tropical compared to the minus forties that we could expect on the Arctic Ocean.

We had also learned that the day-to-day grind of driving dogs meant that we would require a completely different approach to fitness than a mountaineering or manhauling expedition. Heavy sleds topple over and jam in rough blocks of ice, requiring much lifting, pulling, and pushing to get the six-hundred-pound loads moving again. Legs get tangled in dog lines and arms are yanked in all directions. Broken legs and ribs, sprained muscles, and torn ligaments are typical injuries on a long dog-sledging expedition.

Most weekends in March and April were spent ski-touring in the Swiss Alps. An adhesive strip of fine nylon hairs was placed on the underside of each ski, which enabled us to ski uphill with no danger of slipping back. You feel pretty stupid skiing up a ski slope with a perfectly good chairlift directly overhead, but it sure as hell gets you fit.

Nevertheless, our confidence was dealt a major blow when we decided to enter the biannual Patrouille Des Glaciers ski-touring race. The PDG has been taking place since the Second World War when the Swiss Army would dispatch soldiers to patrol its high mountain border with Italy. Often referred to as the "Ironman of the Mountains," the sixty-mile race from Zermatt to Verbier involves a punishing thirteen thousand feet of ascent and another thirteen thousand feet of descent across glaciers and Alpine passes. A series of checkpoints along the route has to be reached within a certain time or you get disqualified. As if that wasn't challenging enough, most of the race takes place in the dead of night when the avalanche danger is less severe. Twelve hours is considered a respectable time. No British team had ever completed the course, and so we thought we would give it a go.

Limbering up on the starting line in the town square in Zermatt alongside the military elite from Alpine nations like Switzerland, France, and Austria, we soon realized we were way out of our league. And so it proved. Our training had been far from adequate, and after fifteen gruel-ing hours we were pulled off the mountain within sight of the final checkpoint. We weren't the only casualties, with less than half the field making it to the finishing line. Still, it was a bitter disappointment and a loud wake-up call for us to step up the pace.

I enlisted Dax Moy, a former Royal Marine and one of the top personal trainers in London, to put together an appropriate fitness regime for George, Andrew, and me. Dax took one look at us before pulling us to pieces. Over the following nine months, he put us through what can only be described as torture. It began with a full body detox when for four weeks we had to strip all red meat, dairy products, wheat, caffeine, and alcohol out of our systems. Our meager diet of fish, salad, and soya milk barely gave us the strength to get out of bed in the mornings, but it helped flush all the toxins out of our bodies before we could get down to the serious physical training that lay ahead. Dax wasn't the sort of guy you would argue with, so we decided that the best approach was to go along with whatever he said.

Months of gym work followed, primarily aimed at building the muscles we would need to lift the heavy sleds up and over pressure ridges. Although they were phenomenally fit for a couple in their early fifties, twenty years of expeditions had taken their toll on Paul and Matty's bodies, and while we knew they would give their all, the three of us accepted that we would probably have to shoulder more of the workload than our Canadian teammates.

Hours were spent on the running, rowing, and cycling machines and we performed all sorts of rigourous stretching routines to minimize the risk of tearing our newfound muscles when we stepped out onto the ice. For the first time in my life I even had something resembling a six-pack. Although we regularly cursed Dax for the punishment he put us through, none of us had ever felt so fit.

Our plans were then dealt a body blow during the summer when Matty e-mailed me to say that she and Paul were getting divorced. There was little detail, but she said that the previous few months had been extremely difficult and that they had decided to go their separate ways. I was gutted, hurt, shocked, in denial. Were we to blame in some way for bringing them together for this expedition when they were clearly competing against each other? Yes, their relationship had at times appeared strained during our training, but I had never attached much significance to it. They had seemed to long for each other's company when apart on expeditions, and each had great respect for the other's polar skills. Would we be able to continue to have normal friendly relationships with Paul and Matty in the future? There were so many unanswered questions.

My overriding emotion was the thought of the devastating effect this would have on the future of our expedition. I found it incredibly frustrating that Paul and Matty's marital problems had brought the expedition to the point of collapse. Apparently they had agreed that, as part of the divorce settlement, Matty would keep the dogs and their home in Iqaluit, while Paul would move south to Ottawa to work as a photographer and lecturer. This inevitably meant that Paul would no longer be part of the team, and it was a terrific blow.

If I was being brutally honest, if it was up to me which of them joined the team, it would have been Paul, and Matty knew this. This wasn't because I thought he was the better dog driver – far from it. They had both been to the North Pole before and both were expert dog drivers, but I knew Paul far better than I knew Matty, and both Andrew and I had forged a close friendship with him in Antarctica in 2002. Furthermore, Peary was Paul's passion, and to travel to the North Pole in his footsteps would have been his dream. How on earth were we going to replace him?

Matty and I spent much of the summer scouring the polar community for somebody to fill Paul's ample shoes. Matty originally questioned the need to find a fifth team member, but I felt that with the odds of making it to the Pole, let alone beating Peary's time, already stacked heavily against us, we could really do with some extra manpower. Prior dog-sledging experience was a key prerequisite. The only problem was, experienced dog drivers are not that easy to find.

We approached people from across the globe, from Paul's former sledging companion, Paul Crowley, to the Brit Geoff Somers who had completed a four-thousand-mile traverse of Antarctica with dogs in 1990 and had helped Andrew and me with our own South Pole preparations in 2002. We contacted the legendary Russian explorer Victor Boyarsky and the former head of the British Antarctic Survey, Paul Rose, but each time the response was negative due to prior commitments. Time was running out.

I telephoned the American Will Steger for advice. Having taken dogs to the North Pole back in 1986 and led the first full-length traverse of Antarctica, Will is the most experienced dog driver in the world today. He had recently returned from an epic three-thousand-mile, five-month dogsledging expedition across the Canadian tundra and suggested we contact a Canadian called Hugh Dale-Harris, who had been part of his multinational team. Will told me that Hugh had cut his teeth working as a guide for Outward Bound, leading kayaking, cross-country skiing, and dogsledging trips for youth groups around southern Ontario. He was in his early thirties, married with a baby daughter, was great with dogs, and laid-back to the point of being horizontal. He was as strong as an ox and never grumbled. "Hugh's your man," said Will. "If you can get him, he'll be great." He sounded perfect.

By a complete coincidence, Matty had met Hugh a couple of years earlier when she was running an Outward Bound white-water rafting course near Hugh's hometown of Thunder Bay. She echoed many of Will's comments, and as they already knew each another, it made sense for Matty to approach him herself. A few days later Hugh accepted our invitation and the team was complete. But who was this unknown? Would he be any good? Would we get on with him? Only time would tell.

THE FINAL FEW MONTHS LEADING UP TO OUR DEPARTURE WERE increasingly frantic. From October 2004 to January 2005, Matty was down in Antarctica, taking Eric and Sarah on a kite-skiing expedition as a way of helping them get over the trauma of their parents' separation. The children had clearly inherited their parent's polar genes, and it was incredible that they should take on such a challenge only fresh out of high school.

But how much would the twelve-hundred-mile journey and the strain of the divorce take out of Matty? I was really concerned that she would be so physically and emotionally drained that the last thing she would want to do within a few weeks of completing a major polar expedition was to pack her bags again and head north with us. There was also the question of what sort of shape the dogs were going to be in with Matty being away from them for so long.

Ten days after her return home to Iqaluit, Matty sent me an e-mail saying, "I am still half in Antarctica, I feel that I am drifting." My concerns at how far behind we were getting with all the logistics were growing by the day. Our departure date from London had been set at 25 February 2005, and there was still a frightening amount to sort out.

I therefore decided to clear my diary and head straight out to Baffin Island in late January to help run the dogs and try to get Matty into expedition mode again. Evenings were either spent at the kitchen table running through expedition logistics or in the workshop building our two replica Peary sleds.

We based our design on a detailed description of Peary's as well as photographs from his final expedition. On a break to New York the previous summer, I had visited the Museum of Natural History next to Central Park, where the Peary meteorites from Greenland and one of his North Pole sleds are on display. I was struck by just how heavily scarred the sled was, war wounds picked up from hundreds of miles of polar travel. It was full of character, and had clearly witnessed countless tales of bravery and hardship during its time on the ice.

What I had found remarkable was that not a single screw or nail had been used in the sled's construction and how it was held together by hundreds of short pieces of cord. This gave the timber frame some elasticity, allowing it to flex and flow with the undulating terrain and preventing it from breaking into pieces. As Peary himself said, solid joints would "smash very quickly under the continuous succession of blows, with the entire weight of the load acting as a hammer at every impact with the flinty ice."

Peary had continually modified his sled design during his years in the

Arctic. Although his sleds had initially been based on traditional Inuit models, by 1909 the front of the runners had been reinforced and raised to help smash a way through the walls of impenetrable ice that guarded the route to the Pole.

The sled was a little over eleven feet long, about two feet wide, and with seven-inch-high runners. Our sleds would have the same dimensions and be constructed in the same way, with the timbers lashed together with traditional Inuit sledging knots.

Building the sleds was like assembling our own kit cars and I took great pride in making them. They were half the size of those used by the likes of Herbert and Steger but, according to Peary, their sleek, lightweight design held the key to his impressive speeds over the Arctic Ocean. He described the Peary sled as "the best type of sled yet built for polar-sea-ice work." I wanted to put his words to the ultimate test.

After a very productive fortnight with Matty and the dogs, I returned to London to find that the house I shared with Andrew had taken on the appearance of a warehouse. Our fellow housemates were losing their patience with the stacks of cardboard boxes that filled every corridor and room, and who could blame them?

New deliveries of equipment and provisions were arriving by the day, from boxes of batteries to power our expedition communications equipment, to ski poles, to 150 pounds of complimentary Cadbury's chocolate, to South African biltong, beef jerky, to thermal underwear. It was total chaos. There was also the logistical nightmare of getting all our supplies onto the flight to Canada.

In mid-February, the week before our departure, George, Andrew, and I were invited to tea at Clarence House by the expedition patrons, the Prince of Wales and Camilla Parker-Bowles, who had just announced their engagement. We had been raising funds for The Prince's Trust, and the Prince wanted to see us before we left. It was a huge honour. We polished our shoes, dusted off our suits, and did our best to look as smart as we could.

Once inside, though, we were immediately put at ease by Camilla, who was incredibly down to earth. We tucked into Duchy Original cookies and enjoyed a lively conversation with the Prince, who impressed us hugely with his knowledge of polar history and the whole Peary debate.

I asked Prince Charles if he could autograph a dogsledging photo for Matty. While passing him the marker pen, I hadn't realized that the lid had fallen off and I accidentally managed to cover the Prince's hand in indelible black ink. I thought I was going to be locked away in the Tower.

We then went outside for photographs. It was the royal couple's first official appearance since the announcement of their engagement, and the press pack snapped away as the five of us stood alongside a mock-up sled and two husky dogs that had been brought in for the occasion. With her thick fur coat, scarf, and fleece gloves, Camilla looked by far the most polar amongst us. The following day the pictures were in all the newspapers.

Barclays Capital was thrilled with the amount of coverage we received, but I wasn't so sure. By throwing ourselves into the media spotlight, we had put ourselves under a huge amount of pressure to make it to the Pole. If the expedition ended in failure, the press would have a field day and our reputations would be in ruins. During my expedition career I have always been much more motivated by success than by a fear of failure, but by setting ourselves such tough goals so publicly, it felt very different. We had to avoid failure at all costs.

Throughout the long preparatory phase of the expedition, I had often sought advice from people within the British polar community. Having never driven a dog team or stepped foot on the Arctic Ocean before, to receive tips and words of encouragement from those who had done it all before was a tremendous fillip to the whole team. It was always interesting to hear their views on Peary. Whether they thought he had simply got his navigation calculations wrong or he had consciously faked his readings, all the people I spoke to were unanimous that Peary got nowhere near the Pole.

A few months before we were due to leave, I phoned Sir Wally Herbert, the man at the heart of the debate, with more Arctic dogsledging experience than anyone in the country. Sir Ranulph Fiennes called him "the greatest explorer of our time," while Prince Charles once said that his "determination and courage are of such heroic proportions that this country should mark his achievements eventually by having him stuffed and put on display."

I was racked with nerves when I dialed Herbert's number, unsure of what he would make of an expedition that was setting out to prove whether it had been him or Peary who had reached the Pole first. His direct tone took me completely by surprise. "Your expedition is bullshit, absolute bullshit. I admire your courage, but you cannot reach the North Pole in thirty-seven days without cheating. Peary was the biggest cheat of them all. Your sleds will be smashed to bits within the first fifteen miles. It would be a miracle if you made it as far as eighty-four degrees north."

The Internet provided a public forum for even stronger condemnation of our plans. One polar website labeled me "The Arctic Don Quixote," and described in graphic detail how our expedition would end in disaster. Anonymous characters emerged from the shadows of the Internet to add to the dissenting voices.

I was amazed at how much reaction our expedition had stirred up before we had even reached the shores of the Arctic Ocean. Some of the attacks were lighthearted, others more vindictive and personal, but for everyone on the team they only made us more motivated to succeed.

Most of what was said or written in the weeks before our departure came from people whom we had never met, but in addition to attacking us, they had the knives out for Peary, too. It was clear that when it came to the old commander, emotions still ran deep. We were determined to prove them wrong. Although I had initially approached the expedition with an open mind as to who was the first person to reach the North Pole, I felt an increasing duty to uphold Peary's name and do everything in my power to reach the Pole within those thirty-seven days.

3. Northern Exposure

GEORGE AND I MET AT HEATHROW AIRPORT
on the afternoon of 25 February 2005, for the
first leg of our long journey to the Pole. With fourteen
pieces of luggage between us, we knew it was going to
be a hefty excess baggage charge. Hugh and Matty
were already in Iqaluit, with Andrew joining us five
days later as he had a few loose ends to wrap up in
South Africa. George had already said his good-byes at
home, but my parents, brother, sister, and my girlfriend, Mary, all came to the airport to see us off.

Mary and I had been together for just over a year.
She had become resigned to the fact that at some point
in our relationship I would be disappearing off to the
Arctic for several months. During the often stressful
planning stages of the expedition, Mary had been a
wonderful, calming influence and a rock of support.

Looking back on those months now, I wish I'd
been able to devote as much time to her as I had to
the expedition. We had grown incredibly close, and
now that I was leaving her behind I felt awful. To
begin with I was concerned about how she would
cope with the worry and uncertainty of what might

be happening to me out on the ice, but I soon learnt that Mary is a strong-willed, independent woman with enormous resilience, and I knew she'd be absolutely fine.

Mary and I normally phoned each other four or five times a day, and although we would be taking an Iridium satellite phone on the expedition, due to the difficulties of charging batteries on the ice we'd be lucky if any of us called home more than once every two weeks. So it was great that Mary had become good friends with Annie and Rowena (George and Andrew's other halves) as the girls would be able to keep each other going during the months ahead.

At the start of an expedition I'm normally so excited that I just want to say a hurried good-bye and leave as quickly as possible, but when the time came to say good-bye to Mary I was overcome with emotion. The tears flowed and I couldn't let her go. It wasn't long before that set Mary off, too. It didn't matter that this was all taking place right in front of my family and half of Terminal 3. I knew I would miss her terribly.

We touched down in Iqaluit the following morning. Our departure date for Resolute Bay was two weeks away, but we still faced a Herculean task in getting all the necessary preparations completed on time.

It was great finally to meet Hugh Dale-Harris. We had chatted on the phone on many occasions over the past few months, and he was exactly as I had imagined him to be: tall, chilled-out, intelligent, hard-working, and exuding a real passion for the North. He was already sporting an impressive polar beard and he couldn't stop laughing. I could tell immediately that he was going to be a brilliant teammate.

Hugh had arrived in Iqaluit a few days before us and had been busy finishing work on the sleds. The day we took them outside for the first time, a weatherbeaten Inuit hunter wearing polar bear trousers came over and peered at them. He took his time as he silently went about checking out the sleds, inspecting our knots and testing the strength of the handlebars, before declaring, "Good sleds." We couldn't have wished for a better endorsement.

There was no shortage of jobs to do: Individual food items had to be stripped of their packaging before being weighed and divided into water-tight daily ration bags, the same needed to be done for the dog food, fuel cans had to be filled, the new sleds had to be put through some rigourous testing, ski bindings had to be mounted to skis, dog whips needed to be made, there was a long list of clothing repairs and modifications to get through, Matty and I had daily meetings with the cargo authorities at Iqaluit Airport, every piece of equipment had to be checked and rechecked, a lot of work still had to be done on the expedition website, Barclays Capital logos needed to be attached to clothing and equipment, there was an endless a stream of media interviews, and the dogs had to be run every day.

During our training in 2004, it had become clear that some of the older dogs in the team (including my old friend Julius) would struggle with weeks of sustained travel. We needed to find some fresh sets of legs. With only a few hundred Eskimo dogs remaining throughout the world, Matty had travelled to Yellowknife on the other side of Canada to find suitable replacements.

Seven new dogs were drafted into the team. They had recently completed a thousand-mile journey across the Northwest Territories. None of them had names and we had great fun christening them. Some, like Seegloo, Marvin, and his brother, Bartlett, were named after members of Peary's team, while Ikki was named after the Inuit word for cold. The final three were Axel, Jacs, and Baffin, the clown in the team. Baffin was easy to identify because of his lopsided left ear, pure white coat, and a chunky metal collar that would not have looked out of place around the neck of an East End gangster.

Hugh had brought along Gloria, his own Eskimo dog from Thunder Bay. Along with Denali, one of Matty's original dogs, this gave us two females, one per team. This was very important for team motivation. Although not as large as their male counterparts, pound for pound they pulled as hard, if not harder. As Peary wrote, "A good team of eight dogs should always have one or two bitches in it. This makes a livelier and better-working team." Governments are always extolling the virtues of businesses having a mixed workforce, so I guess one could say we were doing our bit for equal opportunity.

We quickly learned that if Denali and Gloria were placed towards the front of their respective packs, there was a noticeable increase in sled speed. Both are beautiful dogs, and maybe the testosterone-fueled males in the team were just intent on chasing after the girls.

With some of the older dogs taking early retirement, we were left with a squad of eighteen animals, which had to be whittled down to a final touring party of sixteen, two teams of eight. In the end we chose to leave behind Jacs and Bartlett. Jacs was a quiet, timid dog who was so terrified of the others that he loitered at the back and never pulled. In fact, he was the most useless sled dog any of us had ever worked with.

Bartlett, on the other hand, was a strong puller, but his aggressive behavior often got the better of him and he was always picking fights. It was too big a risk to have such a volatile character on the team, so we decided he also would remain in Iqaluit.

The week before our departure, we received a call from Jerry del Missier's secretary at Barclays Capital. Jerry had been in Montreal on a business trip and as he had a couple of days to spare, he decided to make an impromptu visit to Iqaluit to see how final preparations were coming along. Although I seriously wondered how we would manage to keep Jerry occupied for forty-eight hours and complete the thousand and one things still to do, his visit made me realize just how incredibly fortunate we were to have him, and the bank, as our chief backer. We kitted him out in whatever spare clothing we could find and took him on a two-day dogsledging foray around Frobisher Bay.

The temperatures dropped well into the minus-thirties and it snowed much of the time, so Jerry could have been forgiven had he swapped his cramped place in the tent for a nice warm bed in the Frobisher Inn. But he didn't. Maybe it was his Canadian heritage or his natural competitive instinct, but whatever it was, Jerry proved himself to be a natural. He fully immersed himself in polar travel, never complained, and couldn't have been more enthusiastic about the expedition. It gave us such a thrill that he had made the effort to pay us a visit and it made us realize that when the going got really tough out on the Arctic Ocean, Jerry and everyone at Barclays Capital would be right behind us.

Our last few days in Iqaluit were so traumatic that I have almost completely blocked them from my memory. Last-minute jobs were being added to our to-do list faster than they could be ticked off. The sheer enormity of the project we had taken on had finally dawned on us. We managed to buy some extra time when a blizzard swept through Iqaluit and our flight north was delayed by twenty-four hours, but there was still a mad panic to get everything ready. There was no time to relax or even to write final e-mails home. So frantic had the final few weeks become that I had had no time to think about the expedition itself.

None of us managed more than an hour's sleep during our final two nights – hardly ideal preparation for an expedition to the North Pole. Minds and bodies were shattered and tempers occasionally flared up. One afternoon Andrew and I were in the airport hangar, carefully dividing up our many barrels and bags of supplies and equipment for the different legs of the expedition. The job wasn't big enough for two people so with time short I suggested to Andrew that he go back to help George and Hugh pack the sleds.

"Fine," replied Andrew abruptly, "Give yourself the fun job."

I was irritated, as each task was just as mundane as the other. "OK, if it makes you happier, why don't you stay here and I'll go and work on the sleds," I said.

"No, no, this is what you want to do, so I'll leave you to it."

"Andrew, have we got a problem here?" I asked, "because whenever I've asked you to do something in the last few days, you've snapped back, and every time I express my opinion on anything to do with the expedition itself, you flatly disagree with me, almost without thinking. I've just about had enough. You were never like this on our South Pole trip. I am the expedition leader, I've worked my arse off for two years to put this trip together, and I specifically chose you because I knew that you would make a fantastic teammate. If you've got something to get off your chest, speak now. Otherwise I want this aggressive attitude to stop right here."

I think Andrew was taken aback by my outburst. I'm a pretty laid-back sort of guy and I try to avoid confrontational situations unless absolutely necessary. Knowing how single-minded and competitive Andrew can be, I was becoming increasingly worried that he was trying to undermine my authority. Unless I confronted him the situation could easily have escalated once we were out on the ice.

His response was refreshingly honest. "I'm sorry. I sometimes get a kick out of disagreeing with people. Maybe it's been brought on because we're all so exhausted at the moment. It's not something I'm particularly proud of and I know I've got to stop doing it. It won't happen again."

It was a huge relief. We shook hands and from that moment there hasn't been a cross word between us, discussions on England–South Africa sporting fixtures excepted.

We flew north on 13 March on a First Air commercial flight to the small Inuit community of Resolute Bay, halfway between Iqaluit and our starting point on the north coast of Ellesmere Island. The dogs were ushered into their plastic kennels before being whisked off across the tarmac by forklift truck. They barked like crazy, and I wondered if they had any sense of the great odyssey on which they were about to embark.

All the equipment and provisions were loaded on board, we had checked in, and were waiting to board the plane, when Matty suddenly exclaimed, "Did anyone remember Ootah and Denali?"

Denali had been in heat for two weeks, making the other dogs crazy and almost impossible to drive. Much to the other males' displeasure, Ootah had been given the job of, to put it delicately, making sure Denali came out of heat before the expedition got away. So for our last few days, the two of them had been locked away in a special dog pen by the shore. Probably due to our lack of sleep, we had completely forgotten to add the two lovebirds to the roll call. We collected them from their honeymoon suite in the dog yard and managed to load them onboard just in time for takeoff.

EVEN THOUGH LESS THAN A CENTURY HAS PASSED SINCE THE NORTH Pole was discovered, humankind has been aware of the existence of a northernmost place for thousands of years. As long ago as 3,000 BC, astrologers from Babylonia (southern Iraq today) noticed that the heavens seemed to revolve around a single fixed star.

In fact, the Egyptian pharaohs were so in awe of the Pole Star that the great pyramid of Khufu at Giza was oriented and built in such a way that at night the star remained constantly visible from the bottom of one of the pyramid's deep ventilation shafts.

Meanwhile, in Greece, ancient philosophers observed that the boundary between stars that rose and set each night, and those that always remained above the horizon, passed directly through a constellation dominating the northern night sky called Arktos, or the Bear. They named this invisible line the Arctic Circle, literally the Bear's Circle.

I got my first dose of pre-match nerves an hour into the flight when the captain calmly announced, "Ladies and gentlemen, we have just crossed the Arctic Circle. Welcome to the North." I peered out the window, but all I could see was white. It was as if we were entering an unknown world, a place so remote and inhospitable that many world maps don't even bother including it.

After arriving in Resolute Bay, the plan was for two Twin Otter ski planes, which we had chartered through Kenn Borek Air, to fly us straight up to Cape Columbia. Once the expedition was under way, two separate Twin Otter flights would fly out over the Arctic Ocean to provision us for each leg of the journey.

If all went according to plan, the first resupply flight would touch down beside us when we reached 84°29N, the point at which the support divisions led by Goodsell and MacMillan left their remaining supplies with Peary and returned to land. This was in line with our strategy of replicating Peary's journey as closely as possible. From there, the Twin Otter would continue north before landing at Borup's farthest north at 85°23N, where the pilot would leave our preprepared assortment of provisions, fuel, and dog food to see us through for another ten days or so.

To help us locate these supplies amid thousands of square miles of pack ice, the pilot would attach a small Argos tracking beacon to them. An Argos beacon works not unlike a GPS, constantly updating a website with its coordinates, even if the drifting pack carries the beacon off course. Andrew's father in Cape Town kindly volunteered to keep a track of the cache's exact location and to keep us updated via the satellite phone.

A second flight a few weeks later was then scheduled to fly out to meet us at Marvin's farthest north at 86°38N before continuing on to Bartlett's farthest north at 87°47N where our final supply cache, complete with Argos beacon, would be placed. If and when we eventually reached the Pole, two Twin Otters would then be dispatched to collect us.

The logistics involved in the whole operation were hugely complicated, and we would be leaving a lot to chance. There was so much that could go wrong, whether it be the Argos beacons not working or the pilots being unable to find a runway on the ice. There was also the chance of polar bears pillaging our supplies before we found them or, even worse, we might fail to locate our food caches altogether.

If we missed just one of those resupplies, not only would our chances of making the Pole be severely compromised, but our lives could be put in serious danger. Peary, of course, would have had no such worries because at each of his four resupply points, the support parties that were returning to the ship would have simply transferred their superfluous supplies from their sleds to the sleds that were continuing north.

Our plans received their first setback when we touched down at Resolute Bay. A storm over Ellesmere Island meant that the Twin Otters that were due to take us to Cape Columbia had been grounded and the pilots didn't think they would be able to fly again for several days. We were stranded in Resolute Bay and there was nothing we could do about it.

Resolute Bay is about as far north as you can get while still being able to enjoy some creature comforts. The South Camp Inn is the town's only hotel and caters mainly for government workers, polar bear hunters, and the occasional polar adventurer. It is owned and run by an enterprising character called Ozzie Kheraj, who emigrated from the much warmer climes of Turkey back in the 1980s. Ozzie also happens to be the head of the local police force, the governor of Resolute's only school, as well as the town's mayor. In short, if you need anything during your stay in Resolute Bay, Ozzie's your man.

It's very confusing when people talk of going to the North Pole because many don't realize that there is in fact another North Pole, hundreds of miles to the south. Our goal was the Geographic North Pole, or True North, at 90°N, the northernmost point on the planet, but another pole lies much closer to Resolute. The Magnetic North Pole marks the spot at which the earth's magnetic field points vertically downward. What makes navigation in the High Arctic so misleading is that the dial on a compass points not to the Geographic North Pole but to the Magnetic North Pole. Adding to the confusion, the Magnetic North Pole wanders around the Canadian Arctic by as much as thirty miles a year, caused by the circulation of molten iron within the earth's hot and liquid outer core.

The Magnetic North Pole was discovered by complete luck in 1831. One of the many Northwest Passage failures, led by James Clark Ross, became trapped amongst the pack ice west of Baffin Island for four whole years. To alleviate the boredom, sledging parties were sent out to search for food and a possible way out.

During one of these forays along the Boothia Peninsula (a neck of land protruding north from mainland Canada), Ross noticed his compass behaving erratically near the 70th Parallel, leading him to speculate that he had stumbled across the axis of the earth's magnetic field. Almost by accident, he had found the North Magnetic Pole. To give an idea of how fast it can move, by 2005 the Magnetic North Pole was located just off the west coast of Ellesmere Island at a latitude of 83°N, more than eight hundred miles away.

In recent years, international teams have descended on Resolute Bay to take part in an annual race that sets off from the frozen beach by Ozzie's hotel, finishing some 250 miles farther north at the 1996 position of the Magnetic North Pole at around 78°N.

The Magnetic North Pole is regarded by explorers as being a more straightforward challenge than its polar cousin. Not only is it much closer to civilization, but it drifts amongst the fjords and islands of Canada's Arctic archipelago, where the ocean currents are much weaker than those of the Arctic Ocean. This means the ice is much flatter, there are very few pressure ridges, and there is almost no open water.

Resolute Bay, known amongst the Inuit as Qausuittuq (literally "Place with no Dawn") is located in a protected bay on Cornwallis Island, only 920 miles from the North Pole. The settlement lies beneath a rocky hillock overlooking the ice-choked waters of the Northwest Passage that lured (and often claimed the lives of) so many of the early Arctic pioneers.

The most famous of them all was Sir John Franklin, who in 1845 set off to look for the elusive seaway with two of the fleet's finest ships under his command, 128 men, and enough food to last seven years. They were never seen or heard from again. Over the course of the next fifteen years, dozens of rescue missions (many of which were sponsored by the grieving but ever hopeful Lady Franklin) tried to find the old sea dog and his crew.

Ironically, more men and ships were lost looking for Franklin than those in the original expedition itself, but over time these various expeditions unearthed corpses, abandoned equipment, and other relics that would reveal how Franklin met his end. We now know that when the two ships became trapped in pack ice west of the Boothia Peninsula, Franklin's men attempted to sled hundreds of miles south to the fur-trapping stations of mainland Canada. The party's fate was eventually sealed by a combination of lead poisoning (caused by lead solder on the seams of tin food cans), scurvy,* and starvation.

While they may have ultimately proven the futility of trying to find a viable trading route between Europe and Asia, the many Northwest Passage expeditions in the first half of the nineteenth century were of vital importance to the exploration of the Arctic. Not only were these extraordinary men responsible for mapping hundreds of thousands of square miles of uncharted terrain in the North American high Arctic, but the tales of heroism and bravery of those early Arctic pioneers captured the public's

* A potentially fatal disease caused by a deficiency in Vitamin C. Symptoms include spongy gums, black spots on the skin, swelling of the legs, and bleeding from the nose, ears, and anus.

imagination and reignited the centuries-old quest for the North Pole.

Established as an air base and weather station by the Canadian govern-ment after World War II, most of Resolute's two hundred Inuit residents were relocated from other parts of Canada in the 1950s with the promise of bountiful hunting grounds. The game was never as plentiful as the hunters had been led to believe, and many have since moved south. By 2005, the town's very existence was under serious threat.

Life in Resolute is unimaginably hard. During the winter the sun disappears below the horizon for nearly five months and temperatures plummet to the minus fifties. The bay itself is frozen solid for ten months, leaving a short window at the end of the summer for a single cargo ship to dock and unload the supplies that will keep the people of Resolute going for another year.

As we drove into town along the dirt road from the airport, we were amazed to see children playing outside, seemingly oblivious to the perishing cold. It was −32°C and some of them weren't even wearing hats. There was a church, a school, and even a small supermarket selling everything one could possibly need in the Arctic, from shotgun cartridges to popcicles.

All the houses had snow banked up against the walls to act as insula-tion. Most homes were guarded by a dog on a chain, and several had a macabre assortment of polar bear or seal skins hanging from the drying lines. Resolute was no ordinary town, and we were quickly appreciating that its residents were some of the hardiest people in the world. Heaven knows what they must have made of us, who despite being wrapped from head to toe in the latest polar clothing, were still absolutely freezing.

Matty was confined to her hotel bed for most of our time in Resolute with a nasty chest infection. For everyone's sake it was imperative that she shook it off before the expedition got under way or her participation would be in serious doubt.

There was still a long list of jobs for the rest of us to be getting on with, in particular keeping the dogs active. Unfortunately, the sleds had had to be dismantled so that they could fit inside the cramped fuselage of the Twin Otters. The dogs had to pull something, so we decided the best option was to clip them to the front of Ozzie's truck, leave the gearbox in neutral, and set off along the road between the town and the airport. It was not your average training apparatus, but it worked surprisingly well, and by leaning out of the window to issue instructions to the dogs, we had very little to do apart from turning the wheel and occasionally applying the brakes when we met oncoming traffic.

The one slight mishap during our improvised training sessions occurred when Odin, not the sharpest dog on the team, managed to run on the other side of a lamppost from the rest of the animals and very nearly ended up being pulled back under the wheels when his trace yanked tight. Thankfully, Hugh slammed on the brakes just in time and Odin quickly scampered back into position.

One afternoon we paid a visit to the weather station by the airport. The resident meteorologist, Wayne Davidson, told us that the ice conditions were "the most screwed up" he had seen in his twenty years of monitoring the Arctic Ocean, with leads of open water everywhere. A collection of satellite images going back to the 1980s showed us an alarming year-on-year increase in the amount of leads visible from space. Wayne's view was that this could only be explained by climate change, and that conditions on the Arctic Ocean would continue to deteriorate. "You may well be one of the last teams that try to do this," he said.

Hugh then had us all in stitches when, in that deadpan, very matter-of-fact manner of his, he mused, "I guess we won't really know what the ice is going to be like until we get up there. And then we'll know for sure." I was looking forward to more of Hugh's words of wisdom over the weeks ahead.

Even more disturbing than the satellite images was the graphic painting above Wayne's desk of a man being mauled by a polar bear. "Oh, that was one of my predecessors," explained Wayne. "He spent too much time outside and one day a bear decided to have him for breakfast."

In the end we were holed up in Resolute Bay for five long, frustrating days. In the same way as Peary had done, we had originally hoped to set off from Cape Columbia during the much colder days of early March when the Arctic Ocean is almost guaranteed to be frozen solid.

Nevertheless none of the Kenn Borek Air pilots had flown to Cape Columbia before, so they wanted to wait until mid-March when the sun returned, allowing them enough visibility to find a suitable runway on the snow.

To have our starting date pushed back again, this time due to the weather, was incredibly frustrating. The later in the season we started, the more likely it was that we would encounter warmer conditions and therefore open water, one of the major threats to our plans. Moreover, George, Andrew, and I had all promised our girlfriends we would be home by the end of April.

I always keep a journal when I'm away on an expedition to record each day's events and my thoughts at the time, precious memories that might otherwise be forgotten with the passage of time. I do this as much for myself as for my family, and hopefully one day the children and grandchildren.

After we left Resolute, I began scribbling notes in my journal at the end of every day, which is where the book continues from here. Apart from some historical information that had to be more thoroughly researched back in England, I've tried to keep the journal as close to its original form as possible. In certain cases, it needed to be adapted to make events more easily understood, but these changes have been kept to a minimum. This is our story.

18 MARCH 2005:
Eureka High Arctic Weather Station, −37°C

Over two years since the seeds of the expedition were sown, today was the day that all of that daydreaming, preparation, and training became a reality. Our journey to the roof of the world began with the first leg of a six-hour flight to Cape Columbia, that timeless place on the north coast of Ellesmere Island from where Peary set off on his historic expedition almost exactly ninety-six years ago.

A 4:00 A.M. phone call with the ground crew at Kenn Borek Air confirmed that the weather system appeared to have passed through, and after days of relative inactivity we could finally take to the skies.

I called Mary to tell her that we were off. It was the middle of the night back home and the call went straight through to the answer machine. Typical. Really upset as I'd hoped that we'd get to speak before the expedition got under way. I told her that I loved her and that I would try to call again from the ice.

In the predawn gloom we loaded up the van before taking it in turns to give Ozzie a final bear hug to thank him for looking after us so well during our enforced layover in Resolute.

With so much in the way of supplies and equipment, we had chartered two Twin Otters ski planes to ferry us up to Cape Columbia. I was on the first plane with Matty and Marc de Jersey, the BBC reporter who has been covering our story for the past week. Marc is so terrified of flying that he brought along an emergency supply of Valium pills to help keep him calm during the flight. Seeing him trip as he tackled the first of the aircraft's flimsy steps, I wondered if he needed something stronger.

By the time we had loaded the sleds, equipment, provisions, and dogs onto each plane, there was very little room for us humans. There were dogs in the aisle, dogs under seats, and dogs on the sleds. The smell of dogs in the cabin was overpowering. So convinced was Don, our pilot, that the dogs were going to make a mess everywhere that he demanded to know if they had all been to the loo before boarding the plane. Thankfully they had.

The engines roared into life and we were away. This was the first time that the true scale of the Arctic really hit home. The buildings of Resolute Bay quickly shrunk to tiny specks before disappearing into an ocean of whiteness. The great cliffs and craggy hills of the bay gradually dissolved into the polar landscape, and it wasn't long before our time there was a distant memory.

The dogs, sedated by the warm temperatures inside the cabin, just curled up in whatever space they could find. Ootah and I have built up a close bond over the last few months and he fell asleep with his head in my lap. He's a giant fur ball of an animal and throughout our training he's pulled the hardest of any dog, often starting the sled under his own power. But while he's incredibly affectionate towards us, Ootah hasn't yet gained the respect of the other dogs on the team, probably because he's still relatively young. Despite his size, he often gets picked on, and maybe part of me just feels protective.

Matty and I spent the first hour of the flight discussing our strategy for the next two weeks. Our first resupply is due to arrive approximately twelve days from now, but we've packed provisions, fuel, and dog food for sixteen days in case of weather delays – and all this to cover a distance that if we were driving down the motorway, would only take an hour.

By that time, we hope to be at or close to the site of Peary's Goodsell/ MacMillan Camp at 84°29N. This is just eighty-two miles north of Cape Columbia, but that first leg promises to be the most grueling of the entire expedition. The sleds will be at their heaviest, particularly during the first few days, and the terrain and the cold will be at their most extreme. As the conditions gradually improve and the temperatures warm up, our hope is that our speeds, just like Peary's did, will gradually pick up.

Nevertheless, the 413 nautical miles from Cape Columbia to the Pole is a distance I find so overwhelming and incomprehensible that I'm trying to block it from my thoughts entirely. Dreaming of the day when the Pole arrives would be condemning myself to weeks of unrelenting disappointment. Still, Peary's five major camps are evenly spaced along the route to the Pole and help to split the colossal mileage ahead of us into five more manageable sections.

For now, everything is focused on reaching 84°29N. I'm effectively playing a trick on my mind. Not until we pass our penultimate milestone, our fourth and final resupply at Bartlett Camp, will the focus shift to the Pole itself, by which stage, if all has gone according to plan, the Pole will seem as if it's just around the corner.

Three hours after takeoff, we stopped to refuel at Eureka, a small weather station on Ellesmere Island straddling the 80th Parallel, exactly 600 miles from the Pole. George, Andrew, and Hugh, travelling in the second plane, touched down a couple of minutes after us.

It was noticeably colder than Resolute. As I took my first intake of breath, the super-cooled air stabbed the back of my throat like tiny daggers, sending me into an uncontrollable coughing fit. And to think that it would only get colder the farther north we went. George decided the only way to keep warm and entertained while we waited on the tarmac was to throw snowballs at one another. The game didn't last long as the snow was so powdery it just disintegrated in our hands. On a hillside 400 yards away, a battalion of shaggy musk oxen looked on, thoroughly unamused.

Half an hour later and we were under way again, climbing high into glorious blue skies. The mountain landscape was so unexpectedly dramatic that it took my brain a while to process the spellbinding vista unfolding beneath us. I had anticipated nothing more than undulating snow-covered hills, but there I was, gazing at meandering glaciers, splintered with deep crevasses, snaking their way between row after row of jagged-toothed mountains down to the frozen sea beyond.

This was a land ruled by ice, a complete contrast to the oasis of warmth onboard our tiny plane. The Arctic sun lay just above the southern horizon, tinting this frigid world a subtle hue of oranges and pinks. It was hard to imagine that the place had changed since the dawn of time.

Our flight path took us directly over some of the many ice-choked waterways discovered by some of the Franklin search expeditions. A few of these missions used their presence in the Arctic as an excuse to look for the North Pole, most notably the American Elisha Kane who in 1853 sailed the *Advance* deep into Smith Sound, discovering the large basin off Ellesmere Island now named after him. One of Kane's aims was to over-winter farther north than any Englishman had managed before him because he believed that "the Stars and Stripes ought to wave where no Union Jack had ever fluttered in the polar gale." This he duly did, on Greenland's northwest coast at 78°36N.

After enduring a desperately cold and uncomfortable winter aboard the rat-infested ship (matters were made even worse because Kane grossly underestimated the amount of fuel needed to see out the long polar night and they very nearly froze to death), the men sled north through the uncharted Kane Basin. They discovered the Kennedy Channel, Kane mistakenly believing that the unbroken expanse of open water ahead of them was the gateway to the Open Polar Sea.

Despite his successes, Kane was not a born leader, and his crew despised him. One of the men wrote that he was "peevish, coarse, insulting, the most self-conceited man I ever saw." To make matters worse, Kane was almost always ill. Ever since childhood he had suffered from rheumatic fever and an unpredictable heart, and it was a genuine surprise to his crew that he had lasted so long into the expedition.

The resentment towards Kane boiled over when the ship was forced to overwinter for a second time. Isaac Hayes, (not the 1970s soul legend but the ship's surgeon), had had enough and led a party of six fellow mutineers south in the distant hope of reaching the settlement of Upernavik, 700 miles away on the west Greenland coast. They returned to the *Advance* three months later with their tails between their legs having endured an horrific ordeal in which they suffered scurvy, starvation, and frostbite before being chased for hundreds of miles by hordes of hungry Inuit.

More bickering and desertions followed during the cold, dark months of winter before the sixteen remaining crew abandoned ship and embarked on one of the most extraordinary survival journeys the Arctic had ever witnessed. Manhauling three rowing boats, nearly a ton of food, and four invalids over the frozen sea, the men finally reached open water after a month of bone-crunching toil.

It would be another fifty days before they arrived at Upernavik, surviving on a diet of seagull eggs, a six-ounce daily ration of mouldy bread crumbs, and seaweed. They were at death's door when they spotted a young seal pup in Baffin Bay. Kane noted, "I had not realized how much we were reduced by famine. The men ran over the floe, crying and laughing and brandishing their knives. It was not five minutes before every man was sucking his bloody fingers or mouthing long strips of raw blubber . . . we enjoyed a rare and savage feast."

Six days later they reached salvation. It was Kane's finest hour, and he returned to America as the country's first polar hero. Eighteen months later, his poor health caught up with him and he suffered a fatal stroke aged only thirty-six.

Kane's expedition, whether viewed as a success or a glorious failure, put America firmly on the Arctic map. Next to head north was Kane's chief deserter, Isaac Hayes, who in 1860 set sail from New York aboard the *United States* in the hope of finding the Open Polar Sea and the North Pole. He found neither, although a small consolation was that he extended Kane's northerly record up Smith Sound by a few miles.

After a short lull in polar frivolity during the Civil War, the Americans were back, with the Cincinnati printer Charles Hall next on the scene in 1871. The expedition was formally endorsed by President Ulysses Grant and bankrolled to the tune of fifty thousand dollars by Congress. Hall modestly declared, "I was born to discover the North Pole. That is my purpose. Once I have set my right foot on the Pole I shall be perfectly willing to die."

Unsurprisingly, Hall failed, although he did manage to extend the Smith Sound northing record by another thirty-six miles aboard the *Polaris*, but his words would come back to haunt him. The ship had only recently set in for the winter when Hall collapsed in a fit after drinking a cup of coffee. He was delirious and began vomiting uncontrollably, going so far as to accuse his crew of poisoning him. A week later, he was dead.

The ship began to break up with the summer thaw, so the remaining nineteen men unloaded all the supplies onto an ice floe. Miraculously, they survived for six months on the floe, drifting for a total of 1,500 miles before being picked up by a whaler off the coast of Newfoundland.

A century passed before, in 1968, Hall's body was exhumed from his burial site on the Greenland coast, the autopsy revealing that he had died of arsenic poisoning. He had been murdered by someone on his team after all, although who the guilty party was remains a mystery to this day.

Less than fifty miles to go to Cape Columbia, and with the suspense of our arrival building by the minute, Don called me to the cockpit. The noise of the twin engines was so loud that the only way I could hear him was if he shouted directly into my ear. "Tom, we've got a problem. We've sprung a leak and all the hydraulic fluid that operates the flaps has drained away. We've got no choice but to turn around and make an emergency landing back at Eureka."

"You're kidding," I replied, unsure if this was Don's idea of a practical joke.

"Take a look down there and see for yourself," yelled Don as he opened a panel in the cockpit floor. A bright red liquid that looked like cranberry juice had leaked everywhere. The BRAKE FLUID dial on the flight deck pointed to empty. This was no joke.

"There's no way I'm landing this sucker down there on that ice. Without those flaps, we're going to touch down at a heck of a speed and we could easily lose the front landing gear. I'm so sorry."

As I relayed the bad news to Matty and Marc, the little plane banked to one side and began the long journey back to Eureka. I wasn't sure what filled me with less confidence – the sight of Don anxiously flicking through a manual entitled *DHC-6 Twin Otter Emergency Checklist* or our impending flapless touchdown at Eureka. With over twenty years' experience of flying planes in the High Arctic to his name, I took some comfort from the fact that we had Don at the helm of our stricken little craft. Marc, by now as white as the snows below, poured the remaining contents of his bottle of pills down his throat.

Two hours later we were back at Eureka where we had set off from four hours earlier. Thankfully, the weather remained stable and the landing wasn't as hairy as we had first feared, the plane gliding gently down the gravel runway before coming to rest in a bank of snow. It was a relief still to be in one piece, but we're all bitterly disappointed not to be at Cape Columbia.

We've had more than our fair share of bad luck of late, and this latest delay puts us a full week behind schedule. With our plane now out of commission, and no clues as to how long we might be trapped up here, it's all very frustrating.

We've heard that the second Twin Otter has at least managed to drop Hugh, George, and Andrew off at the Cape, but they're not much use marooned up there without us. All we can do is hope that we can fly north in the morning. Marc is through with light aircraft and has chosen to wait at Eureka until the next flight south.

Another big worry is the next full moon on 25 March. Tidal activity around the world's oceans increases dramatically during the full moon, and the Arctic Ocean is no exception. The Big Lead, which caused Peary so much strife, is much more likely to form during the full moon when the tides produce deep fissures within the pack ice. Given how late we already are, it would be disastrous if we became trapped for days like Peary had been. We need to get well away from the shore and beyond the continental shelf (where the Big Lead always forms) well before the full moon, but everything seems to be transpiring against us at the moment. Although you've got to be patient in this game, I'm finding it hard to stay positive.

The base at Eureka is down the hill, over a mile away from the runway. While it would have been tempting to accept the base manager's kind invitation of pork chops for dinner and a warm bed, there have been reports of wolves in the area in recent weeks, so Matty and I have decided to spend the night with the dogs by the airstrip. Because the dogs have to be tied to the chain, it would be very easy for a pack of wolves to attack each one individually, and we just can't afford to risk one of the team being injured, or worst of all, killed.

The tent is with the others at Cape Columbia, so our only option is to bed down in a simple wooden shed that the scientists sometimes use to store meteorology equipment. It's been dark for hours now and I'm tucked into my sleeping bag on the hut floor, writing by candlelight. Hoarfrost coats the ceiling and the door is so encrusted with ice that it can barely close.

At least we're protected from the worst of the wind, unlike the poor dogs who are curled up outside and chained to a couple of fuel drums. The gun is propped up in the corner of the hut, just in case we need to ward off any unwelcome visitors during the night. It promises to be an uncomfortable one.

George is twenty-nine today and we had planned to have some sort of birthday celebration at Cape Columbia this evening. They'd better not be tucking into the sloe gin without us. It's sad not being with the boys tonight and I wonder how they're getting on.

One positive result of the delay is that it has given Matty and me the chance to discuss subjects other than dogs and ice for a change. The last few weeks have been so tense and stressful for us all that being able to enjoy a good conversation about family, friends, and holidays is very welcome and helps take our minds off of the torture that lies ahead.

19 MARCH
Cape Columbia, −43°C

Throughout the night, the fragile hut walls creaked with the wind like a haunted house. The floor was comfortable enough but sleep wasn't easy thanks to the cold, unremitting draft from under the door. Despite our best efforts to block it, the wind still managed to cloak our sleeping bags with a thin layer of spindrift. Every couple of hours Matty and I took turns checking for wolves but the threat never materialized.

Down at the weather station we were treated to a delicious full English breakfast, complete with hash browns and the largest fried mushroom I've ever seen. I've no idea when we'll be able to enjoy a proper meal again and I was first in line for second helpings. I only felt the slightest tinge of guilt that George, Andrew, and Hugh, cooped up in their tent some 300 miles away, were probably making do with just muesli and powdered milk.

At 8:00 A.M. we received the news that we had been desperately hoping for – the same Twin Otter that had flown the guys north yesterday had decided to cancel its original plans to return to Resolute today in order to take us to Cape Columbia. There was huge relief all round. After a final visit to a civilized bathroom for six weeks, it was back to the airstrip to start loading the plane.

The first of the dogs were safely onboard when I noticed what appeared to be Odin, with his distinctive mane of spiky gray fur along his neck, hiding behind a fuel drum, clearly trying to evade capture. I was no more than ten feet away when Troy (our pilot for the day) screamed, "Jesus Christ, it's a wolf! Get back!"

I froze to the spot, my heart pounding. It soon became clear that this animal was much larger than Odin and the other dogs, with long, skinny legs and a more pronounced snout, stained with blood from a recent kill. I had never seen a wolf in the wild before and I was terrified. Dressed in my red expedition jacket, I couldn't help but think of how Little Red

Riding Hood met her end and wondered if I would suffer the same fate. The wolf held my stare for a brief, chilling, moment before being joined by another six or seven wolves.

The wolf's reputation as a man-eater is unfounded, but they posed a serious threat to the dogs. Secured to the tie-out chain, they would have been easy pickings if the pack decided to attack. With the dogs barking and us clapping and shouting, we did our best to scare the wolves away. The tense standoff lasted for five long minutes before the wolves eventually lost interest and walked away.

Flying north over the spectacular Ellesmere Island landscape for the second day running, faces once again glued to the frosted windows, Matty and I were deep in thought as the moment of reckoning drew closer.

Two years after his return from the Pole, and only seven years after the Wright brothers' momentous first flight in an airplane, Peary predicted that in years to come "the polar regions would be reconnoitred and explored through the air." It would no longer be necessary to sail north a summer in advance, and polar expeditions would only take a matter of weeks. With extraordinary foresight he wrote, "A squadron of airplanes . . . would reach Cape Columbia in a few hours with the whole panorama of Grant Land [the old name for Ellesmere Island] and the American gateway to the pole passing beneath, could alight on the firm level 'glacial fringe' at Cape Columbia, unload their supplies and gasoline, and the supporting machines be back at their base in less than a day." He must have known we were coming.

Before beginning our descent to Cape Columbia, we continued northward out over the frozen sea for a couple of miles to assess the state of the ice. It was my first encounter with the Arctic Ocean, and while I've looked at countless photographs of pressure ridges and rough ice over the last two years, nothing could have prepared me for the chaotic scene stretching away to the horizon.

Wherever I looked all I could see were colossal blocks of ice, piled haphazardly on the surface of the invisible ocean like some sort of never-ending construction site. The one flat pan that I could make out in the distance was no larger than a football field and criss-crossed with narrow channels of inky black water. It was a truly shocking sight, far worse than I had ever imagined. "What the hell have we let ourselves in for?" I asked myself.

Cape Columbia was first visited by an ill-fated British expedition more than thirty years before Peary. In 1875 the Admiralty's top ice navigator, Captain George Nares, was sent north to claim the Pole for Queen and Country. Nothing had been learned from the Franklin disaster; yet again the ships were far too cumbersome and difficult to manoeuvre, the sleds were the same heavy models used by the Royal Navy for decades, rations were woefully inadequate, and the men's woolen suits were so tight they were almost impossible to take off when wet.

But this was the Age of Empire, with Victorian arrogance at its height. There was a general acceptance that when it came to all things polar, we Brits knew better than anyone else how to find the North Pole. Inuit practices such as building igloos and wearing loose-fitting hooded caribou parkas were dismissed out of hand as the practices of savages. Astonishingly, Nares felt the expedition's fifty-five Greenland dogs were best left on the ships. When it came to long sledging journeys across the polar pack, it would be the men who were put into harnesses, not the dogs.

Despite these gross oversights, the expedition did have some success. A combination of good seamanship and a relatively ice-free Smith Sound enabled the ships to become the first to reach Ellesmere Island's north coast. As he gazed out at the vast ocean of jumbled ice blocks before him, Nares correctly reasoned that it was ice all the way to the Pole and that this was as far north as a ship could go.

Nares's second-in-command, Albert Markham, described the scene (the identical view to the one we would be gazing at when we touched down): "Nothing but ice, tight and impassable, was to be seen – a solid, impenetrable mass that no amount of imagination or theoretical belief could ever twist into an Open Polar Sea. We were reluctantly compelled to come to the conclusion that we had in reality arrived on the shore of the Polar Ocean; a frozen sea of such a character as utterly to preclude the possibility of its being navigated by a ship; a wide expanse of ice and snow, whose impenetrable fastnesses seemed to defy the puny efforts of mortal men to invade and expose their hitherto sealed and hidden mysteries."

The following spring, Nares sent out his sledging parties in search of the North Pole, warning the men of the sheer misery ahead of them; "The hardest days' work you have ever imagined, let alone had, would not hold a patch on the work you will have while sledging."

One group under Markham headed north for the Pole while another took their sleds west along the coast of Ellesmere Island beyond Cape Columbia. The polar party moved at a turtle's pace, making just seventy-three miles in forty days. Struggling through waist-deep snowdrifts, having to cross forty-foot-high pressure ridges, and shivering in temperatures down to the minus-forties, Nares's prophecy was becoming horribly true.

Nevertheless, the exhausted men, crippled by scurvy, reached 83°20N, beating Edward Parry's farthest north record that had stood since 1827, but they were still 400 miles from the Pole. It would be another month before they returned to the ship, with Alfred Parr, the one reasonably healthy man left amongst them, covering the final thirty miles alone in a single push to get help for his stricken companions. With three of the ship's crew already dead and many others riddled with scurvy, Nares canceled all plans for a second overwintering and hurried back to England.

The British press and public saw the expedition as a total fiasco and made Nares the scapegoat. THE POLAR FAILURE was how one newspaper headline described him. An expedition that had set off with so much fanfare and optimism returned humiliated. In the back streets of London, the words "North Pole" would become the cockney rhyming slang translation for "arsehole." The British love affair with the frozen north was over. Not until Sir Wally Herbert's trans-Arctic expedition in 1969 would the Union Jack finally be raised at the top of the world.

Cape Columbia is not the dramatic headland one might expect but a narrow apron of flat, inhospitable ground that runs for several miles along the north shore of Ellesmere Island. Like the summit slopes of Everest, the fact that much of this glacial fringe is devoid of snow is a reminder of the gales that frequently batter this remote coastline. From time to time, frigid air from the island's ice cap spills through Ellesmere's mountains, accelerating to a super-chilled downdraft as it pours over the glaciers and out across the open ocean beyond.

With the midday sun hovering just above the southern horizon, our landing strip on the fringe lay in the shadow of the mountains, and it was surprisingly gloomy as we approached. Using snow-filled bin liners, Andrew, Hugh and George marked out a runway last night to make things easier for Troy. After a bumpy landing we came to a halt just yards from the tent, the guys running out to greet us with smiling faces.

It was great to have the team reunited again and there were big hugs all round. Yesterday, their plane had been the one carrying all the dog food and sledging gear, and by the sound of things they had had to endure a pretty rough night with only minimal camping equipment and basic rations. The good news is that they resisted temptation to break into our one bottle of sloe gin alone.

The cold was almost unbearable, and no sooner had Troy waved us off than we dived inside the tent. All four stoves were put into immediate action, on went the kettle, and Matty began preparing a giant bowl of creamy mushroom pasta for everyone.

There were still a few hours of precious daylight left, and while it was too late in the day to pack up camp and try to make some mileage before nightfall, I was determined that we should make the most of our time at Cape Columbia. I opened my fleece pocket and pulled out a black-and-white photo of some igloos and dog kennels, which Peary took during his time here.

As I explained to the team, "This was Peary's base camp at Cape Columbia, named Crane City after the vice president of the Peary Arctic Club, Zenas Crane. His team would have spent their final nights here before confronting the Arctic Ocean. There's no record of anyone having been there since 1909 and all that we know for sure is that it was located somewhere along the coastline behind us. If people are up for it, I want to see if we can find Crane City this afternoon."

"How exactly are we going to do that?" asked Matty. "The place would have been destroyed by the weather and we don't even have any coordinates to plug into the GPS."

Pointing at the photo, I continued, "This twin-peaked hill in the background holds the key. If we follow the shore, hopefully we'll be able to identify that very distinctive hill. With any luck, Crane City will be directly beneath it."

My plans weren't met with the greatest enthusiasm. I got the feeling the others would much rather be spending the time resting before we hit the trail tomorrow.

Eventually everyone agreed to give it a try, and leaving the dogs in camp, we made our way towards the seemingly impenetrable fortress of snow-clad peaks that stretched from east to west as far as we could see. The cold was unrelenting, and we walked at a brisk pace to keep warm.

After more than an hour of searching I was convinced we had found our hill. Everyone gathered round for another look at the photo. Andrew was pretty unconvinced and thought we had been heading in completely the wrong direction. I was far from certain myself, but we soldiered on nevertheless.

Only when we got closer to the hill did the terrain in Peary's photo match perfectly with the topography before us. Although there was nothing to see but snow and frost-shattered rock, we were all absolutely confident that we were standing beneath the twin-peaked summit in the photo. We had located Crane City. We were its first visitors since 25 April 1909, the day Peary and his men passed through on their triumphant return from the Pole. It was an extraordinary feeling to be at that historic place and helped put into perspective the stresses and strains of the last few weeks. We may be a week behind schedule, but it's still only taken us twenty-four days to get here since leaving home. It took Peary eight months.

Pointing at an area of flatter ground in the photo where the igloos had been built, Hugh then said, "Hey guys, I wonder what we'll find in that snowdrift over there." Kicking away the snow with our boots, it wasn't long before we started unearthing artifacts from Peary's expedition: fuel canisters, old sled runners, a rusty baked bean can, and part of a wooden crate that one day probably contained dog food.

Peary has consumed my life for the past two years, and my dreams have taken me to this place many times. I had hoped we might find some evidence of his expedition, but the incredible treasure trove we uncovered was beyond my wildest dreams. Some of the items were so well preserved it felt as if his team were here only recently.

The men may have left nearly a century ago but their ghosts still lingered. I closed my eyes for a brief moment and was overcome with emotion. It could just as easily have been 1909, with Peary, Henson, Bartlett, and the others making the final preparations for their long, treacherous journey across the Arctic Ocean. I could hear their voices and the howls of their dogs, calling out to me from the past. I could picture Henson and the Inuit guide Ootah making repairs to a sled, Peary issuing instructions, and Captain Bob puffing away on his pipe. It was as if they were all still here and would be out on the ice alongside us as we raced to the North Pole together.

Just as Peary and Bartlett had done on the eve of their departure in 1909, Andrew and I clambered a short distance up the scree slope immediately behind Crane City to get a better look at the pack ice and to see if there was a possible chink in its armor. The view was breathtaking. To the east and west, a succession of glaciated peaks and deep fjords meandered their way to the horizon, while to the north, the chaos of the frozen sea stretched away to infinity. The Arctic Ocean is a forbidding jumble of broken ice from whatever angle you look at it, and with the temperatures falling off the bottom of the thermometer we decided that it was time to head down.

Before we left, I put five small rock fragments in my pocket, one of which I will keep for myself, the rest I will give to the others if and when we reach the Pole. In recent years, several expeditions have been accused of cutting corners by being dropped off several miles out to sea, thereby avoiding the most treacherous of the ice conditions that tend to lie closer to the coast. The stones will be simple mementos of our journey, as well as cast-iron proof that we set off from the land.

Our discoveries had energized us all and helped us forget the brutal −43°C temperatures for a short while. With a spring in our step, we set off in a westerly direction to see what else we could find. Our next target was a marker post two miles away, which Andrew and Hugh had spotted from camp this morning. It was located on a rocky outcrop and stood all by itself at what appeared to be the most northerly point of Cape Columbia. The 2,133-foot bulk of Mount Cooper Key lurked a short distance behind, a giant tongue of ice protruding from the saddle between its two summits and down to the shore.

As we approached, it became clear that this was no ordinary hikers' signpost. The timbers were bleached-bone gray, with galvanized iron lines securing each of the four arms to the ground. The main post itself was surrounded by a cairn of large stones. It then dawned on us that we were in fact staring at the very monument Peary erected following his attainment of the Pole. He mentions it in his book, but I just assumed that after being lashed by a century of polar storms, it would have been flattened long ago. A copper plate had been punched with a hammer and nail to produce a basic inscription on each arm, commemorating Peary's geographical achievements during his years in the Arctic and their distance from the Cape.

We stared at the ghostly signpost in silence. The eastern arm pointed to Greenland and read, CAPE MORRIS K. JESSUP, MAY 16, 1900, 275 MILES, the southern arm, CAPE COLUMBIA, JUNE 6, 1906, and the western arm, CAPE THOMAS H. HUBBARD, JULY 1, 1906, 225 MILES. The northern arm pointed purposefully out over the ice-covered ocean, goading us to follow in Peary's footsteps. It was inscribed with the immortal words, NORTH POLE, APRIL 6, 1909, 413 MILES. We were totally overwhelmed.

Standing by Peary's marker post today and finding his base camp has brought this incredible character to life. No longer is Peary a mere name who only appears in textbooks and museums. He is very real and I feel I now know him a little better. This extraordinary day has been the culmination of thousands of hours of accumulated blood, sweat, and tears that we have all endured over the past two years. It feels like we have at last reached the halfway point and all that remains is the journey itself.

The Arctic Ocean lies in wait, barely a hundred yards to the north of us. For the next six weeks we will share this five-million-square-mile frozen wilderness with nobody else but a handful of polar bears, seals, and Arctic foxes, as well as four South Koreans, who eleven days ago set off for the Pole from Ward Hunt Island, thirty miles west of here.

The mood in camp this evening is calm, reflective, with little conversation. There's a real feeling of anticipation, everyone with a thousand thoughts rushing through their heads. For the next month and a half, the five of us and our sixteen canine companions will be out on the open ocean, at the mercy of the ocean currents and polar winds. The cold and the endless walls of ice will sap our strength, we'll need to dig deep into our depleted reserves of energy just to keep going, and at night we'll be sleeping on ice often no more than a couple of feet thick, which could fracture or buckle without warning.

There'll be no respite from the cold, no time to rest, no letup in the perpetual drift of the ice pack, and no feeling of triumph or peace of mind until we reach the North Pole, the top of the world. I wonder if we will do it.

4. Breaking the Ice

DAY 1: 20 MARCH
−32°C, 413.8 Miles to Go

THE ALARM PIERCED THE FRIGID AIR AT 6:00 A.M., but we were already up, going through the time-consuming and perishingly cold process of putting on our many layers of polar clothing. Despite the uncomfortable start, spirits were high. After all the frustrations of the last few days, we felt as prepared as we were ever going to be to tackle the Arctic Ocean and everything it might have in store for us.

It was still dark outside, so breakfast was prepared by flashlight. Over a bowl of muesli and a cup of hot chocolate, the travel plans for the day were finalized. Matty would head out on skis, scouting the route ahead, Hugh and I would follow with the first sled, with George and Andrew bringing up the rear with the second.

In a freshening wind that burned our cheeks raw, we began distributing the equipment and provisions between the two sleds, a job that would have been done yesterday had it not been for the Twin Otter's calamity.

This was the very first time we had tried to pack everything in and as the loads grew in size, I became increasingly anxious that either the sleds weren't going to be large enough to carry everything, or they'd be too heavy for the dogs to pull. We simply could not afford to ditch a load of dog food or cooking fuel, which would leave our carefully laid plans in ruins before we'd even got under way.

Fortunately, our pre-expedition calculations were correct, and we just about managed to cram everything onboard, although by the time Hugh's giant homemade sleeping system (a combination of two inflatable mattresses, an inner and outer sleeping bag, all cocooned within a vast over-bag) was lashed to the top of the second sled, it looked as if it was going to topple over. "Dale-Harris may as well have brought a four-poster bed with him!" joked Andrew.

It was time to unclip the dogs from the tie-out chain and start harnessing them up. As we got closer, both teams erupted into a deafening chorus of uncontrolled howling. As I made my way towards Raven, the lead dog on the first sled, he barked and barked and jumped about all over the place. I had never seen the dogs quite so eager and impatient to get going. They seemed to know they were about to embark on a journey to the North Pole and were so overly excited that they could barely contain themselves.

On the morning of 28 February 1909, Captain Bartlett and his pioneer division set off from Cape Columbia, using pickaxes to break the trail. Support parties led by Borup, Henson, Goodsell, Marvin, and MacMillan followed along at regular intervals. Peary was the last to leave the following morning, bringing up the rear like a general marshaling his troops into battle. Peary being at the back meant the returning support parties could update him with what was going on ahead, and he was able to keep pushing anyone he felt was not pulling their weight. Also, by saving himself and his small polar division from the strenuous work of keeping the trail open, he was able to conserve vital energy for when it would be needed most.

Shortly before 10 A.M. and with Matty already 200 yards out in front, it was our turn to head north. Two years of planning had come down to this moment. thirty-seven days and two hours precisely was the time to beat. In the half-light of the Arctic dawn, we clipped into our skis, pulled our fur hoods down over our heads, and got into position. Butterflies filled my stomach. As Hugh yanked out the snow anchor, I yelled, "OK, Raven, let's go!"

Immediately the dogs fell silent and leapt at their traces as if their lives depended on it. With an ease that belied its weight, the sled sprang into life. We were off. As we hurtled across the easy ground of the glacial fringe, Hugh and I clung to the handlebars like a pair of synchronized waterskiers. "Boy, it's great to be back on the ice!" exclaimed Hugh.

"Sure is! But this ain't gonna last long so enjoy the ride while it lasts!" I replied, wary of what lay ahead. I glanced back to see the other two successfully launch the second team, George grinning from ear to ear. We were under way, and all the problems and pressures of the last few weeks were fast becoming a distant memory.

All that early optimism quickly evaporated into the cold metallic air as we approached the edge of the Arctic Ocean. Last night in the hut by the runway, I read a few pages of Peary's book before bed. For weeks my mind had been so consumed by the practicalities of the expedition that the reality of what we were about to face had yet to hit home. All that changed when Peary described what Day 1 might bring; "Beyond the glacial fringe is the indescribable surface of the . . . tidal crack, that zone of unceasing conflict between the heavy floating ice and the stationary glacial fringe . . . Here the ice is smashed into fragments of all sizes and piled up into great pressure ridges parallel with the shore." For the first time I had a real sense of fear and foreboding.

Right on cue, an almost vertical wall of pack ice loomed up ahead, hugging the shoreline in both directions as far as we could see. It looked like some vast ice fortress, the kind you might expect to see in *The Chronicles of Narnia*. Thrust up against the land by the combined forces of wind and ocean current, the giant pressure ridge made a formidable obstacle. The row of cobalt-blue ice blocks was over forty feet in height and dwarfed our overloaded sleds. It was a truly terrible sight. There was even a moat, a channel of deep powder snow in the lee of the ridge, which made the sleds grind to a halt. We had travelled a mere 500 yards, but already the dogs were panting heavily.

Up at the ridge, Matty had identified a potential cranny in its seemingly impenetrable ramparts, a narrow gateway that, after a bit of widening with the axes, was just about big enough to allow the sleds to squeeze through. The terrain made travelling on skis way too hazardous, so we secured them to the sleds and continued on foot.

With Matty up ahead beckoning the dogs, it still needed the strength of all four of us to lift a single sled into position and force it through the tight crack. Still, those hard-fought yards were highly significant – we had made our last steps on terra firma and were now at the mercy of the shifting ice floes of the frozen sea. It was a sobering thought.

Throughout the day we worked our way over a succession of ridges that Mother Nature had inconveniently aligned at right angles to our route. Skis remained strapped to the sleds all day. It was exhausting work, particularly when the heavy sleds became bogged down in snowdrifts. A single ridge could take as much as half an hour to cross. We even had to skirt around a couple of areas of open water, which none of us had been expecting to see so early in the expedition.

At least our polar work-out was keeping us warm. I couldn't help but feel sorry for Matty who spent most of the day calling on the dogs and waiting for us to catch up to her. She had no option but to stand around in the cold and watch as the four of us and all the dogs struggled to inch the sleds northward. She kept her thick down jacket on all day and could often be seen stamping her feet or swinging her arms around in giant windmills to get the blood circulating to her frozen toes and fingers again.

Raven, with his distinctive black coat and cream spots above each eye, was clearly finding the job of breaking trail through the soft snow too much, and so for the last two hours of the day, Hugh and I volunteered to swap places with Kimmik's team to see if they would fare any better.

It was uncharacteristic of Raven and his brother and right-hand man, Zorro, to be flagging so early. Throughout our training, Raven had proven himself to be a natural leader and extremely popular amongst the other dogs. Not only had he been the most consistent puller on either team, he had also thrived on the responsibility of being out in front and would always put on an extra spurt if the second sled threatened to overtake him.

Zorro lives very much in the shadow of his more gregarious brother. He's too spaced out and laid-back ever to be considered for the role of lead dog, and his coat is so dishevelled it looks like he's been dragged backwards through a hedge, but he makes an excellent second-in-command, positioned slightly behind Raven amongst the pack. They're inseparable and together they form the starter engine of the first team. I just hoped that this deterioration in their performance wasn't a sign of things to come.

There was one alarming moment shortly before we made camp when we met a pressure ridge forming before our very eyes. It had an almost hypnotic affect on me, and for a brief moment I was mesmerized, as the noise of shifting ice blocks rang out like a giant heartbeat. "For fuck's sake, Tom, snap out of it!" cried Hugh. "We've gotta get a move on!"

A natural ramp led up to the one gap in the ridge, but it was closing steadily, like a set of elevator doors in slow motion. Matty, closely followed by the first sled, got through fine, but by the time it came to our turn, the ramp had become caught between the shifting plates of ice and was becoming steeper by the second. George and Andrew were waiting for us on the other side, and we could hear them desperately trying to cajole Raven and the rest of the dogs forwards. They were all pulling their hardest but the sled wouldn't budge. Hugh and I had a real battle to lift it into position before pushing it through in the nick of time. Any later and the sled would have been crushed into kindling wood. Something tells me that won't be our last close shave of the expedition.

By the time we pitched the tent on what seemed to be an area of safe, multiyear ice, it was almost dark. We crawled inside and once the stoves were going, we pulled out the GPS to get the day's mileage. Back in 1909, Peary used a sextant to work out his latitude and distance travelled. A sextant works by calculating the angle between the sun and the horizon at local midday when the sun is at its highest in the sky. This is known as a sun shot and can only be taken when the sky is clear. An accurate latitude reading is then obtained from the celestial almanac, which lists the solar positions of thousands of latitudes around the globe for all 365 days of the year. It's a technique that has been used by sailors and polar explorers for hundreds of years. The GPS has only taken its place in the last fifteen years.

However, I don't trust our own relatively amateur celestial navigation skills to get us to the Pole with a sextant alone, which is why we've brought a GPS with us. Still, there are other ways we can test Peary's much maligned navigation techniques. We'll only turn to the GPS in the evenings to work out our position, and on no account is it to be used for navigation. During the day, just like Peary, we'll rely on the sun, the wind, our watches and, when it's cloudy, our compasses to find our way.

The sun was so low in the sky for the early part of the journey that Peary's first accurate sun shot wasn't taken until 14 March. Each time he or one of his team fixed their position, a wind shelter had to be built and furs laid out on the snow to make sure the man making the observations was comfortable and totally still. The sextant had to be assembled and a series of readings jotted down in a notebook as the sun reached its zenith in the southern sky. It's not hard to imagine what a tedious, bone-numbingly cold chore it must have been for them, particularly as observations could only be carried out at local midday,★ a time when the men would normally be on the trail.

Peary's solution was therefore to take a sun shot every five days. For the intervening period, when they arrived at camp in the evenings, Peary, Bartlett, and Marvin would estimate how far they thought the party had travelled. The average of the three guesstimates would be the distance Peary jotted down in his log book that night.

Henson and the Inuit were also regularly consulted for their opinion, due to their nomadic lifestyle back home in Greenland that required expert navigation. While the Inuit didn't understand the concept of miles, their way of estimating the day's northerly progress was to compare it to the distance between two known points, for example the width of the Kennedy Channel. Based on the ice conditions and the length of time on the trail, they would have had a very good sense of how far they had

★Local midday is the time at which the sun passes directly over the line of longitude (also known as a meridian) at which you are standing. The sun reaches its highest position in the sky at the same time. The origins of the terms A.M. (ante meridiem) and P.M. (post meridiem), still used in twelve-hour timekeeping today, can be traced back to the early astrologers who first noticed this phenomenon.

travelled. So confident was Peary of the technique he and his men had honed after many accumulated years of polar travel that he wrote, "One can tell to within a mile or so how far one walks on the northern ice."

This might seem a fairly rudimentary method for calculating something as important as one's mileage. Indeed, Peary's dead-reckoning of distances has been ridiculed by his critics for years. I want to put his method to the test, and so before we consulted the GPS, I asked everyone to estimate how far they think we have travelled in the eight and a half hours since we hit the trail. We can tell we haven't gone far because Mount Cooper Key still dominates the southern horizon and barely seems to have got any smaller since the morning.

The average of our guesstimates comes to what we think is a very conservative 5.5 miles. There's a collective groan as the GPS tells us the total is in fact 4.1 miles. We're a long way from mastering this dead-reckoning business – a job that's clearly far harder on the frozen ocean than it is on land – and thanks to the keen westerly breeze that has pushed us some distance off course today, only 3.6 of our miles were in a northerly direction. If we carry on at this rate, we won't reach the Pole for another 113 days.

We've fought tooth and nail for every one of those 3.6 miles today and we're all in a sober mood this evening. It's been a brutal introduction to driving dogs on the Arctic Ocean for us all, a real baptism of fire. While today's numerous sled jams and capsizes were to be expected, this has been far more physically draining than I had ever imagined. My muscles ache and my back is stiff from all the heavy lifting we've had to do. It makes manhauling across Antarctica seem like a walk in the park.

The North Pole feels a long way away tonight.

DAY 2: 21 MARCH
−35°C, Seven Miles Behind Peary, 410 Miles to Go

Not the best night's sleep I've ever had. We're no longer protected from Ellesmere Island's wind shadow, and the tent was shaken violently throughout the night. It was also indescribably cold. There was nothing else I could do to insulate myself as, apart from my expedition jacket, I was already wearing every item of clothing I had with me. For hours I lay shivering inside my −40°C-rated sleeping bag, teeth chattering, in the knowledge that more than five long weeks lie ahead with no escape from the deathly cold. The occasional dog whimper from outside reminded me that those of us in the tent were the lucky ones. But it was only some consolation.

With the five of us packed in like sardines, the tent was also horribly claustrophobic. Not only had I pulled my sleeping bag's drawstring too tight around my face in a futile attempt to keep out the freezing temperatures, but thanks to Hugh's giant bed that took up most of our half of the tent, I was crammed up against the tent walls all night and often found myself gasping for air. Condensation from my breath coated the tiny breathing hole in my sleeping bag, giving me a wet face every time I rolled over. Then, to make matters worse, Hugh started snoring. What is it about snorers? No matter how hard you shake them, it makes no difference at all. Hugh was down for the count. All in all, my first taste of the ravages of the polar night were a real shock to the system.

When morning came, Hugh, blissfully unaware of his contribution to my interrupted night's sleep, announced cheerily, "Goooooooood morning! How did everyone sleep?"

"That was a night I'd rather forget," I replied tersely.

"That's an impressive snore you've got yourself, Hugh-Dale," said George.

"Sorry, folks. Nothing I can do about it." But from the cheeky grin on Hugh's face you could tell he was actually quite proud of his efforts. "I guess you'll just have to make sure you fall asleep before me from now on!"

Today's plan was for Raven and Zorro to assume their role leading out the first team. I'd hoped that Hugh and I would be able to get more out of them than we had managed the day before. During breakfast, Andrew said how much he had relished being with the lead sled yesterday afternoon and asked if he could stay at the front. In many ways Andrew is not dissimilar to Raven in that he thrives on being given extra responsibility.

I need to keep Andrew motivated because his unlimited energy reserves are integral to our success. Personal pride just can't get in the way of our goal, so after some thought I volunteered to swap places with him. Andrew and Hugh get on well, and I was sure they would make an excellent team. In 1909, Peary had positioned himself with the rear sled as he felt it was the ideal place for him to gee everyone along, so it's no bad place to be.

It was a pity to relinquish my place on the lead sled at such an early stage, but for the sake of team harmony, it was the right decision to make. Besides, the good news was as it meant I would team up with George on Kimmik's sled. Our priority has to be to get to the Pole as fast as possible – and that's only going to happen with a happy, united team.

There's something deeply rewarding about breaking trail. Even though you're essentially following the scout's ski tracks, you do feel as though you are preparing the trail for the rest of the party to follow, particularly over any awkward terrain. It's just like being the first one to ski down an ungroomed mountainside after a fresh fall of snow.

The real difference between our trail and that made by Peary's party is that we have just two sleds to his nineteen (a number that was whittled down to five as the various support divisions returned to the *Roosevelt*). As Peary's caravan, travelling in single file, crossed a pressure ridge, the ice would have been gradually compacted by the combined effects of the heavy sleds crashing through and the hundreds of dog paws and human feet trampling it down. By the time the final sled had crossed the ridge, the trail would have become almost flat, like a railway cutting splitting a line of hills.

A similar improvement in the trail would have applied in soft snow. The men in the rear divisions would have carefully positioned their sleds so the runners followed precisely in the grooves that the first sled had cut in the snow, where a more compact (and therefore faster) surface could be found.

Even though we only have the two sleds, probably five to ten per cent less effort is required to drive the second sled through than the first. Peary ensured no sled had an unfair advantage by ordering "the leading sled at the end of each hour to drop back to the rear. In this way each driver and team of dogs had an equal share of the work." Because Raven is a much more reliable lead dog than Kimmik, our strategy for keeping everyone at the same speed is to put Kimmik's team in the rear and weigh his sled down with an extra forty-pound sack of dog food.

In all the rush to get ready for the expedition, we had completely forgotten to check that our Winchester 30-06 rifle worked. Due to the polar bear threat, carrying a firearm is of paramount importance on North Pole expeditions, perhaps more so now than ever. As Peary himself had written, "The polar bear has been called the tiger of the North; but a contest between one or two, or even three, of these animals and a man armed with a Winchester repeating rifle is an extremely one-sided affair."

Still, a gun that doesn't work is about as much use against a rampaging half-ton bear as a cricket bat, so after breakfast, Matty used a ski pole to scrape a basic target onto the side of a large ice block near camp. We had a great time as we each took turns blasting off a couple of rounds at the ice. The rifles appeared to be in good working order. We're all experienced shots but it was important to familiarize ourselves with the Winchester, which only Matty and Andrew had ever used before.

Polar bears are one of the greatest dangers to Arctic travellers. They live in a world where prey is incredibly scarce, and they're the top predator on the ice. A carnivore that sometimes has to travel hundreds of miles in search of food can't afford to be a fussy eater. Seals form the bulk of their diet, but they've been known to eat foxes, hares, walrus, and even whales. Even humans are a potential meal for a hungry bear.

The tragedy for the polar bear is that because of climate change, the increasing amount of open water on the Arctic Ocean makes it much easier for the seals to keep out of the bears' way. This means that the bears have to travel farther and farther north in search of food, with the result that most North Pole expeditions now have some sort of encounter with one. Although they saw several sets of bear prints, Peary's expedition met no polar bears during their firty-five days on the Arctic Ocean in 1909.

The polar bear is such a beautiful, iconic animal, but while I would love to see one someday, I'd be happy if it wasn't on this particular expedition. Apart from anything else, I would be distraught if we had to kill one. We are, after all, trespassers in their world. There's an accepted strategy for dealing with a troublesome bear. If its body language suggested that its intentions were more than casual curiosity, first we would shoot over its head, in the hope that the noise of the gun would scare it off. If that failed and the bear continued to pose a threat, we would shoot into the snow by its paws. All the time we would be slapping our skis together and shouting at the top of our voices to act as a deterrent and frighten it off. Shooting it dead would only be a last resort. That is, if it didn't get us first.

Today's progress was a vast improvement on yesterday's. By midday we had left the heaved-up tangle of coastal ice behind and spent the afternoon travelling over a mixture of pans of multiyear ice and pressure ridges. I can now appreciate just what Peary meant when he wrote, "Every one of us was glad to reach the surface of the old floes beyond this crazy zone of ice . . . As soon as we struck the old floes the going was much better."

We were blessed with the much smoother terrain of two recently frozen leads, both of which pointed north. Neither lasted more than about ten minutes, but they provided a welcome change from the endless rows of pressure ridges we've had to deal with so far.

When we visited the weather station back in Resolute Bay, ice guru Wayne Davidson had shown us a terrifying satellite image of the first thirty miles of our route. The whole surface looked like shattered glass, with leads of open water everywhere. It appears, however, that the recent cold weather has frozen over the majority of them because thankfuly we've only seen the occasional small lead since leaving the land. Having said that, Ootah managed to go for an impromptu swim this afternoon when the thin piece of ice he was standing on gave way. Seeing the look of fear on his face as he struggled in the freezing water, I rushed over to help. But he was out before I could reach him, covering me with freezing water as he shook himself dry, seemingly none the worse for wear. They're a hardy bunch, these Eskimo dogs.

We found ourselves bogged down in some deep drifts in the last hour of the day, but we've made much better progress today and everyone was in fine spirits. The way George and I worked together was very satisfying, and Andrew clearly reveled in being with the first sled. Much to our relief, Raven was back to his indomitable best and led from the front all day long, so it looks like we've found a formula that works for everyone. Still, we need to keep pushing. The full moon is just four days away and we've got a long way to go before we clear the edge of the continental shelf, home of the Big Lead.

Travelling on the frozen Arctic Ocean is a fantastic, energizing, but at times terrifying experience. I sometimes have to pinch myself that we're actually at sea out here. I've never been in an environment in such turmoil. You can regularly feel the whole place pulsating, and the security of dry land already feels like a distant memory. The noise and vibrations created as the floes are pulverized against one another send shockwaves through your skis during the day and sleeping bag at night. So mechanical is the racket that at times it's like being on a building site, with a cacophony of hammering, scraping, and general demolition noises filling the air. All pretty terrifying. It's astonishing to think the din is generated by nothing but frozen water.

DAY 3: 22 MARCH
−38°C, Ten Miles Behind Peary, 403 Miles to Go

Another unspeakably cold night. A cruel draft found its way through a gap under the tent door and made matters even worse. Even my bones felt they had turned to ice. The tent walls and our collective body heat give us a paltry one degree centigrade of extra warmth at night. So while the mercury dropped to −42°C outside, inside the tent it was a mere −41°C.

As anyone who has had to share a tent with me on past expeditions would confirm, I find the first half hour of the day a real struggle – particularly after a rough night. I'm invariably the last one to exit my sleeping bag as I savor those last precious minutes of relative warmth. It's been a source of much ridicule from my fellow teammates over the years. Up here in the frozen Arctic, I'm finding the mornings even more of a challenge, and from the time I get up, I spend the rest of the day fantasizing about that blissful moment when I can crawl back into my sleeping bag.

Every night, a blanket of feathery strands of hoarfrost builds up on the inside of the tent, formed as our breath mixes with the frigid air. This morning, I inadvertently brushed my head against the tent roof, showering myself in tiny ice crystals, most of which found their way down my thermal top – not to be recommended.

It's typically the responsibility of the first person who stirs in the mornings (usually Matty), to begin firing up the four MSR Whisperlight stoves for breakfast. Equipment malfunctions are a regular headache on cold expeditions, with stoves routinely the most temperamental items. We've had some worrying trouble with the rubber washers at the top of the bottles. They're not forming a strong enough seal in the extreme cold, causing the bottles to leak. We do have some spare washers that seem to be working better, but for how much longer remains to be seen. Several North Pole expeditions in recent times have come to grief, thanks to faulty stoves, and I'd be devastated if we were to suffer the same fate.

There was another brief moment of panic this morning when we couldn't get the white gas in the frozen fuel bottles to vapourize, meaning the stoves refused to light. With frantic urgency, Matty, Hugh, and I took turns pumping the priming plunger. Still nothing. It was Hugh who applied the magic touch and after ten minutes of trying, the stove eventually spluttered into life, initially with a weak yellow flame, and then a roaring blue one. Huge relief all round.

Frozen fingers were immediately placed over the flames until the sharp pain of pins and needles signaled they had returned to life. Sleeping bags were then packed away into their stuff sacks and Thermarest inflatable mattresses folded into their special L-shaped sleeves. Placed on top of the sleeping bag stuff sacks, they form a surprisingly comfortable chair at mealtimes. With four stoves on the go, as well as cups of piping hot chocolate, two kettles, and five people's breath, the tent soon took on the appearance of a sauna. From then on, it became a game of "dodge the drips" as the hoarfrost thawed.

It had taken us nearly four hours to get going on the previous two mornings. All our chores take twice as long in these temperatures, but we were also clearly out of practice. Our housekeeping needs to become more efficient if we're going to make it to the Pole inside thirty-seven days and before the breakup of the ice. The more time we spend in the tent, the less time we'll have on the trail.

I raised the subject over breakfast and asked for people's suggestions on how we could speed things up. Matty came up with the practical idea of establishing a rota for the five most time-consuming chores, namely feeding the dogs, collecting snow for cooking, preparing breakfast, cooking dinner, and, the worst job of all, washing up. Her plan was met with universal approval, so from now on we'll take turns doing each role, which will give everyone an equal share of the work. In theory, people should rarely be at a loose end, and if someone is taking a break from their particular task for the day, they can keep themselves busy eating, getting dressed, carrying out repairs, or helping others.

Andrew was on breakfast duty today, which involved dishing out the muesli, powdered milk, and sugar into our plastic bowls, filling up the water bottles for the day ahead, and preparing the breakfast drinks. George and Andrew enjoy their coffee in the mornings while the rest of us choose between tea and hot chocolate. Back home, I'm not a great fan of hot drinks, and even up here in the Arctic I only like my drinks tepid at best. Watching me add two sugars and four teaspoons of snow to my mug, Matty joked, "Just how cold would it have to be outside for you to enjoy an ordinary cup of hot tea like the rest of us?"

Our last task in the mornings is the dreaded job of putting on our boots. The whole process can take a good half hour and requires focus and willpower. The boots are always frozen solid and so encrusted with ice that it's as if they're made from concrete. I brushed what ice I could from the outside of both boots before trying to force my foot into the neoprene liner, pulling hard on the canvas outer boot at the same time. But it wouldn't go in. After much stamping on the ground, the boot slipped on and I could immediately feel all that precious warmth being sucked from my toes. The others were experiencing similar discomfort. "I properly hate this bit," George said, grimacing as he grappled with a frozen boot.

Once I'd got the second boot on, it was time to thread the laces through the boot holes on both the inner and outer boots. Despite wearing a pair of thin fleece gloves, it was impossible to finish a whole boot without fingers freezing solid, which would then require a series of vigorous shakes to get the blood circulating again.

As soon as the whole ordeal was over I rushed out into the day and began running on the spot to try and bring my numb toes back to life. Hugh was already outside, going through the same performance. Shaking his head at the overcast sky he said, "This is gonna be a shitty day."

Travelling in cloudy weather in the polar regions is a real test of one's navigation skills. Everywhere you look is gray and featureless, with no differentiation between snow, ice, and sky. Pressure ridges and areas of thin ice become so concealed by the flat light that you don't realize you're about to hit one until the dogs inexplicably stop in their tracks. It's so disorientating and frustrating. Absolute concentration is required at all times, and even if you're lucky enough to spot a piece of ice through the gloom, often there's not enough information for the eyes to process what they're looking at and it quickly disappears again. The flat light gives you headaches and makes you feel nauseous. Peary wrote, "A more ghastly atmosphere could not have been imagined even by Dante himself."

Luckily for Peary, he didn't experience his first flat light until Day 27. The textbooks say that the Arctic Ocean is technically a desert, with clear skies very much the norm, but thanks to climate change, there is now much more in the way of open water than there was in 1909. Because clouds usually form over water, the skies above the Arctic Ocean are becoming increasingly overcast. Like Peary, we don't have the benefit of receiving weather forecasts or satellite imagery. Even if we did, they wouldn't be much use as our tight time frame stipulates that we have to travel in whatever the weather gods throw at us.

And so today proved to be very tough for everyone, none more so than for Matty up in front, who had to test the ground continuously with her ski poles in the same manner a blind person would use a white stick to find their way. By the time we made camp, we were all mentally and physically drained. I wore too much today and as a result my clothes were coated in iced-up sweat. It felt as if we were going uphill all day. Before retiring to the tent, Hugh and I spent a few minutes working on the sleds, tightening the cross-lashings between the handlebars that had become loose, after countless crashes and capsizes.

The route to the Pole is like a never-ending assault course, with the most testing obstacles all coming at the start. Despite being almost impossible to see, today's pressure ridges were monsters. The worst took the best part of an hour of hard toil to cross. Often we had to lift the sleds out of icy ravines that they had toppled into, using the axes to chop a route through the ice or the shovels to clear away snowdrifts. It was a story of much effort expended for very little distance gained.

A quick check of our fuel supplies this evening revealed that we had already gone through more than ten liters of cooking fuel. We had rationed ourselves to three liters of fuel per day until the first resupply comes in, but we've clearly been way too liberal with our fuel consumption so far. The situation was not helped by the leak in one of the fuel cans today, which we think came about after the first sled took a big hit from the final pressure ridge of the day. If we carry on at this rate, we could easily run out of fuel, so we've reluctantly agreed to keep just two of the four stoves on for the last hour of the evening. The drop in temperature is alarming.

There are, however, two crumbs of comfort tonight. Not only have we passed Albert Markham's farthest north record of 83°20 set in 1876, but also now that we're more than twelve miles from the coast, we've reached international waters. If we happened to run into difficulties between here and the Pole, we would be treated just like a ship in distress on the high seas. We've put a full maritime search-and-rescue evacuation plan in place with Kenn Borek Air just in case – all of which is covered by our very expensive expedition insurance policy.

"Because we're now technically in no-man's land, does that mean that if I was to shoot Hugh to get him to quit snoring, I would be immune from prosecution?" asks George mischievously.

"Give it a try and see what happens?" answers Andrew, chuckling away to himself.

"Listen here, you idiots, it took me a while to get to sleep last night and the snoring coming from your side of the tent had to be heard to be believed. So get back in your box!"

Hugh's right; they're all at it now.

Day 4: 23 March
−39°C, Nineteen Miles Behind Peary, 396 Miles to Go

My first decent night's sleep since Resolute Bay. I put it down more to sheer exhaustion than anything else. We started slightly later than normal this morning after Matty accidentally put her boots on the wrong feet and didn't realize it until we were leaving the tent. She was furious with herself for making such a simple, time-consuming mistake and that it happened in full view of the whole team. "That's just the kind of thing I would do," I said, trying to cheer her up. "We'll start loading the sleds while you get yourself sorted."

It must be difficult for Matty being in this testosterone-fueled, all-male team. Because she's skiing out in front on her own all day, away from the dogs and all the action, at times it must feel as if she's almost on a separate expedition. Seeing Matty get so down this morning made me realize that I need to make more of an effort to keep her spirits up and to let her know what a vital contribution she's making.

Even though she's not involved in muscling the 600-pound sleds through the icy rubble, scouting the route ahead is no easy job, and Matty is doing it brilliantly. Even though her insecurities about her age have revealed themselves occasionally, she's still supremely fit and sets an excellent pace for the dogs to follow. She's an integral part of the expedition, and I don't want her to feel like a passenger.

At these northerly latitudes, the sun is up for nearly an hour longer every day, and we're already noticing how much longer the days are. It's mind-boggling to think that we'll have twenty-four hours of daylight within two weeks. We emerged from the tent to be greeted by the most spectacular parhelion, or sun dogs as Peary called them. The morning sky was filled with a myriad of different colours and beams of light, produced by sunlight reflecting and refracting off ice crystals in the atmosphere. The sun hovered just above the eastern horizon, surrounded by three separate orbs, located at nine, twelve, and three o'clock, all linked together by an intense, semicircular rainbow. A horizontal white ring, similar in appearance to an aircraft's vapour trail, encircled the horizon, bisecting the sun and the nine- and three-o'clock orbs. Glittering ice dust filled the air as if a magician had just swished his wand.

Incredibly, a fourth orb, or false sun to give it its scientific name, then appeared in front of me like some kind of biblical vision. Could it be Peary's spirit, I wondered, here to guide us across the floes? It was so close that I felt I could almost touch it and it followed me around wherever I went. On seeing this phenomenon, unique to the polar environment, Peary had mused, "This was the nearest I ever came to finding the pot of gold at the foot of the rainbow."

To witness one of Mother Nature's great celestial displays was a truly awe-inspiring sight. Because we're racing against the clock, so much of this expedition is happening at breakneck speed, and it's sometimes easy to forget about the bigger picture. It's such an incredible privilege to be up here in this unique frozen world, and this was one of those moments to stand back for a moment and soak it all in.

The impossibly beautiful sky provided a dramatic backdrop for the morning's sledging, which was just as well as we needed every bit of encouragement we could find. Just when we thought the going might be getting easier, we stumbled across the largest maze of pressure ridges and rough ice we've encountered so far. It was a whopping four miles long, and with no map to show us where the dead ends might be, it took us most of the day to find a way out. Some of the blocks of ice were piled as high as two-story buildings, and getting the sleds through was a punishing business, with much of the time spent either chopping a route through with the axes or lifting the sleds over the top.

Peary had given us a foretaste of the ice conditions in the early part of our route, writing, "The difficulties and hardships of polar travel over these ragged and mountainous pressure ridges must be experienced to be appreciated. Often, a trail must be hewed out with pick-axes, and the heavily loaded sleds pushed, pulled, hoisted, and lowered over the hummocks and steep acclivities, even unloaded, and the equipment carried over on one's back."

In Henson's words, just to gain a few yards they had to push "from our very toes, straining every muscle, urging the dogs with voice and whip." Descending these ridges is often fraught with danger, and several of Peary's timber sleds were badly damaged as they hurtled out of control back down a ridge.

By the time we pitched camp, it felt as if we'd endured an all-day gym session, and our bodies were screaming out with pain. Even the dogs looked worn out, and their unbridled excitement of the first day seems a long time ago. There's a noticeable change in their behavior and they now take whatever opportunity they can to have a breather. Both teams are finding it much harder to start the sleds than they did in the first few days. It's as if the enormity of the journey ahead has finally sunk in and they've realized that if they're going to make it to the end, they're going to have to conserve their energy.

George and my technique for starting Kimmik's team is for one of us to be at the back pushing hard against the handlebars. The other stands alongside the dogs, pulling one of the two lines that are fixed to the front of the sled's runners. We then call out, "OK, Kimmik . . . ready . . . hike!" If that fails to do the trick, whoever's up in front will then pull the dogs' traces backwards, forcing the dogs to reverse a couple of paces.

With any luck, when the command is given to hike and the lines are released, these few feet of slack will allow the dogs to build up enough momentum to get the sled moving. George then assumes his position on the right of the sled, with me on the left. When we're travelling on skis, one hand stays on the handlebars with the other either holding a ski pole or one of the sled lines, with our skis sliding back and forth.

One of the many frustrations about travelling on the Arctic Ocean is that the surface is so unpredictable and changes every few yards. You might be confronted by powder snow one minute, precariously thin ice the next, followed by a mass of icy boulders and then a treacherous slab of polished blue ice. It means that skis are on and off all day long. They were perfect for the much flatter conditions of our training grounds in Baffin Island, but it's a different story up here on the frozen ocean, and I'm beginning to regret our decision not to follow Peary's example and use snowshoes. While skis are a more efficient way of travelling on flat terrain, snowshoes are far sturdier for going through rubble, and unlike skis, they can often be worn when crossing a pressure ridge, saving precious time.

Removing skis is a thankless task. Ours are similar to cross-country skis in that the foot is only secured by a three-pin toe binding, allowing the heel to lift freely. But to remove each ski involves squatting down and manually releasing the cold metallic plate that holds the boot in place. The skis are then slotted under the tight lashing lines on the top of the sled to ensure they don't slip out when the sled starts moving again. The whole process only takes a couple of minutes, but when you're doing it up to thirty times a day, it can drive you crazy.

On the occasions when there's flat skiable ground on either side of a pressure ridge, rather than going through the rigmarole of securing skis to the sleds for the short climb over the ridge, we launch the skis like javelins right over the top, collecting them on the far side after the sled has nego-tiated its way across.

There were times today, however, when both George and I made a wrong call, opting to keep skis on when the nature of the terrain suggested travelling on foot might be easier. Invariably, a rogue chunk of slippery blue ice, often no bigger than a football, would sweep one of us off our feet, sending us crashing to the ground in spectacular fash-ion. George always seemed to land in a patch of soft snow, whereas I usually managed to slam part of my body into a rock-hard ice block. My language was appalling all afternoon, with the many painful landings being followed with me yelling, "Fucking blue ice!" at the top of my voice.

Wondering what the fuss was all about, the dogs often turned round, Baffin rolling his eyes in despair at the sight of me yet again spread-eagled on the deck.

"That's your fault for being so accident-prone," said George unhelpfully.

Today's battle with the ice has left me nursing an assortment of nasty bruises on both elbows, my left knee, along with an excruciatingly painful bruised coccyx. I'm quickly learning that this landscape has an extraordinary ability both to beguile you and really piss you off. These sharp mood swings are starting to play with my mind.

The fact that we've successfully reached the twenty-five-mile mark is cause for celebration, and before turning in for the night, we each had a couple of swigs from the expedition's one luxury item – the bottle of Gordon's sloe gin. It went straight to my head and helped me take my mind off the turmoil brewing within the ice pack, which will reach its peak when the full moon arrives in two days' time. Another reason to cheer is that we've passed the farthest north record set by an American expedition, that would produce one of the most ghastly survival stories in Arctic history.

1882 was designated the International Polar Year by the world's scientific community. Eleven nations pledged to establish research stations at various locations around the Arctic to carry out the most comprehensive scientific study of the North so far. It was a far cry from the gung-ho approach to Arctic exploration that had prevailed until then.

Fourteen of the fifteen scientific groups returned to their home countries having successfully manned their stations for a year, collecting much valuable data in the process. The exception were the Americans led by the extravagantly named Adolphus Washington Greely.

Like many polar travellers before him, Greely was drawn to the North by dreams of exploration and discovery. In August 1881 his team of twenty-five men was dropped off in Lady Franklin Bay and left alone in a small ramshackle hut to face the coldest, darkest winter on the planet. Greely named his base Fort Conger, which Peary would later his base camp in 1898 on one of his early attempts at the Pole. Greely performed his scientific duties with thermometers and telescopes with great diligence, but deep down he yearned of reaching the Pole, or failing that, to at least claim a new northing record.

Living off food depots left by Nares' British expedition six years earlier, one of Greely's research teams, led by James Lockwood, travelled along the north coast of Greenland by dogsled as far as Lockwood Island (as it's now known) at 83°24N. He had beaten Markham's best by just four miles, and a record that had been British for three centuries was now in American hands. A large rock cairn was built "which will endure for ages," the Stars and Stripes were raised, backs were slapped, and they named the frozen ocean before them the Lincoln Sea. That said, the unfortunate Lockwood would never make it back home to celebrate his triumph.

Due in part to a logistical mix-up back in the United States, the ship that was supposed to resupply the expedition later that summer never arrived. Fortunately, there was enough local game in the form of caribou and musk oxen to keep the men going for another winter.

When no relief ship came the following summer, the mood grew darker, and Greely decided their only option was to leave Fort Conger and take two rowing boats south in the hope of reaching one of the Inuit communities on the west Greenland coast.

The winter of 1883 arrived early, freezing the boats in. Left with no other choice, they made for Pym Island where they used stones and upturned boats to build the most primitive of shelters. A truly awful winter ensued with man after man, including Lockwood, dying of starvation, scurvy, and frostbite. After the sheepskin and buffalo-hide sleeping bags had been boiled and eaten, those still clinging to life resorted to cannibalism, cutting strips of flesh off the frozen corpses half buried in the snow outside.

Things became so desperate that when Charles Henry was caught stealing rations of chopped-up sealskin cord, Greely ordered him to be taken outside and shot dead. One poor individual called Joseph Elison suffered such appalling frostbite that his hands and feet were reduced to gangrenous stumps, his teammates tying a spoon to the end of his right arm to help him eat.

By the time the emaciated party was eventually rescued in June 1884, only six of the original party, including Greely, were still alive.

The mountains of Ellesmere Island still line the southern horizon, but they're getting smaller by the day. It's easy to see how the distinctive twin peaks of Mount Cooper Key, which proudly stand out from the rest of the range, would have helped guide the returning parties safely back to shore in 1909. On catching sight of the mountain for the first time, they must have felt they were nearly home. For us, though, the journey has barely begun.

−37°C, Nineteen Miles Behind Peary, 389 Miles to Go

During Peary's previous attempts to reach the Pole in 1902 and 1906, he had learnt that the ice conditions were at their most difficult between Ellesmere Island and 84°N. To avoid losing critical time in the rough ice for a third time, Peary set off from Cape Columbia with half-empty sleds in 1909. Once the worst of the coastal ice had been passed, several sleds were emptied and sent back to Crane City to bring up the remainder of the supplies, while the advance parties continued to blaze the trail northward.

Not only did this enable the whole expedition to make relatively quick progress through the worst of the pressure ridges, but the endless to-and-fro of sleds created a well-worn trail for those returning to Cape Columbia. Nevertheless, not all went according to plan and during one of their shuttles back to land, both Borup and Marvin became separated from the main party, and it would be several days before they were reunited.

Because we're limited to only the two sleds, we don't have the option of ferrying supplies back and forth. Apart from anything else, it would be very easy for us to lose our two-sled trail, as had happened to Borup and Marvin, but it does put us at a considerable disadvantage because Peary's advance parties set off from Cape Columbia with 350-pound sleds, while ours weighed in at 600 pounds each when we started. It therefore comes as no surprise that after four days on the ice we find ourselves nearly twenty miles behind Peary's position.

On Day 5 of Peary's expedition, however, the curse of the Big Lead struck again, stopping the men in their tracks. Peary wrote: "The white expanse of ice [was] cut by a river of inky black water, throwing off dense clouds of vapour which gathered in a sullen canopy overhead."

Unfortunately, their arrival at the Big Lead coincided not only with a period of mild temperatures, but also with the onset of the full moon and its accompanying spring tides, which combined to keep the quarter-mile-wide channel open for nearly a week. After such a great start from Cape Columbia, the delay must have driven them mad. Henson wrote, "It was exasperating. Seven precious days of fine weather lost; and fine weather is the exception, not the rule up in the Arctic . . . we were ready and anxious to travel . . . but were compelled to inactivity."

Unknown to Peary, they were directly above the point at which the North American continental shelf plunges to the floor of the Arctic Ocean, where strong currents upwelling from deeper waters made it difficult for ice to form. This is why the Big Lead forms so readily. All we can do is keep hoping that the temperatures and tides will be on our side when tomorrow night's full moon arrives.

This morning, as on most mornings, I was followed outside by a shower of rolled-up Thermarests and stuff-sacks bulging at the seams with sleeping bags, clothing, and food. With Hugh on breakfast duty, his final task was to stay behind to help Matty clear out the tent, brush the walls clear of hoarfrost, and fill up the fuel bottles so that they were ready for the evening.

It was a beautiful, still morning, but while it was a relief to be able to stretch out aching limbs, the cold soon seeped through my various layers of clothing that had picked up moisture in the tent. I was chilled to the bone. Hanging about in these temperatures is not a sensible idea, and after jumping up and down a few times to get the blood circulating again, I was off to join George and Andrew to start loading the sleds.

To keep the sleds' centre of gravity as low as possible, the dog food was loaded on first. As was the case in 1909, dog food makes up the largest proportion of the load, and we've brought along over 500 pounds of the stuff for this leg of the expedition alone. The vast majority of this comes in the form of kibble, ground-up beef pellets not dissimilar to the pemmican beef rations Peary fed his dogs. To boost our dogs' calorie intake and to protect their fur, their diet is supplemented with blocks of lard we coated with zinc powder back in Iqaluit. A block of lard gives the dogs the same morale boost as a Snickers bar does for us, although to spice up the taste,

Ikki has taken to peeing on his daily lard ration. Very strange behavior.

The dog food, fuel bottles, our food, kitchen boxes, tent, personal bags, and sleeping systems are all contained within a giant canvas bag that sits in the centre of the sled to balance the load. Lashing the sled bag into position is the morning job I dread most. The only way of ensuring that the lines are taut and knots aren't going to become undone later in the day is to remove our warm sealskin mitts, (which look like giant furry oven gloves), and work in our thin, fleecy inner gloves instead.

As I desperately tried to finish off the first knot this morning, I could feel the warmth being sucked out of my fingers as if I was dipping them in liquid nitrogen. Two seconds later and they were frozen solid. I stopped what I was doing, quickly slipped my mitts back on, and began swinging my arms around furiously to bring them back to life. When circulation was eventually restored, my fingers screamed out with pain – and there were still another five knots to go.

Once the sleds were ready and our fingers had been through the freeze-thaw process more times than I'd care to remember, the final and most important item, the rifle, was slotted carefully under the lashing lines on the top of the sled. Then it was time to harness up the dogs. Some of their bravado from the first couple of days has disappeared and only Kimmik, Baffin, and Ootah greeted us with anything resembling a bark as we walked towards them.

Baffin is proving himself to be one of the characters on the second sled and often has George and me in stitches. Getting him ready in the mornings has become a major performance. No sooner had I grabbed one of his front legs this morning than he collapsed in a heap and began bleating like a distressed sheep. "Baffin, you complete baby, give me your bloody leg. I've never seen such a performance," I said. There was absolutely nothing wrong with him; he was just having his daily early-morning tantrum.

I don't know what our team had with their kibble at breakfast this morning, but they whizzed along all day. As we gradually eat through our supplies, the sleds are becoming lighter and the dogs definitely picked up a gear today. Seemingly innocuous snow hummocks, which would have caused them to stall in the early days of the expedition, no longer pose a problem. In fact, they were so fast today that we regularly found ourselves tailgating the team in front. Each time we could feel we were getting too close, George and I yelled out, "Wohhh" for them to slow down. Pulling all our weight against the handlebars, we turned our skis at right angles to the trail and dug them into the snow. It was no use. Soon Kimmik was trampling over the back of Hugh and Andrew's skis, Andrew to looking back at us with disdain. "Sorry!" I said as we pulled alongside them, still doing our best to slow the dogs down. "Nothing we can do about it!"

Raven glanced across in disbelief before deciding that the only way to stop us was to lead his team straight into ours and take us all out. The whole thing was like watching a car crash in slow motion. The ensuing chaos of dog lines, skis, and sleds took a good five minutes to untangle, with Kimmik getting a serious talking-to for not obeying orders.

The good weather held all day. The ice was kinder to us than it has been, and although there were some huge pressure ridges early on, they didn't pose too many problems. In fact, we were travelling so fast that by the afternoon Matty was unable to keep up with the pace and kept being overtaken. Andrew may not be the most stylish or efficient skier in the team, but he's undoubtedly the fastest. As a child, he was so hyperactive that his parents used to slip Ritalin pills into his food to calm him down. The Arctic Ocean is the ideal place for Andrew's pent-up energy, making him the perfect candidate to swap places with Matty and scout the route ahead. As he skied off into the distance, arms pumping away like fury, I'm sure I even saw a spark fly from under one of his skis. Giving Andrew these extra responsibilities is clearly doing wonders for his morale. His extraordinary reserves of energy are vital to our success – we just need to keep him positive.

I'm so pleased with the way our sleds are holding up. These are the toughest conditions on the planet for driving dogs, and the sleds have taken a serious battering. They had some big crashes today, and the force with which they career into the side of an ice block makes you wince. But other than the odd chip from the sides of the runners, much to everyone's amazement they have so far survived relatively unscathed. Watching them effortlessly cut their way through the choppy terrain like a ship on the high seas fills me with great pride. So much for Sir Wally Herbert's warning that our sleds would be "smashed to bits within the first fifteen miles."

It's been an excellent day, our best of the trip so far. We estimated we had had our first ten-mile day, but the GPS showed we had fallen just half a mile short. Nevertheless, we're back on schedule. All being well, we'll soon have Peary in our sights.

5. The Last Place on Earth

Day 6: 25 March

−40°C, Ten miles Behind Peary, 380 Miles to Go

THINGS DIDN'T GET OFF TO THE BEST OF STARTS when I managed to spill half a kettle of boiling water over my hand while preparing the breakfast drinks. Absolute agony, and I soon had a two-inch blister to show for my clumsiness. Something tells me I wasn't born to be a tea lady.

Today was our toughest yet – the coldest since the start and the most brutal ice conditions imaginable. The ice floes and pressure ridges that characterize the route to the Pole are often described as being like the Grand National, an endless series of fields and fences stretching interminably to the horizon. Unfortunately, the fields today were not much bigger than my bedroom and typically filled with rubble while the fences comprised of individual slabs of ice, varying in size from microwave to coffin to Mini Cooper. Dozens of these sleeping leviathans lay across our path today. It was like trying to find a way through a city razed to the ground by an earthquake. Every yard had to be earned as we hauled our bulky sleds over pressure ridge after pressure ridge. It was a living hell.

I find it almost impossible to comprehend the forces responsible for creating the frozen chaos around us. When one thinks that, just like an iceberg, ninety per cent of a pressure ridge lies underwater, the volume of ice being shunted around at random is colossal. Pans of multiyear ice,★ weighing tens of millions of tonnes, are carried from Siberia across the top of the world by an ocean current known as the Transpolar Gyre. As their inexorable progress is slowed by the land masses of Canada and Greenland, the pans are gradually pulverized as they smash into one another, in much the same way as plate tectonics create mountain ranges.

The speeds at which the Arctic Ocean can give birth to a pressure ridge are truly astounding, and it can take as little as a few hours for a half-mile-long, forty-foot-high wall of ice to form. In fact, on several occasions today we had to take evasive action as ice boulders from freshly forming ridges came hurtling down towards us.

Being up close and personal with something as beautiful and terrifying as a living, breathing pressure ridge makes one realize just how small and insignificant one really is out here. Our motley crew of sixteen highly strung dogs, one tiny woman, and four exhausted and increasingly smelly men shouldn't stand a chance against the might of the frozen sea, but somehow, against all the odds, we're hanging on in there.

With much smoother conditions on the eastern half of the Arctic Ocean, North Pole expeditions these days tend to set off from the Siberian coast. The route may be a hundred miles longer, but with far fewer pressure ridges to contend with and less open water, it's usually a much quicker journey than starting from Canada. We should eventually see a gradual improvement in the ice the farther we get away from the mainland, but right now the days of large, smooth pans seem like a dream.

The conditions were particularly unfriendly today because we're now directly over the continental shelf, home of the Big Lead. This marks

★ Ice thick enough to have survived the previous summer melt.

the natural boundary between the relatively stable land-fast ice off the Canadian coast and the shifting pack ice of the open ocean, which is why it's not uncommon to find a huge channel of open water here. Even though we're craving some sign of warmth, the unseasonably cold temperatures have thankfully locked this volatile zone in frigid suspension – at least for now – but ocean currents from the deep, the titanic force of the Transpolar Gyre (which transports ice from the Russian half of the Arctic Ocean towards Canada), and the tidal influence of the impending full moon have all conspired to make sure the ice is anything but a flat, even surface.

On his return journey from his farthest-north record in 1906, Peary noted identical conditions, "a seemingly endless and indescribable chaos of broken and shattered ice at the place where we had been held up by the Big Lead on our upward march, and it took hours of grim and exhausting work to carry us through it."

We may only be five miles closer to our goal tonight, but five miles is much better than twiddling our thumbs waiting for the Big Lead to close as Peary had in 1909. Still, we're starting to wonder when, if ever, Ellesmere Island's mountains are going to slip below the horizon and disappear from view. It's pretty soul-destroying that they barely seem to have shrunk in the best part of a week.

Today has taken a lot out of us, the dogs in particular, so we decided to camp an hour earlier than normal at 5:00 P.M. In her role as expedition scout, it's Matty's responsibility to find a suitable campsite in the evenings. The sight of Matty in the distance stopped in her tracks, with her ski poles crossed above her head, always comes as a huge relief at the end of nine long hours as it signals another day on the trail is over.

The ideal campsite should be on a pan of flat, multiyear ice. Not only does old, solid ice have the advantage of being much less likely to split during the night, but because the sea salt is gradually leached out of the ice over time, multiyear ice provides us with a source of fresh water. One of our many evening jobs is to collect enough blocks of compacted snow and ice to use for dinner as well as the following morning's breakfast.

The first outside chore every evening is putting up the tent. During our training on Baffin Island, we had real trouble with vapour from cooking and breathing accumulating as increasingly thick layers of ice. Our Hilleberg tunnel tent had a low ceiling and didn't allow the moist air inside to circulate properly, giving it time to condense and freeze. To overcome the problem, we decided that we should make our own tent for the expedition itself, large enough to accommodate all five of us in reasonable comfort and designed in such a way that any ice build-up would be greatly reduced.

We drew a very simple diagram of the tent we felt best suited our needs, based on a model used by the great Fridjtof Nansen for his failed North Pole bid in 1895. It was essentially a double-layered, eight-sided wigwam. The sides were vertical for three feet, high enough for us to be able to sit upright during meal times, before sloping inward towards a central point, seven feet off the ground. There would be a single zipped door on the leeward side of the tent. The tent would have no floor, meaning that while it wouldn't be as warm as the latest expedition tents, the majority of the water vapour would either be absorbed directly into the snow or allowed to escape through a small "chimney" at the top of the roof.

We passed our sketch over to Eric, Matty's son, who as an engineering undergraduate at Acadia University in Nova Scotia is a total whiz at anything to do with graphic design. Eric then produced 3D computer models of our new tent, calculating how much fabric we would need for each of the various panels and how they would all fit together. We decided that with polar bears being carnivorous beasts, attracted to meaty colours like red and orange, unless we happened to meet a vegetarian bear, green would be the safest colour to make the tent.

During our final days of expedition preparation in Baffin Island, Matty had worked through the night on her sewing machine to get the tent ready on time. She's the most incredible seamstress and, as well as assembling the tent, she somehow managed to find the time to make the team five pairs of insulated snow gaiters and five pairs of thin fleecy "wristlets" to be worn under our gloves. We're as reliant on her skills with needle and thread as Peary was on the wives of his Inuit dog drivers, who during the long winter aboard the *Roosevelt,* made the outfits for the entire expedition party.

Another advantage of the Nansen-style tent is that it only takes five minutes to erect. With the tent laid out on the ground, someone crawls inside and props a ski onto a wooden block to stop it from sinking into the snow, with the ski's tip fitting snugly inside the tent roof. It's then all hands on deck as each of the four primary guy ropes are simultaneously pulled tight and secured to the ground with a ski in the snow. The four secondary guy ropes are put through the same process, and eight ski poles are slotted into the tent walls, increasing the tent's overall stability. Snow is then shoveled onto the tent's snow flaps to prevent it from blowing away in the wind.

The next task is to unharness the dogs and walk them over to the tie-out chain, where they will remain until morning. Both tie-out chains are sixty-foot-long steel cables, with eight standard dog clips placed evenly along their length, approximately six feet apart. One end of the chain is secured to the ice with a mountaineering ice screw, twisted deep inside the pan. The other end is looped around whatever sturdy-looking ice pinnacle we can find. If there are none nearby, we'll turn a sled at right angles to the chain, wedge it into a snowdrift, and tie the chain to the sled's handlebars instead.

It's vital that the tie-out chains are firmly anchored. If one of the ends were to come free during the night, it wouldn't be long before the dogs tangled themselves up in a knotted mess of chain, clips, and fur, no doubt trying to bite chunks out of one another at the same time.

Each dog has its own position on the chain, with sworn enemies like K2 and Odin kept well apart and close pals such as Kimmik and Ernie put side by side. Poor old Baffin seems to have fallen out with just about everyone already, so he's stuck on the end, well out of trouble.

Typically, the tie-out chains are placed on either side of the tent, the reason being that were a bear to stroll into camp during the night, chances are it would trip over the dogs, waking them all up. With any luck, the sight of sixteen Eskimo dogs flaring their pearly whites and barking uncontrollably should be enough to scare any intruder away. Our dogs are the best burglar alarm system money can buy in the Far North.

Dinnertime is pandemonium. Each dog is given two pounds of kibble a day. They get two-thirds of their kibble ration, plus their chunk of lard, in the evening and the rest in the morning. As soon as they see us pulling a sack of dog food from the sled, the ravenous animals know that dinner is on its way. They go absolutely crazy, jumping into the air and howling dementedly. Even the quietest characters on the team, dogs like Axel and Gloria, can barely contain themselves.

With so much violent jerking going on, this is the time when the tie-out chain is most likely to come loose. Not only do we have to make sure that we dish the food out quickly, we also try to get all the dogs seated before they receive their ration by saying their name, followed by the command, "Down," in a firm voice.

It doesn't always work, particularly in the case of Ootah who's so excitable at mealtimes that he's totally incapable of keeping still. He has no table manners whatsoever, and no sooner has a bowl of food been emptied out in front of him than he tries to wolf every single pellet of kibble down in one gulp. The result is that his neat pile of dog food is soon spread over a wide area, much of it now out of reach. I've tried explaining to him that he'll have more to eat if he tries eating more slowly, but he never listens.

Things calm down noticeably once the dogs have eaten, and it's not long before they're all curled up in a ball with their tails over their noses. The last one to bed is always Denali, who for a good ten minutes every evening has got into the practice of walking around in circles and trampling down the snow to create a shallow shelter for herself. How these dogs can survive night after night out in the open is quite extraordinary.

With the dogs fed, George and I left the others to prepare dinner while we headed north for about a quarter of a mile to chop a trail through the ice for the first part of tomorrow's route. With axes slung over our shoulders, we must have looked like a pair of lumberjacks heading off into the forest, and it wasn't long before we began singing a woefully out-of-tune version of Monty Python's "Lumberjack Song." It was a light moment in an otherwise difficult day.

DAY 7: 26 MARCH
−33°C, Five Miles Behind Peary, 375 Miles to Go

The full moon is finally upon us, and throughout the night the deafening noise of plates of ice grinding against one another reverberated around the Arctic Ocean. It was as if we had camped in the middle of a giant scrap-metal yard with demolition trucks and cranes crushing everything in sight. As the irritable ice pack grumbled away, I felt very vulnerable inside our little canvas tent. Our current position is particularly precarious as the closer one is to the shore, the more unstable the ice is. Nobody slept well.

When daybreak finally came, the view was almost unrecognizable. Two fresh mounds of ice had erupted within yards of the tent and were continuing to grow, whilst a deep fissure had split our small pan in two. It was as if Sedna, the Inuit goddess of the Arctic, had thrown an all-night party but hadn't bothered to tidy up the mess. It was total carnage, and with light snow falling from a leaden sky, it was clear this would be our toughest day yet.

From camp we followed the trail George and I had prepared yesterday, which mercifully had survived the night's upheaval relatively intact, but we soon found ourselves in a crazy zone of never-ending rubble, which lasted all day. It was like travelling over the surface of an immense lemon meringue pie with lumps, cracks, and waves of snow and ice at every turn. At times like this, there's nothing you can do but put your head down and keep plugging away.

Thanks to the flat light, we had to rely on Raven's keen sense of smell to keep us on the trail. Not only did the front team routinely disappear into the nothingness, but their tracks were virtually impossible to follow. The dogs seem to get a whole new lease of life when travelling through rough ice; their ears prick up and they lift their heads. Some of them, especially Bert and Ernie, even wag their tails. The constantly changing view inside a rubble field and amongst the pressure ridges seems to keep them energized and absorbed by the job at hand. When it comes to large pans of smooth ice, however, they can often appear bored, and it's becoming more of a challenge to keep them motivated on the flat. Not that we've seen a pan in days.

When we come face-to-face with a large pressure ridge, one of us usually clambers up to its highest point to get a bird's-eye view of the surroundings. This is a pointless task when there's no contrast, so we've adopted Peary's practice that if there's no obvious alternative, rather than wasting precious time searching for a better route, the best option is to take a deep breath and plough straight over the top. Several times today Kimmik's sled actually left the ground as it hurtled back down the far side of a ridge, the dogs sprinting for their lives as it accelerated uncontrollably towards them. These are heart-stopping moments for everyone, and it seems only a matter of time before a dog gets clobbered by a loose sled.

It was jaw-lockingly cold all day with the vicious headwind producing a windchill of an unimaginable −63°C. Matty describes days this cold as simply "FF" for obvious reasons. The difference between a minus-sixty day and a minus-thirty day is as extreme as that between an English heatwave and the first frost of the winter. We simply have to keep moving when it's this cold. If we don't, we would just freeze to the spot. During commando training in Arctic Norway, even the Royal Marines are ordered to stop travelling when the temperatures hit −30°C. Each degree below that becomes progressively more horrible. Our only comfort is that Peary, Henson, and the others endured the same suffering and lived to tell the tale.

Throughout the day the fluid in my eyes kept freezing, and I had to force myself to blink regularly to prevent any lasting damage. I had very little feeling in my fingers and my feet were agony. It's much harder to tell when your nose is getting frostbitten because it's almost always numb. So George and I have got into the habit of making regular checks of each other's noses for telltale white marks, which indicate that a period of urgent nasal rubbing is required. The only way of communicating today was by shouting. Human beings were simply not designed for this frigid world.

When we removed our headgear in the relative warmth of the tent, we all winced at the sight of Andrew's nose, which now has a nasty pussy streak running down its length. "Always good to have a few war wounds to impress the folks back home," he joked.

It's as ugly a frostbite wound as I've ever seen, but he actually seems to be quite proud of it. My toes were totally lifeless when I removed my socks tonight and it took a few minutes of massaging over the stove for them to recover their feeling. Luckily, there doesn't appear to be any permanent damage.

The Olympic record for the 5,000 metres is little more than twelve minutes, but it took us a full day's travel to cover that distance today. It's a measly amount when compared to the vast distance that still lies ahead. I keep telling myself that the going will improve as we head north and I shouldn't let our pitiful pace get to me. As long as we're putting one foot in front of the other, each step will bring us closer to our goal.

DAY 8: 27 MARCH
−33°C, *Two Miles Behind Peary, 372 Miles to Go*

The wind actually picked up overnight, but we were so wiped out from yesterday's effort that we slept pretty much straight through. It was still gusting wildly when the alarms went off at 6:00 A.M., so the unanimous decision was made to roll over for another hour. Incredibly, despite the strong winds, according to the GPS we only lost thirty-eight feet to the drift overnight. It being Easter Sunday, over breakfast I tried calling Mary on the satellite phone, but yet again I got her answering machine. It seems we're destined never to speak.

The day began with two big pressure ridges, but gradually the terrain started to improve with more organised pans linked together by the occasional short stretch of rough ice. Windblown snow sometimes reduced visibility at ground level to a few yards, but the sunlit cone of Mount Cooper Key remained in view, floating above the agitated horizon like some distant island.

RIGHT: Climbing the eighteen thousand–foot high Nevado Condoriri in the Bolivian Andes in 1997. These early climbs were an important part of my expedition apprenticeship— and a good test for vertigo. *(Courtesy of Tom Avery)*

Manhauling to the South Pole in 2002 in the footsteps of my childhood hero Captain Scott. *(Courtesy of Tom Avery)*

A twenty year-old dream fulfilled. Andrew Gerber, Paul Landry, Patrick Woodhead, and I at the South Pole after our record-breaking seven hundred–mile journey across Antarctica. *(Courtesy of Tom Avery)*

Commander Robert E. Peary.
(Courtesy of the Peary-Stafford Family)

Matthew Henson.
(Courtesy of the National Geographic Society)

The four Inuit who joined Peary and Henson in the polar party in 1909—Egingwah, Ootah, Ooqueah, and Seegloo. *(Courtesy of the National Geographic Society)*

CLOCKWISE FROM TOP LEFT:

Tom Avery.
(Courtesy of George Wells)

Hugh Dale-Harris.
(Courtesy of Tom Avery)

Andrew Gerber.
(Courtesy of Matty McNair)

Matty McNair.
(Courtesy of Tom Avery)

George Wells.
(Courtesy of Tom Avery)

The U.K.-based members of the expedition, George, Andrew (standing), and I, with our patron HRH The Prince of Wales and Camilla Parker Bowles at Clarence House the week before our departure to the Arctic. *(Courtesy of the Press Association)*

Raven gives the wolves a piece of his mind at the refueling station at Eureka. This standoff had the potential to turn extremely dangerous. With the dogs all secured to the tie-out chain, they would have made an easy meal for the pack of bloodstained wolves. *(Courtesy of Matty McNair)*

Steaming dogs and team members crammed into one of the Twin Otter ski planes for the final leg of the journey to Cape Columbia. *(Courtesy of Hugh Dale-Harris)*

Crane City, Peary's base camp on Ellesmere Island's north coast, a few miles from Cape Columbia.
(Courtesy of the National Geographic Society)

Ninety-six years later, we find ourselves at the same place—the first polar explorers to visit Crane City since 1909. *(Courtesy of Tom Avery)*

I, Andrew, Hugh, and George at Peary's signpost at Cape Columbia, Ellesmere Island, latitude 83°7'N, March 19, 2005, temperature -43°C.
(Courtesy of Matty McNair)

The Arctic Ocean viewed from Cape Columbia. The ice front in the foreground is over forty feet high. Previous expeditions referred to it as the Great Wall of China.
(Courtesy of Matty McNair)

Peary's men crossing a pressure ridge in 1909. Note how many people are needed to lift the sled into position. *(Courtesy of the National Geographic Society)*

Wrestling one of our two six hundred–pound sleds over a pressure ridge, with Matty up ahead beckoning on the dogs. A seemingly minor obstacle like this could take us twenty minutes to cross. *(Courtesy of Hugh Dale-Harris)*

Spectacular parhelion early on in the expedition. Peary called these extraordinary formations "sun dogs." *(Courtesy of Tom Avery)*

I am driving the sled through rough ice in the vicinity of Peary's Big Lead. Our replica Peary sleds endured a daily battering from the ice. *(Courtesy of George Wells)*

George (left) and I enjoy a short reprieve between pressure ridges. Our dogs were an inspiration and never gave up. From left to right: Ootah, Bert, Ernie, Apu (obscured), Baffin, Axel, Kimmik (our lead dog), and K2.
(Courtesy of Hugh Dale-Harris)

Hugh, George, Andrew, and Matty during one of our breaks on the trail. There was little time or appetite for conversation during these brief pit stops. It was a case of consuming as many calories as we could in the few minutes before fingers and toes began turning numb. *(Courtesy of Tom Avery)*

With the onset of the Arctic spring, the ice pack began cracking open like an eggshell. *(Courtesy of Tom Avery)*

If the ice was too thin, we would use the sleds to make a bridge between two sturdier areas of ice. Here George (right) and I help Bert across.
(Courtesy of Hugh Dale-Harris)

RIGHT: George drying his boots following his impromptu swim in the Arctic Ocean. *(Courtesy of Tom Avery)*

BELOW: Hugh rushing over to rescue a sinking sled from the icy clutches of the Arctic Ocean. Five dogs ended up in the water, and had it not been for the quick thinking of Kimmik, Bert, and Ernie, they could all have drowned. The water here is over two miles deep. *(Courtesy of Tom Avery)*

Andrew, George, and I supervise yet another hairy descent from a pressure ridge as Gloria leads the team away from danger. *(Courtesy of Hugh Dale-Harris)*

Once a storm had passed, the dogs were often so blanketed in snow that some were impossible to see. Here, a yawning Zorro (who was always the last one to get up in the morning) emerges from a snowdrift. *(Courtesy of Hugh Dale-Harris)*

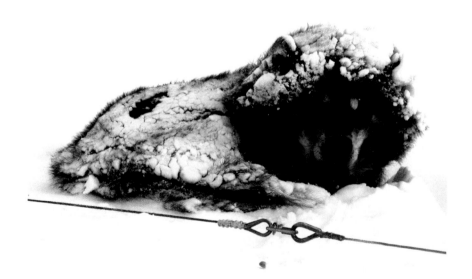

I am pulling
Ernie out of the
freezing waters of
the Arctic Ocean.
I lost count of the
number of times I
had to rescue this
particular dog
from a watery
end. *(Courtesy of
George Wells)*

As the ice pack disintegrated, we had to fight tooth and nail for every inch of
northerly progress. *(Courtesy of Tom Avery)*

The terrain improved markedly during our dash toward the Pole, just as it had for Peary in 1909, and our speeds increased dramatically. In another throwback to Peary's expedition, we rolled the clock to take advantage of the twenty-four-hour daylight. This photograph was taken at local midnight, the time when the sun is due north. *(Courtesy of George Wells)*

All was going perfectly until, with less than three miles to go, a vast area of open water and rough ice stopped us in our tracks. To make matters worse, we were fighting a drift that was carrying us away from the Pole at a rate of more than seven miles a day. I was convinced we were going to drift right past the Pole and miss it altogether. *(Courtesy of Hugh Dale-Harris)*

Ooqueah, Ootah, Matthew Henson, Egingwah, Seegloo, and Robert Peary (behind the camera) become the first men in history to stand at the North Pole, April 6, 1909. *(Courtesy of the National Geographic Society)*

George Wells, Matty McNair, Tom Avery, Hugh Dale-Harris, and Andrew Gerber become the fastest team in history to reach the North Pole, April 26, 2005. *(Courtesy of Hugh Dale-Harris)*

Andrew and George flank me as we face the press on our return to Heathrow Airport. *(Courtesy of Leo Avery)*

Reunited with our girlfriends at last. From left to right: Andrew, Rowena, me, Mary, Annie, and George. *(Courtesy of the Press Association)*

The storm blew itself out during the morning, the clouds dispersed, and for the remainder of the day we were blessed with perfect travel conditions – cold, clear, and calm. Having been cursing the Arctic for days, today there was nowhere else I would rather have been. The weightless, blood-red orb of the sun spent the day rolling its way along the southern sky in an all-day sunset. Vapour clouds billowed from the breathless dogs like smoke from an old steam engine. The frozen river of fog lingered in the stagnant air, snaking its way back along our route and glowing purple in the watery twilight. It was as if time had frozen still. There are times when the Arctic Ocean can be the most beautiful landscape on earth.

Being up in front scouting the route ahead, it's logical that Matty should be responsible for group navigation. With the GPS stowed deep inside one of the sleds, we find our way in exactly the same way as they did in 1909. Because the ice is constantly on the move, a map of the frozen sea, were it to exist, would be completely useless as it would have to be updated every few hours.

On clear days, all we need to plot our way north is the sun and a wristwatch. Ever since the ancient cartographers began drawing the first maps, latitude and longitude meridians have crisscrossed the earth in a grid of imaginary lines. The latitudes are a series of ever-shrinking lines, lying parallel to the Equator, the North and South Poles at 90°N and 90°S respectively, while the Equator is at latitude zero.

Lines of longitude (also known as meridians) circle the globe in giant rings, converging as they pass through the Poles. Because it takes twenty-four hours for the earth to complete a full 360° revolution, 15° of longitude therefore translate to an hour of time. This is reflected in an apparent movement of the sun across the sky of 15° per hour. Since we're travelling more or less along the 70th Meridian, and our clocks are five hours behind GMT (Greenwich being the home of zero longitude), local midday will therefore be at 11:40 A.M. Local midday is important because wherever you are in the northern hemisphere, this is the moment when the sun is due south and one's shadow points directly at the North Pole.

During expedition preparations in Iqaluit, we drew basic compass dials onto our skis with a marker pen. By placing the tip of a ski pole in the centre of our makeshift sundial at various times during the day, the perpetual movement of the sun will help us work out where north is wherever we are on the Arctic Ocean. To maintain a northerly course at 8:40 A.M., for example, the ski pole's shadow should be kept at an angle of 45° to the left of our skis, while at 5 P.M. the shadow should be at 80° to the right of the skis.

Of course, we're just estimating these angles with the naked eye, but it's a surprisingly accurate method. Even if the drift carries us miles to the east or west, as long as we know when local midday is, we simply recalibrate our angles accordingly to help us find True North. Just like Peary, we never try to second-guess the drift by purposefully heading off on a different course – we always do our best to head due north.

Having said all that, during the afternoon, Matty appeared to be taking us farther and farther to the east. By my calculations, we were travelling a full 45° off course – so far astray that I started to question my own mental arithmetic.

"Mate, she's definitely going the wrong way," I said to George for about the tenth time. "I've got to stop her. We're losing a big chunk of our mileage going this way. We've worked so hard to get this far but precious yards are being lost."

I knew it would dent Matty's confidence for me to question her decades of navigation expertise, so I held off for ten minutes in the hope that she might change tack. Had the day been drawing to an end, I might have let it drop, but there was still more than an hour to go.

"I can't take this anymore, I'm off."

I took a couple of ski poles from the top of the sled and skied off in pursuit of Matty, 200 yards beyond the first sled.

I was sweating by the time I caught up with her. "Matty!" I yelled out as I approached, "You're going the wrong way!"

She stopped and turned round, surprised to see me so close. "No we're not," she replied defensively.

"The Pole's that way," I said, gesticulating with a ski pole.

After consulting her compass, Matty shrugged her shoulders and said, "Oh well, silly me. Must have been daydreaming."

I was hopping mad, but while I wanted to give her an earful for switching off, a harmonious team is more important than the few hundred yards that our detour had cost us, so I chose to bite my lip instead and quit while I was ahead.

The dogs were in flying form all day, so it came as no surprise when the GPS told us that despite our roundabout route, this had been our first day of double-digit mileage, 11.1 of them to be precise. Our canine friends were obviously relishing the improvement in conditions and the lighter loads, which are reducing by more than fifty pounds a day as we get through our supplies. The sleds are noticeably faster and more nimble than they were a week ago.

Everyone is in great form this evening after our record day, which for the first time has brought us ahead of Peary, who was still pinned down at the Big Lead. It was the perfect excuse to finish the last of the sloe gin. I hope I remembered to pack another bottle in the next resupply or I'm going to be very unpopular.

The fact that it's Easter is another reason to celebrate. I'm not particularly religious, but I do love my chocolate, and so after dinner I handed out the five Cadbury's Cream Eggs that I'd been saving in my personal kit bag for this moment. Andrew's disappeared in a single mouthful and he was soon demanding to know if I had any more secret supplies.

This evening's gratuitous excess is in stark contrast to the stories of near-starvation usually associated with polar expeditions. It might seem folly to bring supplies with us not known for their nutritional qualities, particularly when weight is so tight, but I've always found on my expeditions that the odd little treat along the way can do wonders for team morale. Strange as it may seem, these luxuries could make all the difference between success and failure.

My feet have been giving me grief for a few days now, so this evening I decided to lance the two bloodied blisters on my heels and one on my right big toe. I've now taped them up, which will hopefully relieve some of the pain. Our arms and backs are stiff from the daily effort of working the sleds, but it's nothing more than we anticipated.

On our last night together in London, Mary gave me a package of letters and cards to open at various stages of the expedition. After this morning's missed call, the thought of crawling into my sleeping bag to open her Easter card kept me going all day. Her cheery words bring both a smile and a tear or two. We're only a handful of miles into this 413-mile odyssey and the moment when we'll be reunited feels light-years away.

Day 9: 28 March
−33°C, Nine Miles Ahead of Peary, 362 Miles to Go

A day of two halves. The morning was a continuation of yesterday's flat pans before we hit a more organised series of pressure ridges and frozen leads at midday, which slowed us down considerably. Nevertheless, another record mileage represents a good day's work. My feet were less painful than they have been, and in mid-afternoon we caught what we hope will be our last glimpse of land for a month, sixty-odd miles to the south. Finally, it feels as if we've been cast adrift on the open ocean.

The sun shone on and off all day, which meant Matty had to keep switching between navigating by compass and shadow. Using a compass to find one's way in the Arctic is much more complicated and stressful than might be imagined. This is because the compass dial points not to the Geographic North Pole, but to the vicinity of the Magnetic North Pole, some 350 miles west of our current position. This means that when Matty takes a bearing, she has to factor in a magnetic variation of almost 90°. This deviation will continue to grow, and by the time we reach 89°N, sixty miles shy of the Pole, compasses will need to be adjusted by nearly 110°. From 89°N to the Pole, the variation accelerates at such a rate that for the final days of the expedition, the compass will end up pointing almost due south.

In 1909 our understanding of the earth's magnetic field was more limited than it is today, and so on the few occasions when Peary adjusted his compass bearing to take account of the declination, he had to rely in part on magnetic data he had collected himself during his previous expeditions around the Arctic. Thankfully, polar explorers today are given a helping hand by the Geological Survey of Canada, which publishes up-to-date magnetic variations for specific latitudes and longitudes. We check this information most days to ensure our compasses are always pointing at True North.

Because the flat light washes out all contrast from the landscape, it's almost impossible to take a bearing off a distant ice feature before it disappears completely. This is when the compass comes into its own, but it only gives an accurate reading when held horizontally, so Matty continuously has to look up and down as she skis. I think she enjoys the solitude of being out in front, away from her male teammates, but today's overcast sections would have been no fun at all for her. Peary wrote, "The endeavour to keep a direct course for any length of time under such conditions imposes such a strain on mind and body that travel sometimes becomes impossible. In addition to this, the feelings of fatigue and heaviness which are the result of the fog . . . make travelling still more difficult." After yesterday's detour, Matty was fully focused all day today, and thanks to her efforts we've stayed right on track.

The evenings are a time for us to unwind after a long day on the trail, but it takes the best part of an hour of tedious housekeeping before we can relax completely. Matty is always the first inside, leaving the four of us to unpack the sleds, sort out the dogs, and untangle their traces while she fires up the four stoves to warm the tent and begin melting snow.

The last thing I do before diving inside the tent is to remove my large red expedition jacket and stuff it into the sled bag. During our three-week training expedition to Baffin Island with Paul and Matty, the jackets we had used were very prone to icing up. It may be ridiculously cold up here, but the Arctic Ocean is actually one of the most humid environments on earth, so sweat is much more problematic than it is in the drier climate of Antarctica. And iced-up clothing is a sure-fire way to get hypothermia.

Concerned that our jackets would turn to chain mail after a few days on the Arctic Ocean, in March 2004 I approached Mountain Hardwear, the outdoor clothing company that had supported my expeditions for the last six years, to ask if they might be able to design something more appropriate for the expedition. They agreed and put their top designers in

Hong Kong on the case – the last place one would expect to find polar clothing experts.

Gore-Tex loses its ability to breathe below about −25°C, so they suggested using a synthetic fabric called microfibre, which is the best material available for wicking moisture away from our assortment of sweaty, rather unpleasant undergarments. It doesn't matter that microfibre isn't waterproof because a rainstorm on the frozen sea in March and April is about as likely as a blizzard in the Amazon rainforest. Nevertheless, it is windproof, and to protect our nether regions from the cutting winds, I asked for the jackets to be extended halfway down our thighs.

A Velcro strip was sewn to the hoods so we could attach a fur ruff, and the jackets themselves were fitted with extra-large zips that could easily be operated with mittened hands. The finished item is superb, and the small amounts of frost build-up we find after a day of heavy sledging can easily be removed by taking off our jacket and giving it a good shake. Andrew's thick mane of body hair clearly makes him sweat more than the rest of us because the inside of his jacket seems to be permanently caked in ice.

Fingers are invariably frozen by the time the outside chores are completed, and as soon as we dive inside the tent we desperately try to thaw them out over the stoves, screaming with pain when they finally come back to life. My fingers have been through the freeze-thaw process so many times now that it's as if they have been stung by a thousand stinging nettles.

Frozen sweat is much more of a problem in our footwear, and once our fingers are functioning again, we take turns with the nylon brush to sweep away the great accumulations of rime, granules of ice that build up inside our overboots and between the laces. It can take forever but it's time well spent – the more ice-encrusted the boot is, the harder it will be to put back on in the morning. Outer mitts, inner gloves, wristlets, ski masks, and hats are all frosted up after ten hours on the trail, so they're hung up to thaw out in the roof of the tent like cured meats at a butcher's.

While all this activity is going on, we each hazard a guess at the day's mileage. The average of our estimates this evening was ten miles, so there was a collective cheer when the GPS told us that not only had we finally passed the 84th Parallel but also that we had clocked 11.3 miles today – a new record distance.

Every evening promptly at 7:30 P.M. we report our current position and travel status to Tim Moffatt back at Kenn Borek Air HQ in Resolute Bay. This is partly to help them coordinate our various resupply flights and partly for safety purposes. If something were to happen to us out on the ice, Kenn Borek Air, with their small fleet of Twin Otter ski planes, would be the only people who could put together any sort of emergency rescue effort. Peary's team, of course, had no such luxury. Having said that, the potential killers out here – polar bears, drowning, hypothermia, or an unstable pressure ridge – would finish us off in a far quicker time than it would take to scramble an aircraft many hours of flying time away. This was tragically proven last year when French solo skier Dominick Arduin fell through the ice three days into her North Pole expedition, never to be heard from again despite numerous air searches.

Keeping a Twin Otter on permanent standby would be ridiculously expensive, so there's the added risk that one might not be available for days. Compounding any potential delays, incredible flying machines though they are, these aircraft can only take off and land in good weather. In order to land safely they need a large, flat pan of multiyear ice. In 2003 the record-breaking British explorer Pen Hadow spent nine increasingly desperate days awaiting rescue near the North Pole. Modern-day expeditions, although marginally safer than they were a century ago, are still fraught with danger.

Using one of our two Iridium satellite phones, the scheduled call always begins in a very formal, almost military way: "Tim, it's Tom." The similarity of our names always makes Andrew and Hugh snigger.

"Hi Tom, give me your position."

"North, eight four, spot zero nine, spot five seven one."

"Thanks. I repeat. North, eight four, spot zero nine, spot five seven one."

"Correct. Now our longitude. West, six nine, spot two six, spot six five three."

"Thanks. I repeat. West, six nine, spot two six, spot six five three."

"Correct."

Once the formalities are out of the way, I usually give Tim a brief update on our progress and the current state of the weather and ice. Tonight he told me that plans for our first resupply were on track and that, weather permitting, in two days' time a Twin Otter will be touching down on the ice alongside us with a week's worth of supplies, at or very close to the same position that Peary's first support party turned back in 1909.

Tim also gave me two bits of very disturbing news. The first concerned the members of a Japanese scientific expedition on Ellesmere Island's north coast who were extremely fortunate to have escaped with their lives after a hungry polar bear strolled into their camp last week. The scientists woke up just as the adult male's paw burst through the tent canvas. Still inside his sleeping bag, one of the men reacted immediately, grabbing the rifle and shooting the bear dead, with only its silhouette to aim at.

The other piece of news from the Arctic grapevine involved two young English skiers, Matt Hancock and Matt Coates, who we had got to know during our preparations in Iqaluit a few weeks ago. They were planning on skiing 250 miles from Ellesmere Island to the Magnetic North Pole but had to be evacuated just two days into their expedition after developing severe frostbite in their hands. After two years of planning and sacrifice, to have your dreams shattered so abruptly must be heartbreaking and we're all deeply disappointed for them. It's a reminder of the fickleness of one's fortunes out on the ice.

One of the great things about our satellite phone is that it can receive text messages, so there's a barrage of messages waiting for us every evening from friends and family. Unfortunately, we can't send replies, but their words of encouragement and news from back home do wonders for our spirits. The only disappointment is that my beloved Brighton and Hove Albion lost 1–0 at home to Reading over the weekend.

Suppertime is the moment I look forward to most during the day. Typically dinner begins with a Cup-a-Soup and crackers. We have a selection of main courses to choose from, produced by Harvest Foodworks, from chili con carne to meatballs in tomato sauce to spaghetti Bolognese. They're all tasty and packed with calories. They consist of small chunks of freeze-dried meat, powder, and either pasta or rice, which expand to a full bowl of food when mixed with hot water. By lobbing half a slab of butter into the mix, the calorific content (and taste) increases further still.

Dessert is either a slice of shortbread or one of Matty's homemade chocolate brownies, which have me salivating just writing about them. I'm sure Gordon Ramsay would be appalled at the basic nature of our expedition cuisine and the total absence of any fresh produce, but it fills a very big hole in our bellies and sends us to bed with a warm, satisfied glow.

Pasta carbonara was the highlight of tonight's menu. It was delicious, although George (chef for the evening) forgot to stir the thing, and about a dozen burned-black tubes of penne pasta were stuck to the bottom of the pan. Annoyingly, I was on washing-up duty, a task made even harder with only snow and a worn-out Brillo pad to help me. Irritatingly, it took me over twenty minutes to scrub the pan clean.

Evening conversation typically centres around the dogs and which ones have got in to mischief during the day. It's almost always Baffin. Post-dinner is a good time to write diaries, read some of Peary's journal, or make any repairs – I've already had to sew a patch onto the palm of my right mitten and it looks like the left one will be worn out very soon.

Sleeping bags remain in their stuff sacks until bedtime because of the problems associated with moisture from cooking and breathing. Once trapped between the down feathers of the bags, any steam would quickly condense and freeze, reducing the insulating capacities of the sleeping bag and increasing its weight. As soon as the stoves are turned off, the temperature drops like a stone. Within three minutes it plummets from a couple of degrees above freezing to −40°C, leading to a mass panic as we try to squirm into our sleeping bags before the cold takes over.

Moisture remains an important consideration until morning. Humans lose an average of a pint of moisture in sweat every night, which in this cold would quickly build up as ice inside our double-layered sleeping bags. This is not a prospect that fills any of us with much excitement, so to get around it we're all using a plastic waterproof inner bag called a vapour barrier liner or VBL, which is supposed to prevent any moisture from getting into the sleeping bag itself.

Having said that, I've already got a few ice chunks lurking within the down of my bag, and their size and numbers are increasing. Trying to spend eight hours lying still within the clammy confines of what is effectively a giant condom, with chunks of ice protruding into one's thigh or midriff, is about as unpleasant an experience as the Arctic provides.

The first few hours of the night are usually the warmest, but as our metabolisms get to work on the dinner in our stomachs, the cold begins to creep back in to our bodies like some evil spirit. I'm plagued by frozen feet almost every night. The cold is sapping an average of 2,000 calories from our shivering bodies every night, and by morning everyone is usually curled up in the foetal position, rubbing arms and legs like mad to generate warmth. I've yet to sleep straight through.

The full moon may have passed, but the ice on the restless frozen ocean is always in a fragile state. Every night we're faced with the very real risk that the pan on which we've camped could disintegrate beneath us while we lie in our sleeping bags. It's a sobering thought, and probably the single part of this whole experience that fills me with the greatest fear. Socks, thermal underwear, hats, and fleeces are all worn while we sleep, in part to ward off the cold, but also in case we need to make a speedy exit in the middle of the night to save dogs, sleds, and everything else.

Peary's sleeping systems were far more versatile than our own. The caribou fur parkas that his team wore on the trail were designed in such a way that once the men bedded down for the night "both arms and hands are drawn inside the coat . . . The coat thus becomes the upper half of a light, well-fitting one-man sleeping-bag." Furs took the place of our inflatable Thermarests, and yet more furs were draped over their legs. Reading Peary's journal in bed the other night, I stumbled across the following passage which I wish I had read six months ago: "This is the reason why I have never used a sleeping-bag when out on the polar ice. I prefer to have my legs and arms free, and to be ready for any emergency at a moment's notice . . . What chance would a man in a sleeping-bag have, should he suddenly wake to find himself in the water?" Hindsight is a wonderful thing.

Day 10: 29 March
−35°C, Twenty-one Miles Ahead of Peary, 350 Miles to Go

A quiet and uneventful night in the tent, a welcome respite from those alarming tales of marauding polar bears and disintegrating campsites.

Over breakfast, I tried Mary again, this time at work. "I'm terribly sorry but Mary's just stepped away from her desk," said one of her colleagues. Unbelievable. Anyway, I finally got through on the third attempt, the first time we'd spoken in almost two weeks. It was amazing to hear her voice again. She said she was devastated to have missed my call on Easter Sunday. I had apparently phoned when all the family were at home watching the boat race on TV. But Granny Hope's hearing is not what it was and the volume on the TV was turned up so loud that nobody had heard the phone ringing. We all feel very detached from the rest of the world up here, but it seems that life without us back home is carrying on very much as normal.

George and Andrew managed to speak to their girlfriends on Easter Sunday and yesterday Hugh spoke to his wife Amy, while Matty got through to both Eric and Sarah. It's so cold outside that phone calls to loved ones can only be made inside, in full earshot of everyone else. The rest of the group chats amongst themselves, but it's inhibiting and makes it impossible to have any sort of private phone conversation.

Mary wanted a full debrief, of the conditions, how I was coping, how the dogs were, and how was everybody feeling. I just said that everything was fine and that I was really pleased with the way the expedition was going. I didn't want to let her in on the full horror of our first nine days on the ice. Even though she was putting a brave face on it, I could tell that she was concerned and I didn't want to worry her unduly. I hoped that by saying things like, "It's nothing like as cold as I expected," and "I'm sleeping so well," and "My body feels great," would help put her mind at rest. I wanted to tell her how much she meant to me but us Brits aren't very good when it comes to expressing our feelings, particularly in front of an audience. As soon as I hung up, I regretted that I hadn't plucked up the courage to say how much I missed her and that I was counting the days until we would be back together.

Now that we've broken through the psychological barrier of the 84th Parallel, there's been a noticeable change in the terrain. Gone are the big pressure ridges and frozen leads we've grown used to, and after the grueling slog of the first sixty miles, today provided our first chance to set a steady pace with far fewer interruptions.

The only major problem today was the state of the snow, which to begin with was so sugary that the dogs frequently sank right in up to their bellies. Even our skis became submerged and we ground to a snail's pace, men and dogs pushing and pulling the sleds with all our strength.

Mid morning, we saw what appeared to be a series of hills on the horizon. At first I wondered if it might be an ice island, a giant iceberg many miles across that could have calved off one of Ellesmere Island's many coastal ice shelves, an increasingly common phenomenon these days due to global warming. As we approached, however, the wall of ice continued to grow, looking more and more like the White Cliffs of Dover. "We've discovered a new island!" exclaimed George.

An hour later, our frozen Atlantis had sunk back into the Arctic Ocean, never to be seen again. It had been a mirage, an extraordinary optical illusion known as ice blink, caused by the light from distant pressure ridges refracting over the horizon. I had read about ice blink during my Arctic research but had never expected it to look so real. It also helped explain something Peary believed he had seen almost a century ago: after returning to the *Roosevelt* from his farthest north record in 1906, Peary then embarked on a two-month, 600-mile survey of the north coast of Ellesmere Island "to fill in the unknown gap in the coast." His insatiable appetite for geographical discoveries was as strong as ever and he found new mountains, fjords, and headlands. On 26 June he spotted "snow clad summits of a distant land in the northwest, above the ice horizon." He named this new island Crocker Land after one of his sponsors. A later expedition in 1914 proved that no such island existed.

I had always wondered why Peary would fabricate a discovery like that, particularly as he had made countless other Arctic discoveries over the years and put dozens of his supporters' names on the map. Some of his biographers have suggested that this was purely done to help sway a wealthy supporter into backing another attempt on the Pole, and evidence that Peary lied about his achievements. Having now had my own eyes deceived by ice blink, I can see exactly why Peary was convinced he had sighted a distant land.

By afternoon the surface firmed up, but in the bitterly cold temperatures the snow had taken on the texture of sandpaper, a dry, abrasive surface offering the sleds minimal glide. A sled on wheels would have been far more practical. Despite our efforts to push from behind, the sleds kept stalling, prompting the frustrated dogs to look back at us as if to imply that this was all our fault. Kimmik even shook his head. "Maybe they think we've been sitting on the sleds?" suggested George. It was demoralizing for us all, particularly as the terrain was flat.

Since leaving Cape Columbia, we've been chopping and changing the teams around as part of our never-ending search for the fastest and most efficient way to travel. Last week, Ernie and Kinnik had been larking about at the front of the line, so we now have Ernie running on a much shorter trace where we can keep a closer eye on him. He's behaved impeccably for the last two days and is pulling harder than ever.

Gloria has been a real sensation since Hugh brought her into the team, and she was rewarded for her efforts today with a promotion to one of the front lines. Relations between K2 and Baffin became so bad that it was distracting the rest of the dogs on the team, so today George and I transferred K2 to the front sled, swapping him for the powerhouse of the pack, Ootah. It was great to be reunited with my old friend again and the difference in our team's performance was immediate, with Ootah frequently starting the sled on his own.

Baffin has now picked a fight with every dog on our sled, but has been roundly defeated every time. He now finds himself firmly rooted to the bottom of the dogs' social ladder, alongside Axel who's so terrified of the other dogs that whenever a scuffle breaks out, he runs the other way and hides behind the sled. Apu, the old campaigner of the team, is very much the boss dog and runs on a short trace at the back, always growling whenever one of his canine companions shows signs of slacking off. The dogs see George and me as being at the top of the hierarchy, although I'm sure Apu would disagree with that.

Fights are a regular part of dog sledging and can lead to serious injury, or even death, if they get out of hand. Scraps are most likely to occur when the conditions are at their most taxing and the dogs are on edge. The moment a fight erupted this afternoon, George and I unclipped from our skis and ran towards the dogs, shouting "No, no, no!" It's never easy to make oneself heard above the din of barks and howls, and the whip is usually treated with much more respect than our voices.

A surge of adrenaline and anger swept through me as we ran over, and within seconds the entire team (minus Axel) was knotted together in a giant ball of bloodstained fur, saliva, and tangled lines. They were like sharks in a feeding frenzy and it was imperative to pull them apart as quickly as possible. But as George found to his cost a few days ago, putting one's arm into the centre of a dog brawl, with teeth snapping at anything that moves, is extremely foolhardy. Wading in with kicks and punches is the only effective way of bringing them under control. Once pulled away from the melee, the dogs are told in no uncertain terms to remain where they are or they'll be punished. Apu was having none of it, and no sooner had I turned my back than he dived in for another round.

Amid all the commotion, I hadn't noticed Axel making his cowardly dash to safety, and his trace sent me crashing to the ground as it pulled tight around my legs like a tripwire. My face ended up just inches from Bert's flaring gums. I had no intention of being pulled into the fight myself so I rolled away fast and leapt to my feet.

The fight was over as soon as it had started. A number of dogs emerged with fresh cuts on their faces, but it was Baffin who was the worst off. He had been the target of the attack and was limping badly. Being an outsider with a cocky swagger about him, the rest of the dogs had clearly decided to put him in his place once and for all. I just pray that his injuries are not long-lasting and that he's finally learned his lesson. I want all of us to reach the Pole – both humans and dogs.

I took Apu, who instigated the whole fracas, to one side. My body was still shaking from the adrenaline rush of the fight and I was fuming. Apu knew he was in trouble and he tried his best to hide amongst the other dogs. He cowered as I yelled into his face and struck his snout firmly with the whip handle. I was furious that his behavior was potentially putting the expedition in jeopardy.

Although we never hit the dogs so hard that it causes them any damage, I hate beating them, and only do it as a last resort. But it's the only way to bring them into line and to prevent them from causing potentially fatal injuries to one another. Baffin was also partly to blame, but seeing him lying in the snow, licking his wounds, I couldn't help but feel sorry for him and so this time chose to let him off.

Later in the day, we came across the first open water of the expedition, a narrow lead snaking its way through an area of rough ice like a mountain stream. The two-foot-wide channel of black water looked innocent enough, but it was the thin ice on either side that posed the greatest risk. Ensuring the dogs crossed in exactly the right place was paramount, so I left George with our team and went ahead to help the front sled. Sensing the danger, the dogs were very skittish, and before we had had a chance to make a plan, they took off across the thin film of new ice bordering the lead. The sled was heading straight for the water, with Andrew and me being pulled along on our skis behind it. "Let's flip it!" Andrew screamed, terrified that we would join the sled in a watery grave.

We leaned all our weight on to the left-hand handlebar, causing the sled to capsize and stop just shy of the water. One of the runners broke through the thin ice but the load stayed dry. Disaster, however, hadn't been completely averted as the sudden jolt caused both Marvin and Zorro to lose their footing and slip into the lead. Thankfully, Hugh and Matty were on hand to pull them out, and they were soon rolling around in the snow to soak up the water in their fur and shaking themselves dry. We were soon under way again, Marvin and Zorro back in the harness as if nothing had happened.

These dogs never cease to amaze me. Their indestructibility helps put our own sufferings into perspective.

DAY 11: 30 MARCH
−32°C, Twenty-nine Miles Ahead of Peary, 342 Miles to Go

Today marked the end of the first phase of the expedition, as later in the day our first resupply was due to arrive. A Twin Otter, loaded with the various cardboard boxes and canvas bags of provisions that we had carefully prepared weeks ago, took off from Eureka at first light. With clear skies and light winds, the conditions were perfect for flying, and when I spoke to Tim on the satellite phone after breakfast, he told me to expect to see the plane around midday.

We broke camp earlier than normal to try to chalk up the maximum possible mileage with our near-empty sleds before the plane came in. Coordinating our resupplies is far more problematic that it was for Peary, who, when the time was right, would have just given the command for a few sleds to be emptied and their loads redistributed amongst the remaining sleds. Those dogs, sleds, and men that were now surplus to requirement were then sent back to the ship on minimal rations, while the remaining party continued north.

For us the great headaches are twofold: finding a runway for the Twin Otter, not an easy job in this world of leads and pressure ridges, and trying to make ourselves seen amongst millions of square miles of pack ice. If either of these two vital pieces of the jigsaw were to fail, we could find ourselves trapped on the ice with only a few days of emergency supplies remaining.

The GPS and satellite phone were kept close at hand today, and throughout the morning I updated Tim at Kenn Borek HQ with our position and current weather conditions, vital information he then relayed to the pilot, Troy.

We'd been on the go for over four hours when beyond the southern horizon we heard the familiar drone of a Twin Otter. The dogs pricked up their ears and stood still.

"Sorry guys, we're not going home for a long time yet," said George despondently.

Flying low, the little plane passed a couple hundred yards to the east of us. Despite Hugh's valiant attempts to attract Troy's attention with a series of elaborate star jumps, the plane continued on its way. This had always been the plan. When speaking to Troy last night, I had asked him to continue north for a further sixty miles to place a second depot of fuel and provisions, complete with Argos tracking beacon, at a latitude of approximately 85°23N, before coming back to look for us. Troy's detour gave us an hour to find and prepare a runway.

In all our previous phone calls and meetings with the Kenn Borek team, we had always been told that the pilots needed at least 400 yards of smooth, thick ice to land safely. The Twin Otter's extraordinary ability to land and take off over short distances has made it the aircraft of choice in these high latitudes. The Maldives are the only other part of the world where they operate, ferrying tourists to the various islands, floats instead of skis enabling them to land on the water.

Would we be able to find a runway long enough? I wondered. I always try to take an optimistic view on life, but last night I was racked with worry at the thought of the Twin Otter being unable to land at either camp. Not only would it be disastrous for the outcome of the expedition, but the cost implications of the Twin Otter making an aborted trip would have been huge.

Fortunately, the terrain had been improving throughout the morning, and by complete fluke, we soon stumbled across the largest pan of multi-year ice we had seen since leaving Cape Columbia. However, when Andrew paced out the pan at only 320 yards we were faced with a dilemma – to make do with what we had, or to continue our search and risk ending up with no runway at all. We decided that this one would have to do.

The next hour was a total panic as we feverishly set about preparing the runway. All bumps in the surface were either flattened with shovels or chopped away with axes. Snow-filled bin liners were placed at regular intervals on either side of the runway to show Troy where the smoothest stretch was. The real problem was an old frozen lead that split the runway in two. It had been partly filled in with windblown snow but still required a lot of shoveling to make it safe. It was hardly Heathrow Airport, but up in the Arctic you have to make do with what you've got.

As a reward for carrying out their lead dog duties so brilliantly, Raven and Kimmik were let off their lines and given a run-around. Relishing their first taste of freedom in weeks, they danced around the other dogs, mocking them for still being tied up. We soon realized this was not such a clever idea when five minutes later they returned from the far side of the pan, each clutching one of the runway markers in their mouths. They obviously thought they were helping.

Fresh from successfully dropping off the second resupply and the Argos tracking beacon at Borup Camp (which we hope to pick up in five or six days' time), the Twin Otter came into view, tilting its wings to show that it had spotted us. We all waved back and hollered excitedly. But the ski plane simply passed us by. It then banked to one side and returned, ready to make what I presumed would be its final approach. The Twin Otter glided in again, but Troy was clearly not happy with the runway we had made him and again he pulled up. He was so close we could see him shaking his head in the cockpit. Worryingly, he didn't come back.

We then watched in disbelief as the tiny speck of the aircraft circled continuously a couple of miles to the east of our position. I was becoming increasingly irritable and couldn't keep still, conscious that the Twin Otter would be running low on fuel and would soon need to return to base. Troy had to make a decision. I had visions of him landing far away and of us spending hours needlessly crossing pressure ridges to retrieve our supplies. Or worse still, what if he decided to jettison our carefully packed provisions from the plane? There was no parachute to break their fall. Fuel cans would split and food bags disintegrate on contact with the ice. It didn't bear thinking about.

Ten minutes later, our hopes were raised when the Twin Otter came our way again, flying lower than it had done on its previous fly-pasts. This was it, the moment of truth. The plane swooped down, briefly touching its skis on the snow before a roar of the engines took it back into the skies. I couldn't believe it.

Troy then came in for yet another go. We all held our breath as the plane cleared a nearby pressure ridge by a matter of inches before hitting the deck hard. The engines were slammed into reverse as the Twin Otter bounced its way along the uneven surface at breakneck speed, clouds of snow being kicked up into the air. A ridge of sastrugi sent the aircraft lurching to the left, a wingtip narrowly avoiding the ground, before the plane finally came to rest in a snowdrift at the end of the runway.

We all clapped and cheered as the plane taxied towards us. The dogs erupted into a collective howl, heads pointing skyward and steam billowing from their mouths. It was the most extraordinary piece of flying any of us had ever seen.

Hugh, Andrew, and I rushed over to greet our brave pilot.

"Hey Troy, how you doing?" I asked enthusiastically as the cockpit door opened.

No response.

"That was some landing you pulled off there!" Hugh exclaimed.

Troy just looked at us, shrugged his shoulders, and climbed down the steps.

"What did you think of our runway?" asked Andrew.

Troy took a second to think about the most diplomatic answer he could give. With no expression on his face, he simply said, "Short."

Troy explained that the weather at Eureka had deteriorated and asked if it would be OK if he and his copilot John stayed with us until the storm had blown itself out and it was safe for them to fly. "All we can offer you in return for your hospitality is this bag of oranges," he said. Mouths watering at the prospect of fresh fruit, we invited them into our tent with open arms.

We hadn't had any human interaction for nearly two weeks, and it was great to catch up with Troy and John again. Hidden away amongst the contents of our resupply was a chocolate cake that Ozzie's wife had made for us in Resolute Bay. It was delicious, and along with the oranges, a welcome change from our staple expedition diet.

Troy told us that off the coast of Ellesmere Island, they had noticed a vast expanse of open water over a mile wide and stretching from east to west as far as they could see. It was the Big Lead. How lucky we've been to have slipped through when we did. Peary was held up there for six long days, and even though our progress has been slow, we've managed to eke out a two-day lead.

The guys also told us that we stank to high heaven. George asked, "What do you think of my beard?" which is still pretty feeble after two weeks of meticulous cultivation.

With brilliant comic timing, Troy paused for a moment and said, "Short." We all fell about laughing.

While Matty made cups of tea for the two pilots, the four of us spent the remainder of the afternoon repacking the sleds with the supplies for the next leg of the journey. Any unwanted equipment was arranged into piles to be sent back with the plane. Keen to do his bit for the team's weight-saving efforts, Baffin selflessly gave up the heavy-duty steel chain he had worn religiously around his neck since the start of the expedition, and from now on will wear a standard collar like the rest of the dogs. He seems to have recovered from yesterday's scrap with Apu, which is good news.

At 5 P.M., Troy and John got the all-clear from Eureka. We waved good-bye as the plane rose into the sunset. Suddenly we were alone again. The silence was deafening.

We're thrilled to be where we are right now, a mere five and a bit miles shy of the exact spot from which Goodsell, MacMillan, and their respective support parties were sent back in 1909. Reaching this campsite is all that has consumed my mind for the past few weeks, and there were many times when I wondered if we would ever get here.

Incredibly, we're still right on schedule and with a healthy lead over Peary it would be easy to be complacent. However, the highs and lows of our time on the ice so far have shown me the importance of taking every day as it comes and to expect the unexpected.

Nevertheless, we've definitely turned a corner. We'll go to bed early tonight and start out first thing in the morning, with the hope of putting in a big day. With any luck, the most demanding miles are behind us now, although the breakup of the pack will become an increasing threat to our progress over the weeks ahead. Attention now turns to Borup Camp. As for the Pole itself, it still feels light-years away.

6. Cold War

DAY 12: 31 MARCH
−33°C, *Thirty-five Miles Ahead of Peary,*
336 Miles to Go

OUR HARD-EARNED THIRTY-FIVE-MILE LEAD over Peary needed protecting. Having been held up by the Big Lead for the best part of a week, the giant river finally closed up and on the twelfth day of their expedition Peary and his men were on the move again. Had it not been for this unfortunate delay, there's no way we would be two days ahead at the moment. But the Big Lead would represent his last major holdup, so we know we have to keep pushing.

After yesterday's afternoon off, the dogs were raring to go. No sooner had we left the tent than the Arctic silence was shattered by the din of sixteen barking animals. Once we were under way, George and my team was so overpowered that we kept catching up with the front sled. So we gave them Axel to balance things out more, leaving us with seven dogs to their nine.

The ice conditions weren't much to write home about, particularly in the morning, and the lack of any decent pans, coupled with a huge increase in sled weight, made it difficult to get into any sort of rhythm. Even though a full 413 nautical miles separate Cape Columbia from the North Pole, driving dogs across this frozen bomb site is often reduced to a game of inches. A fraction too far to the right or the left can make all the difference between a sled sailing through a narrow gap between jagged blocks of rubble or being stopped in its tracks by the edge of an ice wall or deep snowdrift.

Before we can even think about getting the sled moving again, skis have to be removed to improve our stance for the backbreaking toil of digging up the drifts or chopping at any protrusions of solid ice. I suppose all those months in the gym were meant for moments like this. More often than not, the only option is to bend our backs and heave the sled clear of the hazard. Before you know it, half an hour has gone by and you've only made two yards.

Now that we've been resupplied, the sleds have more than doubled in weight, and several times today we had to call on extra manpower from the front sled, a favour we returned when the others became trapped. Only when the sled is in position and free from any obstructions can the call to pull be made to the dogs. It always takes a huge effort from everyone to get the deadweight of the sled moving again, dogs pulling their hearts out while George and I shunt from the rear with all our might or pull the sled lines up in front. False starts, of which there are many, are usually met with a chorus of agitated barks.

This all means that we need to be incredibly precise when driving the sleds, and that is where an innovative appendage on our Peary sleds comes into its own. When designing their sleds, Peary and Henson fixed a bow-shaped strip of bent ash between the front of the two runners. Not only did this upturned handle make the sleds sturdier, it also helped the men aim the sleds much more accurately.

Our own attempts to warp a piece of ash into shape in Matty's workshop in Iqaluit failed miserably, and we ended up having much more success in bending strips of thick PVC. They've been an excellent substitute. There's no record of the name Peary used for his steering contraptions so we've simply called ours *amituks,* the Inuit word for thingamajig.

Our amituks have already saved us countless hours messing about in the rough ice and we've found them to be a much more reliable way of steering than swinging the handlebars from side to side. When approaching an obstacle, one of us skis up to the front of the sled and yanks the PVC hoop one way or the other to make sure the sled takes the course of least resistance, thereby mitigating the need for lengthy delays when the sled gets jammed. But it can be dangerous up front, where one risks being wedged against an ice boulder or getting a foot trapped under the sled runners, neither of which are to be recommended.

The amituks are not without their limitations. Later this morning, George and I came around a corner to be confronted by a deep trench. The seven dogs avoided it by quickly changing tack. But there was no time for either of us to get to the amituk, so we tried frantically to turn the sled from the rear. While the dogs are capable of cornering at lightning speed, the lumbering sled, simply cannot. The handlebars are as unresponsive as an oil tanker's rudder, and we just couldn't get it to change direction fast enough. Moments later the sled disappeared into the ditch with a sickening thud, dragging Ootah in with it.

The other dogs, George, and I peered over the lip to find Ootah with his leg raised and peeing all over the sled bag. The sled was on its side, but mercifully there was no major damage. The lashings that secured the handlebars were noticeably looser but they could be retied later in camp. The sled was far too heavy for us to lift out on our own so we signaled to the others to come and lend a hand. A full thirty minutes passed before we were finally under way again.

My mood was soured by the delay, and it didn't get any better when I managed to get flattened by the sled. It had become jammed between two large slabs, so I went ahead to pull the amituk to try and set the sled free. It worked, and the sled was soon on the move, but my mind was still preoccupied with the delay in the trench and I hadn't removed my skis. Big mistake. As the sled flew through the narrow gap, I couldn't jump clear in time. The sled momentarily rocked to its side and I got clattered on the coccyx by the handlebars with so much force that I was thrown headfirst into a deep fissure in the ice. Instinctively I put my hands out to break my fall and in the process managed to sprain my right wrist.

George, who had been recording my embarrassing Charlie Chaplin-esque accident on the video camera, came rushing back to pull me out. I was in absolute agony. I still had some movement in my fingers and just prayed that nothing was broken.

I'm sure that one day that videotape will bring us much amusement, but out here on the ice we stopped laughing at one another's misfortunes a long time ago. We've all spent much of this expedition on our backsides. Often the only thing to cushion a fall is an unforgiving block of rock-hard ice, and we've all got impressive cuts and bruises to show for it. Our tired bodies are feeling the strain, having been yanked in every direction by both sleds and dogs. None of us had ever imagined that dog sledging to the North Pole would be so punishing.

Another worry is that one of our Iridium satellite phones has succumbed to the cold and has stopped working. Until we pick up the Argos tracking beacon at Borup Camp next week, the one phone still in decent working order is our only means of letting the outside world know where we are and what kind of state we're in. Were the second phone to pack in, too, Kenn Borek would have no option but to assume the worst and send a plane out to bring us home – even if we were absolutely fine.

After everything we've put into this over the last two years, to be pulled off the ice because of something as mundane as a faulty telephone would be utterly devastating. I remember the story of Margaret Thatcher's son Mark disappearing for a week in the Sahara Desert during the Paris-Dakar Rally before eventually being rescued by his mother's search party. I don't want to suffer the same fate. Having to explain our failure to sponsors and the media would be the ultimate humiliation, and the tabloids would have an absolute field day.

Consequently, we need to do everything we can to preserve the second phone. From now on it will only be used for evening calls to Tim Moffat in Resolute Bay. There will be no personal calls, and the only text messages will be the ones we receive from Andrew's father updating us on the position of Borup Camp as it drifts around the Arctic Ocean. It also means that until we get another phone flown in, hopefully with the next resupply, I'll have to break one of my commitments to Barclays and stop writing dispatches for the expedition website.

Using nothing more than an Iridium phone, a PDA palm-held computer, a digital camera, and a few cables, every day for the past two weeks I've been able to send a few hundred words of text, a photo, and the occasional video clip back to the Barclays server in London. With the sun so low in the sky, solar panels are totally redundant up here, so everything is powered by AA lithium batteries. They don't last long in the cold so we need a weighty forty-eight batteries for each leg of the journey.

Sending a dispatch to the website can take up to an hour, and I'm often typing away in the confines of my sleeping bag long after everyone else has gone to sleep. It's been a real labour of love, particularly after a brutal day on the trail, but sharing our faraway polar bubble with so many people has given me great pleasure. I often wonder what they all make of our journey across the ice. Is it changing opinions on Peary and Henson? Are we opening people's eyes to the beauty of the Arctic or inspiring them in their day-to-day lives? There will no doubt be some who thoroughly disapprove of our expedition, but we can't expect to keep everyone happy.

All the information gets uploaded onto a very professional-looking website and sent as an e-mail to the tens of thousands of Barclays' employees across the world. The website has a live map plotting our progress against Peary's and a special "Dog of the Day" section where the day's star performer is rewarded with a write-up and a photo on the home page. We're getting thousands of hits a day, and it's been a great way for friends and family to follow our progress. Until now.

In the way that communication blackouts during the lunar landings led wives and families back home to fear the worst, we're all worried about the impact our sudden radio silence will have on our nearest and dearest. Being away from them for so long is something we're all finding difficult, but moments like this remind us that these expeditions cause more stress and anxiety for those we leave behind. I feel horribly guilty for putting Mary and my family through all of this but I cannot imagine how tough it must have been for the families of Peary's men, who were away from home for years with no contact whatsoever with the outside world.

I don't quite understand how, but despite the heavy loads, the delays, and my fall, we managed 11.3 miles today and beat our previous record by a whisker.

DAY 13: 1 APRIL
−36°C, Thirty-one Miles Ahead of Peary, 325 Miles to Go

It took me a while to fall asleep last night, due in no small part to Hugh and Andrew's snoring duet. I was still awake at midnight, gazing up at the tent roof when it dawned on me that the sun was still out, tinting the top of the ski that props up the tent a deep shade of orange. The days have been lengthening rapidly since we left Cape Columbia, and it's been a long time since we needed headlamps. But to go from eight to twenty-four-hours daylight in a matter of days of is quite extraordinary.

I woke up feeling as though I'd gone twelve rounds with a prize fighter. Ninety miles of manoeuvring the sleds over rubble fields have taken their toll on our backs and necks, but after yesterday's fall I was stiff all over. Everything seemed to hurt, particularly my coccyx. At least the anti-inflammatory pills Matty prescribed last night had some effect, and the swelling in my wrist has calmed down.

Throughout the time we've known the dogs, they've been at their happiest when running across an ice floe at full pelt with a heavy wooden sled rattling along behind them. As Peary himself had once said, "The Eskimo dog was born to pull." But nine hours on the trail no longer seem to fill the dogs with the same levels of excitement as it did a week ago. Once they're on the move they're fine, but getting them going after breakfast is becoming more and more labourious, like starting a car on a frosty morning. At times they just couldn't care less. Their barking has become noticeably more subdued. For the last few days we've given them half a scoop of kibble in the mornings and reduced the size of their dinner ration as a way of putting some fire into their bellies for the day ahead. There've been some signs of improvement but not as much as we'd hoped.

So reluctant were the dogs to get to their feet this morning that it was as if they were all nursing bad hangovers. Matty and the first sled had already left camp, but George and my team were just wandering about aimlessly, completely ignoring our increasingly desperate pleas to take up the slack in the sled lines and pull. While I shoved my weight against the handlebars, George was out in front, beckoning Kimmik towards him by slapping his thighs and calling, "Come on Kimmik, come!"

It took all his powers of persuasion to convince the dogs to get into first gear, but it was too late. The other team was already several hundred yards away, a gap that was too big for our demoralized team to close. Moments later, they stopped pulling. Andrew had to ski back to cajole our dogs forwards, but more precious minutes had been needlessly wasted. It was nobody's fault, but it was a clear reminder that the dogs' spirits need to be maintained by keeping the teams close together.

We'd only been on the move for half an hour when Ootah had to stop to be sick. This didn't worry us unduly as it could easily have been due to indigestion, brought on by the speed at which he scarfs down his breakfast. However, as the day wore on, Ootah's performance deteriorated and his line was slack for much of the day. We just hope that he was having an off day.

I find I'm far hungrier now than I was at the start and have definitely lost weight. I have to pull my trousers belt in much tighter than I used to. I spent much of today daydreaming of food and fantasizing about my perfect meal – roast lamb, Mum's amazing roast potatoes, leeks, and carrots drowned in gravy. Just like Peary, we're each consuming a ration of two and a quarter pounds per person per day, giving us a daily energy intake of approximately 6,000 calories. The problem is that we're burning somewhere between 7,000 and 10,000 calories every single day out here, a caloric deficit that not even Weight Watchers would recommend. We're effectively starving ourselves, but if we want to keep our sled weights down, we have no other choice.

Our days are divided into four sections of between two and two and a half hours in length. At the end of each section we stop for a fifteen-minute pit stop, designed to give the dogs a breather and to give us our latest caloric fix. These breaks follow the same routine every time; skis are removed, the dogs are sat down, and their lines untangled while Matty pours out five mugs of hot orange Tang from one of the thermoses filled up during breakfast. On windy days we huddle behind one of the sleds for shelter, wrapped up in our down-filled over jackets. Mouths begin to water as a dozen ziplock food bags are opened and laid out like a spread on a buffet table. It's then every man and woman for themselves as we delve into the assortment of treats and pour them down our throats with mittened hands.

Pit-stop fodder includes high-calorie foods that burn their energy gradually throughout the day – things like chunks of cheese, dried fruit, nuts, sesame bars, slices of salami and biltong – but we also need more immediate stimulants like fudge, cookies, flapjacks, and chocolate. I had remembered from the South Pole expedition the frustration of chewing one's way through a frozen chocolate bar, so when Cadbury's agreed to donate the expedition's entire chocolate supply, I ordered boxes and boxes of bite-sized Heroes that could be sucked rather than chewed. They would also add some variety to our diet and would hopefully reduce the risk of us losing any teeth.

The one to watch out for at these pit stops is Andrew, whose slim build belies the most prodigious appetite of any man I know. Several times already on the expedition, one of us has had to tell him to return some of the goodies from his overflowing hand back to the bag. As hunger levels grow, I can see Andrew's craving stomach is only going to become harder to satisfy.

I always look forward to these stops, but after a few minutes of relative inactivity, the precious warmth in our bodies begins to ebb away. When fingers and toes start turning numb, that's the signal to hit the trail and get the blood pumping again. In temperatures as low as these, continuous activity is the only way to keep frostbite at bay.

Poor Ootah brought up his kibble again this evening, only this time it was mixed with blood. I gave him a dose of antibiotics, which Matty had dug out of the dogs' first-aid kit, and spent a few minutes by his side, stroking him and talking quietly into his ear. I told him I wanted him to make it to the Pole. He's a shadow of his former self at the moment and I'm just praying that he gets better.

The temperatures today were off the scale, never more than −36°C according to the thermometer, but more like −50°C once the windchill was factored in. Throughout the day I kept wiggling my toes to stop them from succumbing to the cold. Mary's never been particularly complimentary about my toes, but she'd have a lot to say if I returned home with stumps on my feet as Peary had done.

Despite the bitter conditions, I actually felt the warmth of the sun's rays on my face for the first time on the expedition. Spring will soon be on its way. While the brief moment of warmth provided a welcome respite from the hostile conditions, the sun is public enemy number one out here. As the days grow longer and the sun climbs higher in the sky, its ultraviolet rays will weaken the ice pack, making it more susceptible to breaking up. Until now, all but two of the leads we've encountered have been frozen solid, but the Arctic Ocean won't be held in frigid suspension for much longer.

Another record distance today – 13.5 miles. Only the small matter of 312 more to go.

DAY 14: 2 APRIL
−35°C, Thirty-one Miles Ahead of Peary, 312 Miles to Go

We're running the dogs on a simple fan-hitch, the same traditional Inuit system that Peary used. Each dog is connected to the sled by a series of traces, which vary in length from about fifteen to thirty feet. When they're on the move, the dogs spread out like a fan, with the dogs on the longest traces in the centre of the pack. Like restless football managers who constantly tinker with their team formations, we're forever swapping the dogs around to try to get the maximum performance from them.

Kimmik has been reinstalled as lead dog on the longest trace with Bert and Ernie as his two wingmen. We're back to a team of eight now with Gloria, Baffin, and a struggling Ootah on the midlength traces, and Axel and the veteran Apu bringing up the rear.

The more conventional tandem hitch widely used in Alaska and Lapland, where the dogs are clipped in pairs along a long central trace, would be completely ineffective on the polar pack. While the more regimented order of the tandem hitch eliminates the problem of tangles, the dogs would be much more constrained and strung out over a long distance. Not only does this reduce the team's power, but in areas of rough ice, the chances of a dog becoming pinned against a slab of ice or disappearing into a crack would be greatly increased. With a fan hitch, the dogs can more or less run where they want, and were the sled to get stuck, they can give themselves a better footing to get it going again.

The major hassle of the fan hitch is that over time the traces can become badly knotted, particularly in rough terrain where dogs are jumping across each others' lines. Untangling the traces is a chore carried out during pit stops when the dogs are all sat down. It's as unpleasant and cold a job as lashing the sleds in the mornings. Mittens have to be removed for fingers to loosen the knots, and it's not long before they're totally numb. George and I often have to finish each other's handiwork while the other frantically tries to bring his frozen fingers to life.

While crossing a pressure ridge this morning, Axel was jumping all over the place and managed to get his trace in a major mess. I went up to try and untangle him, but he was in such a bind, yelping in pain with part of Ernie's trace wrapped around his back legs. The quickest way of freeing him was to unclip him from his trace, pull it clear, and then reattach him again – nice in theory, but in practice, a total disaster. No sooner had I detached him he seized his opportunity, leaping across the other lines, and his collar slipped from my cold hands. As he made his determined bid for freedom I dived headlong towards him, but he squirmed his way free.

"Axel, get your sorry arse back here or else!" I screamed, beating my fist against the snow, but Axel had other ideas and was on his way back towards Cape Columbia.

"So long, Axel!" cried out George as the fugitive disappeared towards the horizon, and with that, we continued north with seven dogs instead of eight.

We always knew that Axel would return. Realizing the futility of his actions, and that his only chance of survival was to stay with us, five minutes later he turned around and started following us. For a while he trotted along just out of our reach. It was going to take great cunning to recapture him, so we just ignored him and carried on driving the team forwards. Peary wrote, "To catch a loose dog sometimes requires more or less time and ingenuity . . . Our usual method of capturing one of these polar wolves was to coax him within reach by throwing out morsels of meat to him, then throw ourselves upon him and quickly bury his head in the snow. Sometimes a dog is too wily to be caught in any such way and has to be lassoed and choked almost senseless before he can be put back in harness."

Like a loose horse at the Grand National, Axel then decided to run out ahead of the other dogs, which initially seemed to spur them on. He soon tired of this particular trick and resumed his original position amongst the pack, pretending that he had somehow managed to reattach himself to his trace and was pulling the sled like everyone else. He hadn't, of course, and the other dogs knew this, continually looking back and barking their disapproval at him. Axel was becoming a nuisance, but each time George and I tried to grab him, a quick sidestep was all he needed to evade our clutches.

Nearly an hour later we stopped for a break. This was our chance. We used Peary's technique and managed to entice Axel towards us by throwing a few peanuts in his direction. George then surreptitiously sneaked up behind him before launching himself into a rugby tackle. He landed right on top of him and quickly wrapped his arms and legs around the struggling Axel like an octopus taking down its prey. The rest of us watched in amusement. "You could have picked on someone your own size!" said Matty.

Axel didn't put up much of a fight, and much to the other dogs' delight, he was soon clipped in again. We then all winced as in a moment of madness, Axel decided to lick the aluminium karibiner that linked the traces to the pituk.* He squealed in pain as his tongue stuck fast to the frozen metal like a magnet. We rushed over to help the poor dog but thankfully he managed to free himself. A small flap of frozen tongue remains attached to the karabiner, which should deter the other dogs from making the same mistake in the future.

We were pitching the tent this evening when Hugh spotted the vapour trail of a Boeing 747 high in the skies above us. The tiny plane was heading in the direction of the North Pole, the most direct flying route between New York and the Far East.

"Just picture the scene up in first class at the moment," said Andrew. "They'll be stretched out in their flatbeds watching the *Bourne Supremacy,* drinking champagne, and eating like kings."

"Bastards," muttered George, gazing forlornly at the jet stream, which had been tinted a vivid orange by the low sun.

We're all missing our creature comforts at the moment and would give anything for a decent meal, a bath, and a comfortable bed. Our relentless battle against the ice can really get us down sometimes, but given the chance none of us would have swapped places with anyone on that plane. In fact, there's nowhere else we'd rather be than right here in this spectacular world of snow and ice.

Incredibly, flying machines were cruising the skies above the Arctic Ocean years before Peary ever set foot on the frozen sea. In July 1897 the Swedish balloonist Salomon Andrée was making the final preparations for possibly the most imaginative and totally ridiculous of all polar adventures. His romantic vision was to fly his hydrogen balloon, the *Eagle,* with two companions from a small island off Spitsbergen all the way to the Pole and on to Canada.

Huge crowds sailed north from Scandinavia to watch the launch. After a shaky takeoff that saw the balloon's basket dragged through the

---

* The pituk is a length of cord, loosely strung between the two sled runners, to which the dog traces are attached.

sea for half a mile, the *Eagle* climbed majestically to an altitude of 1,600 feet before speeding off into the distance at more than twenty knots. Two days later a carrier pigeon landed on a Norwegian sealing ship, carrying a message from Andrée, reporting that all was well onboard and that they had already covered 300 miles. But the trio was never heard from again.

Not until 1930 was the mystery of the *Eagle*'s fate solved when the skeletons of the three balloonists were discovered on White Island, just fifty miles east of their takeoff point. The men's journals and a roll of undeveloped photographic film were also recovered, which shed light on the crew's chilling end. They revealed that three days into the voyage the men had been forced down by the accumulation of ice on the balloon's canopy. They had flown over 500 miles and reached 82°56N.

With no other option but to abandon the stricken balloon, the men marched south, reaching White Island after eighty days of indescribable misery, eating whatever wildlife they could shoot along the way. By this stage they were so exhausted and suffering from chronic diarrhea and stomach cramps that they couldn't even muster the strength to build a proper shelter. Andrée's diary entries, becoming increasingly illegible and shorter, came to an abrupt halt a week later. The advancing winter eventually did for them all.

Ootah was sick again and spent the day hobbling along like a wounded soldier. This is becoming a real concern. Better news is that we managed 14.7 miles today, our third record day in a row, and we're now beyond the 85th Parallel – a full four days faster than it took us to cross the previous degree. At this rate, the new bottle of sloe gin that arrived with our first resupply will be empty within days. I don't think Peary would approve, who said, "Liquor should have no place in a polar ration." Our good progress is all down to the smoother surface, fewer pressure ridges, our improved efficiency, and a lack of open water. Long may it continue.

Following his countless misdemeanors today, Axel was unanimously voted our Dog of the Day.

Day 15: 3 April
−37°C, Thirty-four Miles Ahead of Peary, 297 Miles to Go

I couldn't be happier with our mileage since Goodsell/MacMillan Camp, and last night I floated the idea of adding a couple more hours on to our day today to try and make a single push to Borup Camp. According to the text messages from Andrew's father, our resupply was 19.2 miles away, only 4.5 miles farther than our record day. Rather than making two shorter marches, wouldn't it be better to cover the distance in one go? I suggested. I was conscious of the fact that we'd travelled fourteen days in a row and doing one big day now would give everyone the opportunity to take a well-deserved rest day tomorrow.

I also felt that a long march would spare us the time-consuming hassle of breaking camp, packing up the sleds, and harnessing up the dogs and then setting up a new camp a couple of hours later. Peary's claims of being able to travel twenty miles or more in a single day lie at the heart of the controversy. We have no idea what the coming days will bring, and with the ice and weather so benign at the moment I felt this could be our only opportunity to get close to that important landmark. Nonetheless, everyone was tired last night and, other than George, there hadn't been much appetite for my idea.

For the last three days, our daily mileages have been almost identical to Peary's. On their fifteenth day, Goodsell and MacMillan returned to the ship, while the remaining expedition members stayed in camp to divide up the loads and carry out repairs to sleds and equipment. While their rest day would help us extend our lead over Peary today, we're acutely aware that he was saving the team's energy for a sprint finish to the Pole in a few weeks' time.

It was another insanely cold day today. The old frostbite wounds on my cheeks that I got going to the South Pole have opened up again. Last time they turned a shocking shade of black, and I was left with two bright pink scars that lasted over a year. They proved useful conversation-starters at dinner parties, but freezing the flesh on one's face isn't much fun, so I've patched them up with zinc oxide tape in the hope they don't deteriorate further. More of a worry are the three fingers I froze in Antarctica, which were very sore today. They just don't seem to have the circulation that they once did.

After a difficult first hour the terrain improved significantly with a series of large, flat pans. With not a cloud in the sky, the Arctic Ocean was at its dazzling best. Skiing along as the sled glided silently through the soft snow, I turned to George and said, "Are you thinking what I'm thinking?"

"These conditions are awesome, aren't they?"

"They're unbelievable. I really think we should keep going all the way to Borup. We'll be there in no time."

At the final break, I asked Matty to dig out the GPS and find out how far away we were. There were just seven miles to go, a distance we would expect to cover in around four hours at our current speeds.

"Guys, I think we should try to knock these miles off tonight and take a well-earned rest tomorrow," I said. "Our dogs are on great form and—"

Before I had even finished, I was interrupted by Andrew. "No I don't think we should. I don't see the point. I think we should just stick to the schedule and get there tomorrow. And besides, we're almost out of water."

"That's not a reason," I replied. "We'll just be a bit parched when we get into camp."

He then started explaining his theory that the body recovers more quickly after a half day's rest than a full day. "And besides, I don't really feel like spending a whole day resting in the tent." I really don't understand him sometimes.

Matty said that her back was giving her some grief, but if there was agreement she was happy to carry on. Then Hugh came up with the much more valid argument that he felt the front team was on the wane, and I reluctantly backed down and suggested we find an early camp. When we were under way again, George laughed and said to me, "It's got to be tough being the leader when there's disagreement in the team. I don't envy you one bit."

Things would be so much tougher without George by my side. He's been a part of my expeditions for nearly a decade now and has always been an invaluable sounding board and rock of support. Yet, even though I am equally close to Andrew, we have always had the occasional argument. Thankfully, they only seem to happen on expeditions. Besides, there are probably traits in me that get on his nerves. For the sake of our friendship, it's going to be best if I can resist the urge to get riled up every time he disagrees with me.

Driving these dogs is a delicate balance. We want to make the most of the kinder conditions while we can, but we musn't to push the dogs too hard and pay the price later in the expedition. These thoughts were confirmed when poor old Ootah, who had been pulling strongly all day, was sick late in the day. Maybe my over-exuberance had been getting the better of me after all. We're in an endurance race, not a sprint, and we should pace ourselves accordingly. Getting to the Pole in less than thirty-seven days would be incredible, but the ultimate goal is simply to get all twenty-one of us to the end, in safety and good health.

DAY 16: 4 APRIL
−33°C, Forty-eight Miles Ahead of Peary, 284 Miles to Go

Even though there were less than six miles to go to Borup Camp, the dogs were a pain in the backside the whole way there. Whether they were rebelling after yesterday's heated discussion on the ice or they had got out of the wrong side of bed I don't know, but whatever the reason was, motivating the dogs was a real struggle. They can be a real joy, but there are times when they are absolute hell. This morning was one of those moments, and George and I repeatedly lost our temper with them.

The conditions were a continuation of the smooth, flat pans and frozen leads we have grown used to over these past few days, interspersed with sporadic blue ice blocks that jutted out of the uniform terrain like giant tombstones. At least the skies were clear, which made the job of finding our resupply more straightforward than it would have been in a whiteout.

Throughout the morning Matty made regular consultations of the GPS, which indicated that we were gradually homing in on our target. I was concerned that the depot of food and fuel could be impossible to find because the text message updates from Andrew's father had shown that it had drifted more than half a mile since Troy and John had dropped it on the ice five days ago. If the Argos beacon had developed a glitch or somehow become detached from the 510 pounds of supplies, it would have been like trying to find a needle in a haystack and we would have been in serious trouble.

At the first break, George and I climbed a pressure ridge to see if we could spot the blue barrels and red-and-white sacks of dog food amongst the icescape. We had been taking turns scouring the horizon with the binoculars for some time when George pulled down his fur hood and shrieked, "I can see Borup Camp!"

His eyesight must be better than mine because even when he pointed it out to me, the cache was still almost impossible to see through the binoculars. With the sun now much higher in the sky, the glare can blur one's vision.

Matty was first to the depot, which was piled high in the centre of a large pan. I couldn't believe how something as complicated as trying to locate a tiny stash of food amongst millions of square miles of pack ice could have gone so smoothly. Someone must have been looking down kindly on us. Deep scars in the snow, only partially drifted in, showed where Troy's Twin Otter had taken off and landed. The good news was that our fears of a polar bear ransacking our precious supplies as they lay unguarded on the ice hadn't materialized.

As a reward for getting us to our second resupply so quickly, once camp was set up all the dogs were given an hour-long run-around. Because we're a day ahead of schedule now, we actually have more dog food than we need for the next leg of the expedition, so we dug a long, shallow trench in the snow and filled it with the entire contents of a forty-pound bag of kibble.

The unexpected treat proved extremely popular, and the dogs were soon lined up like hungry pigs feeding from a trough. That is, everyone except Odin. With a line of long spiky hair running down the length of his body, Odin is the dog that most closely resembles a wolf. He's a real streetfighter and always getting into trouble, so when he decided to make an unprovoked attack on Seegloo halfway through their lunchtime feast, we had no option but to reattach him to the tie-out chain while the others carried on eating. Matty gave him a serious dressing-down.

It's been nearly three weeks since any of us had a decent bath, and we're all smelling revolting. Until now, our only way of washing has been to put a small amount of tepid water into a ziplock bag and give ourselves a quick sponge bath. When it comes to cleaning our privates, a call of "Privacy" is the signal for eyes to be averted, although Andrew gave everyone a horrible shock the other day when he forgot to give the call until after he had pulled his trousers down. But sponge baths burn valuable fuel and don't really do the job. Far more effective is the snow bath. Popular in Scandinavia, where a naked frolic in the snow is immediately followed by a relaxing sauna, I've found snow baths to be the best way of maintaining a reasonable level of cleanliness on a long polar journey.

The bitter temperatures thus far have made snow baths unthinkable, but with next to no wind and the polar sun shining brightly, Hugh and I decided to take the plunge this afternoon. We emerged from the tent giggling nervously and wearing nothing but boxer shorts and our down-filled tent booties. "This is a very bad idea!" joked Hugh. The dogs just looked on, wondering what the fuss was all about.

We wanted the ordeal over and done with as quickly as possible, so we grabbed handfuls of powdery snow and began scrubbing away like madmen. The snow felt more like coarse sand than soapy water and refused to melt on contact with our bodies. It was −33°C, after all.

The next sixty seconds were a blur of arms and snow, accompanied by the occasional high-pitched squeal when the snow came into contact with a particularly sensitive area. This was the first time we had seen our bodies in the light of day since Resolute Bay, and we were shocked at how emaciated we already looked. We were also covered in bruises, and I counted seven on my right leg alone. This expedition is taking a far greater toll on us than I had ever imagined.

Unable to take the cold any longer and shivering feverishly, we dived back into the warmth of the tent. There were a few difficult moments as we struggled to put clothes back on, an almost impossible task with numb fingers. Ten minutes later we were dressed, thawed out, and feeling wonderfully refreshed. Some may view snow baths as sadistic, but I find them strangely enjoyable.

The rest of the afternoon was spent relaxing in camp, making repairs to the sled bags and our mitts, drying clothes, and gorging ourselves silly on our surplus food rations. We also took time to tend to our growing list of injuries and ailments. The frostbite on Andrew's nose has gone septic, and George's eyelids have become puffed up with windburn. The kettle burn on my hand is struggling to recover and both my nostrils have now split open, which is excruciating. I've also developed a hacking cough that has awakened me and my fellow tentmates on each of the last four nights.

Despite applying copious amounts of lip salve since Day 1, all of us, bar Andrew, have split lips, which after forming a basic scab overnight, proceed to rip apart when we take our first mouthful of muesli in the morning. The skin on our hands has cracked like leather and is covered in tiny cuts that reopen the moment they snag on our fleecy clothing. We're not a pretty sight. The one salvation is that our toes, although blistered, seem to be frostbite-free.

Still, despite the considerable discomfort, spirits remain high. While we've had more than our fair share of pressure ridges and rough ice to contend with, the ice pack has remained locked together. There's been almost no open water. The cold has kept a stranglehold on the Arctic Ocean since we left Cape Columbia, and the warmest temperature we've witnessed so far was the −32°C on that first morning. Nevertheless, we've gradually acclimatized to the unseasonably frigid conditions, and while we're constantly windmilling our arms around and running up and down on the spot in a desperate bid to stay warm, the cold hasn't held us up too much.

Tonight we're camped less than a mile from where George Borup, the "tenderfoot" of the team as Peary called him, was sent back to the ship on 20 March 1909, with three Inuit, two half-empty sleds, and sixteen dogs, his expedition over. A crestfallen Borup later wrote, "I would have given my immortal soul to have gone on . . . I never felt so bad in my life as when I turned my footsteps landward, and I hope I never will again. Still, it was all part of the game. When the Captain of your eleven orders you to go to the side lines, there's no use making . . . frenzied pleas to be allowed to go on."

Borup had done everything that Peary had asked of him. He wrote, "I regretted that circumstances made it expedient to send Borup back from here . . . His whole heart was in the work, and he had hauled his heavy sled along and driven his dogs with almost the skill of an Eskimo. But with all his enthusiasm for this kind of work, he was still inexperienced in the many treacheries of the ice; and I was not willing to subject him to any further risks . . . It was a serious disappointment that he was obliged to turn back; but he had reason to feel proud of his work – even as I was proud of him."

Many of Peary's detractors have suggested that Peary was a ruthless, coldhearted man who viewed his support divisions as mere tools to get him to the Pole. In my view, hearing Peary gushing with paternal pride and compassion over his team members (he gave equally glowing reports of Goodsell, MacMillan, Marvin, Bartlett, Henson, and the Inuit) demonstrates a much softer, caring side to his character than he is given credit for. Equally notable is the fact that in all their own books about the expedition, none of Peary's companions ever had a bad word to say about him, even though all of them, bar Henson, endured the heartache of being sent back before the Pole. Peary was an incredible leader of men.

Tomorrow we embark on the next leg of the journey to Marvin Camp, seventy-five miles to our north. Incredibly, we've actually managed to extend our lead over Peary to nearly four days. We're counting on Sedna, the all-powerful Inuit goddess of the sea, to keep the ice in check. Whether the ice will behave or not, only time will tell.

7. Snow Patrol

THINGS BEGAN VERY SLOWLY THIS MORNING. This was mainly thanks to a zone of rubble that took a good couple of hours to negotiate. We were hampered by the sleds being back to full weight, and the dogs appeared to be thoroughly disillusioned by it all. Even small hummocks between the ridges produced enough drag for the sleds to stall out. The dogs are now so weary that, even when the going's easy, George and I usually have to get the sled moving ourselves before they even consider taking up the strain. How we're going to keep them going for another three weeks, I have no idea.

Just about the last thing we need right now is an injury to one of the dogs, so when Baffin decided to ambush Ootah, who is still distinctly off colour, maul his front right paw, and leave it bleeding badly, it sent George into a rage. George is normally such a passive guy, and in all the years I've known him, I don't think

I have ever seen him lose his cool. So it came as a complete surprise when he removed his skis, marched over towards Baffin, and threw himself on top of him. Punches rained down on the notorious troublemaker as George screamed into his ear, "Don't you ever do that again, Baffin! You are a very, very bad dog!"

The poor animal then whined in pain as George proceeded to clamp his jaws down on Baffin's ear. He held his bite for a good couple of seconds before I told him that that was probably enough. Baffin emerged from the scrap completely unscathed, but I had never seen a dressing-down like it. "That bloody dog has been pissing me off since Day 1," said George as he clipped his skis back on. "He only pulls when he feels like it and he's always picking fights. We've let him off way too many times. He needed to be taught a lesson."

George is the last person I would expect to explode in the way he did, but these extreme conditions are pushing us to the very limit. The message seemed to have got through however, and Baffin was a model sled dog for the rest of the day, keeping out of trouble and giving his all.

Later in the day, we were just about to stop for our second break when we hit the polar equivalent of the M1 – a completely smooth highway stretching all the way to the shimmering horizon. The frozen lead was perfectly straight and wide enough to accommodate a dozen lanes of traffic. Even better, it was completely solid. There was just one minor problem – it headed northwest, a full forty-five degrees off course.

"If only it pointed north," lamented George as we all gathered together for hot Tang and snacks, "we could reach the Pole by the end of the week."

It was one of the most spectacular sights we had seen on the trip so far, and coincided with a perfect Arctic day of clear blue skies and no wind-chill. Then as Matty clambered down the two-foot bank to begin skiing across to the other side of the lead, I suddenly had a flashback to my GCSE maths. "Hang on a sec, Matty. I don't think we should dismiss this route out of hand."

"But it's going to take us completely off course."

"I know, but what's the point in burning ourselves out by bashing our way through rough ice, when we could hitch a free ride on this thing and speed along at five miles an hour?"

I then took a ski pole and drew a right-angled triangle in the snow.

"Let's call this side due north, and the longest side, where the lead is pointing, northwest. Now, if I remember Pythagoras correctly, we'd need to travel about 1.4 miles along the lead to make one mile of northerly progress. That seems a fair trade-off to me. What do people think?"

To my surprise Andrew, Hugh, and George seemed confident enough in my grasp of geometry to endorse the idea, but Matty thought the lead pointed more west than north and needed more persuading. "I tell you what, Matty, if this ends up costing us mileage, you can lay the blame squarely with me, but I'm convinced we're on to a winner here. And you never know, it might eventually end up veering north."

She paused for a moment as she analyzed my woeful artwork. "Whatever you say, Tom," she sighed, still clearly unhappy about the decision.

So off we went, and for one carefree hour, which I shall remember for the rest of my life, we cruised along in complete solitude, everyone lost in their own thoughts. Invigorated by the wide expanse of smooth terrain ahead of them, the dogs trotted along effortlessly, as if the sleds weren't even there. In fact, the dogs were so fast that Matty was unable to keep ahead of them and ended up joining Hugh and Andrew at the back of the first sled. Clinging to the handlebars, we made long, easy strides with our skis as the sleds floated across a surface as flawless as a skating rink.

For weeks now, we've yearned for an escape route that would take us away from this frozen chaos. We may not have been going in the ideal direction, but for a brief moment the lead transported us away from the harsh realities of the journey and reminded us of the breathtaking majesty of the Arctic Ocean. We've become so engrossed in the day-to-day grind of inching our way north, that it's easy to forget how lucky we are to witness these incredible panoramas that nobody has ever seen before.

The icescape is never repetitive or tedious because the views are changing all the time. As we glided along on our merry way, the dark, steely surface of the frozen lead began to change. An untold number of pure white frost flowers carpeted the lead like feathers. Formed by salt leaching out of the ice, they sparkled in the bright sunlight like diamonds, their tiny leaves fluttering in the faintest puff of wind. It felt as if we were on another planet.

Eventually the lead petered out and it was back to the slower going of the old ice. But fortune was clearly on our side today because during the final session Matty found a series of interconnecting frozen lakes, this time heading almost due north for three or four miles. Disappointingly, a much coarser layer of frost flowers meant the sleds didn't run quite as smoothly as they had done on our magic lead earlier in the day, but nobody was complaining.

It came as no surprise when the GPS told us we had smashed our mileage record and clocked a total of 17.5 miles of northerly gain in nine hours of travel. Peary's best mileage to date was a day of fifteen miles. It all felt so effortless; we hadn't had to take skis off once during the final two sessions, and I felt vindicated for suggesting the detour in the first place.

Up here in the Arctic, you've got to take full advantage when you're dealt a good hand. Peary had a difficult time of it today, battling through rough ice and only making eight miles on his seventeenth day. I'd never fully appreciated just how much of a role luck plays on a North Pole expedition. Had we been travelling on a course a few hundred yards farther east today, it's conceivable that we could have missed our two frozen highways altogether and ended up in a vast rubble field, or cut off by open water.

People say that because there's nothing new to explore up in the Arctic, modern polar explorers should instead call themselves "adventurers" or, a term I really can't stand, "trekkers." I disagree completely. No map, satellite photograph, guide book, or past expedition report would help us find our way around here. The Arctic Ocean is such a volatile and rapidly changing environment that physical landmarks are formed, destroyed, or transported about in the blink of an eye. The only way to get to the North Pole today is to do as the original pioneers did and search for the best route as we go.

On the other hand, despite our record day and the continuing improvement in the conditions, relations amongst the team members are becoming increasingly fractious. We've been on the go now for seventeen consecutive days without a rest and living on top of one another in the cold, cramped quarters of the tent. Everyone's shattered and starting to get on one anothers' nerves.

After being jumped on by Baffin this morning, Ootah spent the rest of the day limping along, barely able to keep up with the other dogs, his trace completely slack. He kept looking back at George and me with his big soppy eyes as if to say he couldn't take much more of this. Over dinner, Matty suggested flying in a couple of spare dogs at the next resupply to boost the team's power. "That's a total cop-out," I protested. "When we started planning this expedition, we set ourselves a target of replicating Peary and trying to reach the Pole in thirty-seven days with teams of eight dogs. By increasing the size of each team to nine dogs, we're basically admitting that we're giving up."

Andrew leapt to Matty's defence. "Look, for me, it's all about trying to get to the Pole as quickly as possible. The dogs are exhausted and we could do with the extra power that Bartlett and Jacs would give us."

"But Peary only had eight dogs on each sled," I retorted. I wasn't going to let the integrity of the expedition be compromised.

Both George and Hugh backed me up. Hugh said, "We had a plan. I think we should stick to it."

Having let me get my way earlier in the day at the frozen lead, Matty dug in her heels. No side was backing down, and with the discussion becoming increasingly hostile, it took a compromise solution from Hugh to break the tension. "Bartlett and Jacs are no use to anyone sitting in the dog yard in Iqaluit," he said. "Why don't we have them flown up to Resolute, where they can wait on standby? I'm sure Ozzie would look after them for us, and should Ootah, or one of the other dogs, become too sick to carry on, then we can do a straight swap at the next resupply."

It was a sensible suggestion, we all went along with it, and it didn't compromise the goals of the expedition. Of the 133 dogs that left Cape Columbia with Peary in 1909, only forty would be selected for the polar party, which gave Peary a large pool from which to select the strongest and freshest animals. Although I desperately hope that Bartlett and Jacs are never needed, the approach is essentially the same as Peary's.

The argument left me drained so I stepped outside to escape our self-imposed togetherness for a short time. It was a calm, windless evening, and I was able to spend a minute with each of the dogs without getting too cold, airing my frustrations. Everyone has their own motives for doing this expedition. My own motivation comes from trying to set the record straight on the old commander's behalf, and the best way to do this is by simulating his journey as closely as possible. That said, I cannot expect everyone to be driven by the same things as I am and I should consider myself fortunate that everyone still seems determined to reach the Pole within thirty-seven days.

The dogs listened to me patiently. I also told them we couldn't have got this far without them and gave special attention to Ootah, who has battled on heroically. It's heart-wrenching to see him like this and I just want him to pull through.

Day 18: 6 April
−35°C, Fifty-three Miles Ahead of Peary, 260 Miles to Go

6 April – the day that Peary reached the Pole. It also happens to be George's girlfriend, Annie's, birthday today, and the smooth bastard has pre-arranged for a bouquet of flowers to be delivered to her office. "I always forget things like birthdays, anniversaries, and Valentine's Days," he confessed over breakfast, "so there's no way in hell she'll believe they're from me."

With the sun now above the horizon throughout the night, provided the clouds stay away, its rays warm the tent like a greenhouse. It may have been touching −40°C outside the tent last night but inside it was an almost tropical −17°C. The amount of fuel needed to warm the tent has halved in recent days, which will help reduce the sled loads in the closing stages of the expedition. Even better news is that the mild temperatures prevent our sweat from freezing inside our sleeping bags, and last night was my first without my claustrophobic vapour barrier bag. It's a fantastic feeling of freedom finally to be out of that straitjacket.

Over breakfast Hugh had everyone in hysterics when he confessed to having wet his bed last night. When it comes to answering late-night calls of nature, we've each brought along a wide-brimmed pee bottle, which, after a careful bit of bodily manoeuvring, can be used safely inside one's sleeping bag. This is a much easier task for men than it is for women, so if things can't wait until the morning, Matty has little choice but to go outside in the snow.

Having filled up his bottle last night, Hugh apparently then paused for a few moments before reattaching the lid. During those brief seconds, he made the fatal error of dozing back to sleep, only to wake a few minutes later after accidentally emptying the entire contents of the bottle all over himself and the inside of his sleeping bag. Our sympathy was mixed with incredulity. I would have been mortified had it been me, but true to form, Hugh just laughed off the whole incident. As he rinsed out his soiled thermals in a pan of hot water, he chuckled, saying, "And Tom, if you want to include my misfortune with the pee bottle in the expedition book one day, I'd be honoured. It might serve as a warning to stop me making the same mistake again."

Hugh's little accident, and the manner in which he dealt with it, helped diffuse any tension in the group still lingering from the previous evening. After giving Ootah some more antibiotics, we agreed to monitor his situation during the day and make a decision about his two possible replacements this evening.

There were no leads today, frozen or otherwise, just a succession of wide-open pans interspersed with the occasional pressure ridge. A total absence of wind made it feel considerably warmer than the −35°C that registered on the thermometer this morning, and at the breaks we didn't even need our superwarm down parkas.

Gloria has done an excellent job as our lead dog for the last five days, but without the brawn of her male companions, she's no sled-starter. George and I could sense that Kimmik was itching to assume his original role again at the head of the pack and so we swapped them around at the first break. The change was immediate, and the dogs were running strong for the rest of the day, Ootah included.

Ootah even managed to join in one of our impromptu team howls. Occasionally, when the dogs are sat down, waiting for the front sled to clear an obstacle, they spontaneously burst into song. It's an incredible spectacle to see the dogs point their snouts skyward and howl in unison like a pack of wolves, steam billowing from their mouths. The sound is so comforting, in stark contrast to the threatening, staccato noises of the ice that regularly pierce the silence of the frozen ocean.

The Eskimo dog still has one paw firmly in the wild, and these collective sing-alongs seem to reinforce their bond with the Arctic. Ernie and Apu are usually the chief choirmasters, but for the past week, George and I have tried starting the whole howling business off ourselves. At first, our efforts received no more than a look of bewilderment and derision from the dogs, but now, to our amazement, they join in wholeheartedly. It's as if they've finally welcomed these strange two-legged creatures into their inner circle. We're now part of the pack.

There will be some who think that taking dogs on expeditions, and the way they're treated, is a cruel game. But the dogs, like the five of us, are thriving on the challenge of sledging across this vast frozen wilderness. Fatigue, cold, hunger, and general hardship all come with the terrain, for dogs and humans alike. Our survival up here is very much intertwined, but so, too, are our successes. Whether we make it to the Pole or not, it's that magical bond we had with our animals that I will look back on with the greatest nostalgia in the years to come. It's truly awesome.

We took another sizeable bite out of the remaining distance to the Pole today. We covered 16.5 miles in eight and a half hours of travel and are now tantalizingly close to the 86th Parallel. More troubles for Peary today means that we're now a full sixty miles, a whole degree, ahead of him.

Even though he was sick yet again this afternoon, Ootah was in great spirits all day, and during dinner it was agreed that it would be best to leave Bartlett and Jacs where they are in Iqaluit. We're going to try to make it to the Pole with the team we started with.

The dogs were full of energy today, although a couple of times the sled stalled completely when they decided to take turns peeing on almost every single protrusion in the surface. Very frustrating. In the same way that domestic dogs urinate on trees to mark out their territory, our animals are becoming increasingly competitive about being the last one to shake a few precious drips out onto an irrelevant piece of ice. A bit of collective peeing is all very well, but it's getting beyond a joke. At this rate, it's going to take us til Christmas to reach the Pole.

Unlike us, Peary's Inuit were masters with the whip and would have been able to crack a warning shot directly above the dogs' backs if they sensed the sled was slowing down. We somehow managed to lose two of our three whips within the first three days of the expedition and now have to make do with our voices, which are nothing like as effective as a hard leather whip. Even if we hadn't managed to lose our whips, if our training was anything to go by, chances are we would either hit ourselves on the backside or trip as the coils became entangled in our skis. Aiming the whip while on the move is a skill that takes years to perfect.

Were we to be travelling back along the same route a few weeks from now, with the dogs' keen sense of smell, it would be surprisingly easy for them to find their way back to Cape Columbia – even if the pee stains had since been buried by snow. Turning for home gave Peary's dogs, and those of his various support parties, a new lease on life as they could sense the expedition was nearing its end. Coupled with the fact that they could easily sniff out the homeward trail, all the various divisions made it back to Crane City in a much faster time than in their outward marches.

One of the greatest challenges we face in the first ten minutes of the day is staying clear of dog shit. At times there's so much of it that it's like trying to go for a run in Battersea Park, a mecca for all South London dog-walkers. When one of the dogs needs the bathroom, the sled doesn't stop for them – it would just take too long to wait for everyone – so they have to do their business on the move, which is not an easy task. The sled quickly catches up with the poor dog, forcing it out to the side as it shuf-fles along on its backside, trying desperately to keep up with the team. It's not long before the dog has drawn alongside us, giving us despairing looks and begging us to slow down. But the dogs have the final laugh because once they've finished, they sprint forward to rejoin the others, invariably causing any muck they've deposited on their trace-line to flick into the air and land on us. Thankfully, it soon freezes solid and can be brushed off, as can frozen dog urine, but being soiled by one's animals is the ultimate humiliation.

Sometimes the dogs will gang up on us and we're faced with the prospect of three or four of them taking a crap at the same time. The surface is soon littered with brown landmines that are impossible to avoid, and despite our best efforts to get out of the way, the sled and our skis inevitably slide straight through some of them, leaving a long dirty skidmark in the snow. When dog muck freezes to skis and sled runners, it reduces their drag considerably. All we can do is stop and scrape the frozen excrement off with the axe. Oh, the glamour of dogsledging to the North Pole.

The winds have now shifted around to the east. What began as a gentle puff picked up significantly as the day wore on, which explains the increasing number of freshly formed leads we saw later in the day. With temperatures still in the mid minus-thirties, the good news is that it's still cold enough for them to freeze over again pretty quickly.

During the day's third session, we had almost crossed one particular refrozen lead when a floating ice boulder caused the second sled to flip over onto its side. Since he is lighter than I am, and therefore less likely to break through the three-inch-thick ice, George volunteered to climb back down onto the lead to right the sled. I was up in front with the dogs, trying to encourage them to pull the sled to safety, when I heard a noise like a gunshot. I quickly turned round to see George standing motionless on the ice, with a look of sheer horror etched across his face. "The ice is splitting and the sled's going in," he whispered.

"Forget the sled," I yelled, "Just save yourself!"

A growing pool of dark water stained the ice like an oil slick, and one of the sled's runners began slipping under. George's right ski was already submerged. I rushed back to the edge of the lead as George tentatively shuffled towards me. He grabbed my outstretched hand and I was able to pull him off the lead before the crack caught up with him. The dogs must have sensed the panic in our voices and leapt into action, pulling the capsized sled a short distance up the bank and out of harm's way.

Further adrenaline-pumping mishaps ensued at the next two leads, but luckily it was only the sleds that got wet. Even though we were fully prepared for thin ice and had waterproofed the contents of the sleds accordingly, it's unbelievable how quickly this place can change.

Having enjoyed three perfect days, the ice is definitely on the move again, and all afternoon we could hear it muttering to itself as it began to break apart. We searched for more than an hour for a suitable campsite, but wherever we looked, thin ice or open leads blocked our path. With the dogs totally spent, we had no option but to pitch the tent on a tiny pan, barely eighty feet across and bordered on three sides by menacing lanes of black water. Our only hope is that it will refreeze or close overnight and that we will be able to get away from here in double-quick time.

To our great surprise, we clocked another 16.1 miles today, a huge distance given our troubles late in the afternoon. That's over fifty miles in the last three days, way beyond our wildest dreams. Ootah seems much better, which is a great relief. Thoughts are already turning to our next resupply at Marvin Camp, just twenty-six miles to the north of us. The first two resupplies went like clockwork, but with the ice and weather conditions deteriorating, picking up our final two caches is unlikely to be so straightforward.

During my evening call with Kenn Borek HQ, Tim's colleague Mickey Riley told me that they had been tracking a weather system that was heading our way. "There's a cloudbank, a good three hundred miles across, which we need to blow through before we'll be comfortable about flying," he said.

I also had a brief chat with Rod Fishbrook, the pilot, and reiterated the importance of trying to drop the final cache, complete with Argos tracking beacon, as close as possible to the latitude of Bartlett's turn-around point at 87°47N. "You got it," he said.

I've got a horrible feeling in the pit of my stomach as I'm writing this tonight. We're surrounded by open water and the ice is creaking and groaning like the timbers of an old ship. All we can do is sit tight and pray that fate doesn't deal us the same cards as Peary had in 1909 when the pan on which they had camped split in two. On the night of 28 March, Peary woke to the noise of "someone yelling excitedly outside." He wrote, "Awakening my men, I kicked our snow door into fragments and was outside in a moment. The break in the ice had occurred within a foot of the fastening of one of my dog teams, the team escaping by just those few inches from being dragged into the water. Another team had just escaped being buried under a pressure ridge . . . Bartlett's igloo was moving east on the ice raft which had broken off, and beyond it . . . there was nothing but black water. Our two igloos, Henson and mine, were on a small piece of old floe, separated by a crack and . . . it was clear that it would take very little strain or pressure to detach us and set us afloat like Bartlett's division."

By complete luck, Bartlett's igloo eventually drifted into the far side of the floe, allowing him and his dogs to jump across to safety. Soon everyone was reunited and they moved camp to a more secure-looking pan, but it could all have been so different.

We're definitely in a vulnerable position tonight, and I don't have much faith in our feeble little pan lasting until the morning. Only time will tell.

Day 20: 8 April
−29°C, Sixty-one Miles Ahead of Peary, 228 Miles to Go

I slept badly. The ice pack complained throughout the night, each scrape or boom sending me bolt-upright in my sleeping bag, ready to make a speedy exit from the tent. Andrew, George, and Matty were up most of the night, too, but despite the frightful din, Hugh somehow managed to sleep through everything.

The GPS revealed we had drifted more than a mile northward overnight, which would explain yesterday's bumper mileage. This is all thanks to the winds, which turn the pressure ridges into giant sails and set the ice pack in motion. Looking back on how much effort we had to exert to make a single mile of northerly progress during the early days of the expedition, to cover the same distance while cocooned in our beds feels almost like cheating. "Let's just kick back here for a few weeks and let the winds carry us to the Pole," mused Andrew.

Nonetheless, due to the fickleness of the polar winds, we know that it's only a matter of time before the goddess Sedna claws it all back again. We cannot afford to relax. Typically, a helping wind will drive the ice floes apart, which is why it was a miracle that our pan had somehow managed to remain intact throughout the night.

Over breakfast, we realized that the drift had carried us beyond the farthest north record of the brilliant Fridtjof Nansen, one of my all-time polar heroes. In 1888 Nansen made the first coast-to-coast crossing of the Greenland ice cap. Even though the six-week journey propelled the photogenic Nansen to stardom, he considered his Greenland crossing as a mere training excursion for a far more daring expedition to the North Pole.

Rather than viewing the frozen wastes of the Arctic Ocean as his enemy, Nansen planned to sail his ship right into the heart of the icepack north of Siberia and let the currents carry him westward over the Pole and on to Canada. He built a bizarre-looking vessel called the *Fram*★ with a rounded underbelly. When pressure was applied to both sides, rather than being crushed by the ice, the *Fram* would simply be forced upward, "slip like an eel out of the embraces of the ice" and rest on the surface.

The *Fram* set sail from Oslo in June 1893, entering the pack northwest of the New Siberian Islands in October, where she became instantly frozen in. Over the course of the next eighteen months the little ship gradually zigzagged her way across the polar sea. By early 1895 Nansen

---

★ The *Fram* would later be used by the ship's captain and one of Nansen's original Greenland team, Otto Sverdrup, on a mapping survey of the Canadian High Arctic in 1898–1902. It was during the early stages of Sverdrup's expedition that he had had his brief encounter with Peary. In 1910, Roald Amundsen then sailed the *Fram* to the coast of Antarctica before embarking on his historic dog-sledging journey to the South Pole.

was growing increasingly concerned that they were being carried off course and that the Pole would eventually pass them by.

Nansen couldn't take the tedium any longer and decided it was time to make his audacious dash to the Pole. Along with Hjalmar Johansen, he left the *Fram* in March 1895 with three dog teams, two kayaks, a three months' supply of food, and headed off into the unknown. The Pole was just 350 miles away, but the drifting ice was now carrying the men south. It was a losing battle, and after four weeks they abandoned their attempt at 86°13N. Even so, they had broken the previous record by almost three full degrees.

The two men were now faced with a terrifying race against the clock. Due to the uncertainties of the shifting ice pack, they had no hope of retracing their tracks back to the *Fram*. Their only option was to head for the closest land, the Franz Josef Islands 400 miles to the south. It would be four more months of sledging and kayaking before they finally made landfall, the men being forced to eat their dogs to survive. With winter fast closing in, they dug a shallow pit where they sat for nine months of unimaginable boredom, living off seal and polar bear meat.

The following spring, they lashed the two kayaks together and set sail in the hope of reaching Spitsbergen. Calamity struck almost immediately when the poorly moored kayaks floated away from an iceberg they had climbed to get their bearings. Seeing their sole means of transport drifting off into the distance, Nansen promptly dived into the freezing water. He eventually caught up with the boats but barely made it back to the berg alive.

Three days later they came under attack from a pod of walruses. During the mayhem, a walrus tusk punctured a hole deep into the side of one of the kayaks and the men had to paddle frantically for the nearest land before they sank.

By extraordinary good fortune, they came ashore within a mile of a British party that happened to be surveying Franz Josef Land. They were the only people amongst hundreds of thousands of square miles of ice, yet somehow their paths had crossed. The pair was eventually returned to Norway, but Nansen's narrow escape from the icy clutches of the North left him with such an indelible scar that he vowed never to return to the Arctic again.

The meandering lead bordering our small pan had refrozen overnight, enabling us finally to escape the maze of icy rivers. Soon afterwards we ran into a zone of monstrous pressure ridges. After an hour of slow, exhausting progress, up and over the great walls of ice, we were through, but our troubles were only just beginning.

The cloudbank Tim had warned us about last night rolled in, giving us our first flat light in a week and washing out all definition in the landscape. A lead fifty yards across then blocked our route, and even though it was iced over, Matty deemed it too thin to cross. Being the only one of us with prior Arctic Ocean experience, Matty is very much in charge when it comes to selecting the safest place to cross. The theory goes that the darker the ice, the thinner it is, but with a dog team exerting more downward pressure on the ice than a single skier, making the right judgment is far from straightforward.

We followed the lead's shore for twenty minutes before coming to what looked like a potential crossing point. The ice had overlapped in the centre of the lead, which we hoped would make things sturdier. Matty drove a ski pole through the ice, as far as the pole's basket. No water bubbled up through the hole, indicating the ice was at least three inches thick. "Don't follow until I say so," she said as she gingerly skied across to the other side, making further prods of the ice as she went.

With Matty safely across, next it was the dogs' turn. We took great care to lower the sleds onto the lead's surface, rather than having them crash down the three-foot lip at high speed. First to go was Raven's team. Hugh pointed the sled in Matty's direction and let go. Our hearts were in our mouths as the driverless sled trundled across the lead, Matty beckoning them towards her. The dogs could clearly sense the danger and almost seemed to be tiptoeing. Puddles seeped out from the sled's tracks.

Unlike freshwater, which sets like glass when frozen, a thin layer of frozen seawater has a much more rubbery consistency, and to our great alarm the lead began flexing under the combined weight of the dogs and sled. With the ripples in the ice amalgamating to form a more organised bow wave in front of the sled, I thought it was only a matter of time before it broke through into the water. Incredibly, the dogs and sled made it to safety and shot up the bank on the far side. The bow wave producing a gaping hole in the ice as it crashed against the shore.

The second sled crossed slightly farther down, and then it was our turn to ski across. The delicate skin of newly formed ice warped with every stride, and I was utterly petrified. I kept telling myself to concentrate and keep moving. Stopping in the middle of the lead or not gliding my skis smoothly across the surface could easily have fatal consequences. How had Matty found it so easy? I wondered. Then it dawned on me that I probably weighed almost double what she did, and because our skis were the same length I was actually applying nearly twice as much pressure on the ice. The experience would probably be like trying to walk across the River Thames, with only a layer of soggy cardboard for support. I kept my eyes focused on the far bank, trying to forget, not very successfully, that the ocean beneath my feet was nearly two miles deep. Three anxious minutes later and I was across, soon to be joined by the others. We were all overcome with relief.

As the day wore on, we encountered more and more leads. We wanted to head due north but the ice was having none of it, sending us on a series of wild goose chases as we searched for a way through. One particular lead had begun to fracture in the centre. The two sleds bouncing over the brittle ice and the four of us following along behind must have weakened the flimsy structure further, because when George, the last in the party, started making his way across, he very nearly came a cropper when a table-sized slab of ice became detached, rocking from side to side under his weight. George's arms windmilled around wildly as he tried desperately to recover his balance, but he eventually made it to dry land.

Another lead, which was far too thin to cross, appeared to be swinging around to a more northerly direction. For more than an hour we sledged along its bank, only to find ourselves boxed in at a cul-de-sac where the lead had splintered into four open tributaries. There was no alternative but to make a U-turn and look for another way through.

These endless detours were incredibly frustrating, and we felt as though luck was turning against us. It took a moment of inspiration from Andrew to get us out of this particular fix. We had been travelling southwest for more than a mile when Andrew spotted a small island in the centre of the lead. It was just ten feet from the main bank, with a similar gap separating it from the far side. "The sled will easily straddle the lead," said Andrew. "We could just use it as a bridge."

The dogs were unclipped from the first sled, and with Hugh and Andrew pushing down on the handlebars to keep the runners elevated, they were able to work the sled so it spanned the crack. Matty, Andrew, and Hugh clambered over the sled to the island and called the dogs over the ice towards them. The ice was no more than an inch thick, and the three stragglers in the group, Zorro, Seegloo, and Marvin all broke through into the water as they ran across. Fortunately, Matty and Andrew were on hand to pull them out by their collars, the dogs thanking their rescuers by showering them with icy water.

The dogs in the second team were panicked, watching their colleagues falling in, so we decided it would be a wise precaution to unharness them and get them to crawl across the sled bridge one by one. Kimmik was initially reluctant to cross, but once he was over, the remaining dogs followed suit. That is, everyone except Apu, who was obviously fed up waiting and decided to shuffle across to the far side of the lead by himself, avoiding the island altogether. The wily old campaigner is the only one of the dogs who has been to the North Pole before★ and obviously has a sixth sense when it comes to crossing precariously thin ice. Had anyone been able to catch a sight of the five of us, fifteen dogs and our two sleds crammed onto the tiny island wondering what to do next, and Apu giving us disparaging looks from the far bank, they would probably presume that it was Apu who was calling the shots.

The gap to the far side of the lead proved straightforward to bridge, and fifteen minutes later we were all safely across. Although I long for the

★ Apu had been part of Paul Landry and Paul Crowley's dogsled expedition to the North Pole in 2000, and he had accompanied Landry again when he skied to the Pole with the South Korean Swee Chiow in 2002.

days of endless flat pans again, it was exciting work and a refreshing change from the challenges of crossing pressure ridges. With Matty at our side instead of way off in the distance where she normally is, this was probably the first time on the expedition that we all had worked together as a single unit. Even though we take our breaks together and share the same tent, on the trail itself we tend to carry on independently. Seeing my team working so effectively as one gave me a warm feeling of pride.

Almost immediately, the next lead blocked our path. These never-ending watery moats are getting us down. Just when we think we're out of trouble, up ahead comes the next lead, and the next, and the next. It's driving us crazy. Matty scouted to the west for five minutes and Hugh skied off to the east, but the lead only widened in both directions. We would have to cross here.

The ice appeared to be more solid than the previous lead, but the crossing was made all the more problematic by a six-foot vertical wall on the far side. Andrew, Hugh, George, and I quickly built up a sweat as we lifted each sled over the top as Matty called on the dogs. They were extremely apprehensive and leapt at their traces frenetically, their desperate barks filling the air. We were nervous, too, because any slight slip could cause the sled to crash down and puncture the ice we were standing on.

Another lead five minutes later proved equally challenging. This one was covered with a thin layer of newly formed ice, interspersed with natural stepping stones of rubble ice. I was the last to cross, but the force of dogs, sleds, and people going before me had obviously caused the flimsy structure to weaken. I had only just got going when, to my sheer horror, one of the floating islands collapsed under my weight. For a split second I was peering into the black abyss of the Arctic Ocean. With no time to think, I instinctively lunged for the nearest stepping stone. Luck was on my side and it held firm. But my leg had gone into the slushy waters up to the thigh and my trouser leg was already freezing solid.

The others had moved on and had disappeared behind a wall of ice, so no one had seen me go in. I was beginning to hyperventilate. The fear of falling through the ice had haunted me since I first started planning the expedition, and now I was living that nightmare. I got back to my feet as fast as possible. I remembered Peary saying that the best way to treat a wet leg was to keep walking and use one's body warmth to dry out thermals and trousers from the inside. I could always scrape the thick layer of ice off the outside of my trousers later in the tent. My leg was weighed down by ice and my teeth were chattering uncontrollably. But the fear of frostbite got the adrenaline pumping and spurred me into action as I sped off in pursuit of the others.

Towards the end of the day, we came to yet another lead. There was a great temptation to pitch camp, but we decided to cross it, as leads have a nasty habit of expanding during the night at the moment. It took half an hour to negotiate, by which time every one of us was dog-tired. We collapsed inside the tent, too shattered to speak. What a day. Although we had probably covered more than twelve miles, if one was to strip out the detours, our efforts amounted to just 7.6 miles of northerly progress. I made a check on my leg, foot, and toes and thankfully they seemed OK.

The Twin Otter is due in two days' time, but if the winds continue to pry the ice pack apart like this, it's going to be a struggle to find a decent runway for them to land. We're all totally spent, and the ever-present worry of thin ice is fraying our nerves. The ice pack, which has been locked in frigid suspension all winter long, is beginning to disintegrate.

Day 21: 9 April
—31°C, Fifty-seven Miles Ahead of Peary, 220 Miles to Go

We've been going for three weeks straight without a break and we're all feeling it. Our backs are now so stiff from working the sleds that when we step outside to start the new day, we're completely bent over double. The next few minutes are like a speeded-up version of the evolutionary development of man as we gradually crank ourselves up from hunchback Neanderthals to fully upright Homo sapiens. Poor Matty is faring even worse and has been complaining of a painfully sore shoulder for a while now. To think we were fit as fiddles when we set off from Cape Columbia.

Although I tend to avoid gyms like the plague, I do try to keep myself in reasonable shape between expeditions. I'm careful about what I eat and usually go running several times a week. There's a very picturesque five-mile circuit I do near where Mary lives in South London that takes me through playing fields, around the lake and golf course of Wimbledon Park, up a couple of steep hills, past the All England Lawn Tennis Club, where the world-famous tennis championships are held, and then home again. When there's an expedition on the horizon, I ramp things up significantly and will add circuit training, weights, and stretching exercises to my fitness regime. I find it much easier to work towards a target, rather than trying to stay in peak condition just for the sake of it.

Andrew couldn't be more different; he goes running before breakfast every morning to keep his pent-up energy in check. It's fairly typical that he'll finish his run by throwing up. Then there's George, who is one of those annoying individuals who somehow manages to stay fit without doing any training whatsoever. He was one of the unhealthiest people I knew at university, and seemed to survive on a diet of baked beans on toast, kebabs, and Guinness. When we ran the London Marathon together in 1997, he arrived at the starting line reeking of alcohol and complaining of a hangover. I managed to complete the course in under four hours, with George only just behind me.

As for Hugh and Matty, with Canada's great outdoors on their doorsteps, they probably lead the most active lifestyles out of all of us. But three weeks in the Arctic has been a great leveler. And now we're equally exhausted all the time.

Getting the dogs going at the beginning of the day is becoming progressively more difficult. After breaking camp, Matty skis off into the distance while we try to get our dogs in gear and follow her tracks. Both Kimmik and Raven's teams are now equally uninterested in towing a sled across the polar wastes, and who can blame them? They've all visibly lost weight and appear shattered and pretty fed up with it all. When we tried to gee them along this morning, we had to physically pick some of them off the ground, so reluctant were they to get to their feet. With hundreds of miles still to go, it's difficult to see how we're going to avoid burning them out altogether. They need a rest day as much as we do, but our schedule is so tight that we can only afford a day off if we get hit by a storm.

Despite the hardship, I'm sure that life on this expedition is more bearable for our dogs than it was for Peary's, whose Inuit were hard task-masters. Their way of maximizing the dogs' performance was to discipline them with voice and whip. The dogs knew that if they stepped out of line, they could expect to be punished severely. Occasionally, one of the Inuit would go on ahead and callously pretend that he was stalking a polar bear or chopping up seal meat to entice the dogs towards him. The men's relationship with their animals seemed to be more like master and slave than expedition companions.

While there are times when we need to be firm with the dogs, essentially we're trying to make the journey one big game for them. The soundtrack to our day consists of a never-ending stream of hollering, excitable tongue-rolling, high-pitched "yee-hoo"s, and enthusiastic claps of our hands, which, apart from first thing in the morning, seem to have the desired effect of spurring the dogs on. On flatter terrain, George and I will often take turns skiing just ahead of the dogs, encouraging them with dog calls. But three weeks in the same one-sided conversation that goes something like, "That's it, Kimmik, that's it. He's a good boy Kimmik, good boy. Come on then, Kimmik, hup, hup, hup, yee-hoo," has left us totally brain dead. I'm sure the team can now pick up on the lack of motivation in our voices, and at one point today Apu looked back at me as if to say, "Give us a break and quit patronizing us with your silly noises."

It took us most of the day's first session to negotiate a vast rubble field. When we regrouped at the first break, I asked Matty how the terrain looked up ahead. "More of the same, I'm afraid," came her reply.

Ever optimistic, I climbed a small pressure ridge nearby in the hope of finding a better way through. "Have you seen those pans over there?" I asked, full of excitement.

"What pans?" replied Matty from the bottom of the ridge.

"There are at least three interconnected pans over there which will only take us a couple of minutes to get to. I'd say there's well over a mile of easy terrain if we take a slight detour. Come up here and I'll show you."

I tried not to show it, but I was disappointed with Matty. Had she just kept skiing blindly northward, we would have missed the pans altogether, resuming our exhausting battle with the rubble instead. Once Matty had made it to the top of the ridge, I put it to her gently, "It's a pretty awesome view from up here, isn't it? You're doing a brilliant job up in front, but next time the sleds get held up in crap terrain and you're having to wait for us, it would be a huge help if you could climb one of these things to see if there was a better route up ahead."

She agreed, and we were soon on our way again, enjoying the easy conditions the three pans provided. I need to tread very carefully with Matty. Not only does she take criticism extremely personally but her mind is all over the place at the moment. I'm sure that skiing out in front all day she is regularly distracted from the tedium of breaking the trail; which may be why she sometimes seems to have tunnel vision. During conversations over dinner, she often talks about her break-up from her husband, Paul, and the impact it's had on her and the children. Now that Eric and Sarah have left home, it's going to be especially tough for her to return to an empty house at the end of the expedition. This morning while we were loading the sleds, Andrew apologized for his tendency to take Matty's side during team disagreements. "I think she's pretty lonely," he said. "I guess I just feel sorry for her." We need to keep her spirits up.

The rest of the day was a blur of rubble ice, squabbling dogs, and a wind that cut our faces like razor blades. Windblown snow accumulated on my eyelashes, and I kept having to blink to prevent them from freezing shut. A paltry 8.5 miles was all we had to show for our day's efforts. The only blessing is that Peary was having a rest day today, having just sent back Borup's division, so we've actually managed to extend our lead over him. Unfortunately, all that is set to change because tonight's campsite is totally surrounded by towering blue-ice pressure ridges, and the view to the north looks equally uninviting. We're supposed to be resupplied tomorrow, but whether the plane will be able to land is another matter altogether.

Today's Dog of the Day prize is shared by three incredible dogs. During one of our many lead crossings today, the second sled broke through the ice, soon to be followed by five of the team, everyone except Kimmik, Bert, and Ernie. The incident happened in the centre of the lead, and it would have been a struggle for us to get close to the dogs without weakening the fragile surface further. We then all watched in utter amazement as the three dogs somehow found the strength to haul not only their fellow dogs out of the water but the stricken sled as well. Had it not been for their quick thinking, the sled could have easily ended up dragging them all under. It just doesn't bear thinking about.

DAY 22: 10 APRIL
−26°C, *Sixty-six Miles Ahead of Peary, 211 Miles to Go*

A disastrous morning. We woke to find that the Arctic conveyor belt has switched into reverse and overnight we drifted 1.5 miles to the south-west. So massive were the towers of ice that blocked our route from camp that it took us more than an hour of backbreaking work to progress just one hundred yards. It was devastating to think that this represented ground we had lost in our sleep.

The sleds have taken a battering over the last few days and one of the napus on the front sled (the wooden crosspieces that straddle the two runners and hold them together) snapped clean off after colliding with a slab of ice this morning. It seems only a matter of time before one of the sleds suffers an even more serious accident. At least they're light. How the likes of Will Steger and Wally Herbert managed to muscle their 1,200-pound sleds through ice like this is beyond me.

Towards the end of the first session, the mother of all pressure ridges reared up ahead of us, rising out of the ice pack like some medieval city wall. Half an hour later, we had managed to get the sled near the top of the gigantic monolith. We were poised for the descent when Ernie completely disappeared from view. With our hearts in our mouths, George and I raced forwards to discover that he had fallen down a deep crevasse within the ridge. To over disbelief, Ernie, completely unfazed, proceeded to spread his paws against either side of the narrow crack and shuffle all the way up like an expert rock climber. These animals are something else.

At midday I called Mickey at Kenn Borek HQ on our one functioning satellite phone and updated him with our current position. "Rod will be taking off from Eureka very shortly," he told me. "He's planning to drop the cache at Bartlett Camp and then come to you. He'll be with you around three-thirty. You located a runway yet?"

"We're working on it," I replied.

If we couldn't find a runway before Rod's arrival in three and a half hours' time, he would be forced to abort his mission altogether and come back another time, leaving us with no food for days and a very large bill for an extra flight. Once again, the only alternative would be to drop our precious supplies from the plane, which would be pointless because everything would be pulverized as soon as it crashed into the ice.

The next few hours became increasingly stressful as we searched in vain for a potential runway. The pituk on the front sled then snagged on a particularly vicious shard of ice that sliced it in half. With nothing to connect them to the sled anymore, the dogs sprinted free, leaving Andrew and Hugh with no engine to propel their sled. The dogs were eventually recaptured, but a vital fifteen minutes had been lost.

With the situation becoming increasingly desperate, I decided to take matters into my own hands, and while waiting for Hugh to retie the pituk, I clambered up a nearby pressure ridge. It was a clear, breezy day and the sun was so high in the sky that the reddish hue we had grown used to in the early weeks of the expedition had been replaced by the deep blue of a summer's day. About a quarter of a mile to the northeast of us I spotted the largest pan we had seen in days. It was the only piece of smooth terrain I could see in all directions and it stood out from the menacing shadows of the angular pressure ridges, glistening brightly in the afternoon sun. I breathed a huge sigh of relief and cheered, "Great news guys, we've got ourselves a runway!"

Matty changed direction and we headed straight for the pan, reaching it in little more than twenty minutes. But there was still much to be done.

We had barely an hour to prepare the runway, and a mad panic ensued as we laid out the snow-filled bin liners to mark the best landing spot, leveled off any deformities in the surface, and phoned Mickey for a second time with the pan's coordinates. Fortunately, the runway was nothing like as lumpy as the last one we had to build. Right on schedule, the Twin Otter touched down smoothly at only the second attempt.

We went over to welcome Rod to Marvin Camp and to help him unload the plane, but his attitude was in sharp contrast to the jovial Troy, and he was abrupt from the start. "You owe me a bottle of whiskey for that landing," he protested. "That was way too short and uneven."

I apologized but assured him that it was a vast improvement on our previous effort. "How did you get on putting down our cache at Bartlett Camp?" I asked.

"There was no way I was going up there," he scoffed.

"You're kidding," I said incredulously, my heart rate increasing dramatically.

"I didn't think it was important. I got to within about twenty miles but the weather to the north of here is sucked in all the way to the Pole. Besides, you've hardly got any provisions for that resupply anyway – only a few sacks of dog food, an Argos beacon, and a couple of bags of other stuff. Surely you can just take it all from here. Anyway, I was told that if the weather at 87°47 didn't look good, I could just bring all the gear to you here."

From the tone of his voice I got the impression that Rod was being far from straight with us and I blew my top. "Who the hell said that you could just give us both resupplies here? There's no way we can fit everything on the sleds. Just the other evening I gave specific instructions that the second load was to go in as close to 87°47 as you could get. We've been meticulously planning this whole operation with Kenn Borek for nearly two years now. You knew the drill, Rod. And as for the weather being bad, the skies look pretty clear to me. You only had to fly another seventy-six miles north of here. I can't believe the weather would change that quickly. You've put our whole expedition in jeopardy."

I don't think Rod had any idea about our expedition goals. He was probably so used to ferrying whole planeloads of supplies between Canada's Arctic communities that he couldn't understand the logic of an extra 150-mile round-trip to drop off what to him seemed like an insignificant load. It was unlike me to lose my temper like I did. But out here my patience levels are being pushed to the limit by the stresses of expedition life, our exhausted state, and because there's just so much at stake.

"Listen, this isn't my problem. If you've got any issues, you need to raise it with the guys in the office. I don't have the time to talk anymore. I want to get the hell out of here in case the weather changes. Do you want this second load of stuff or not?"

The extra load was no use to us here, so I told Rod to take it back with him and to do everything he could to get it to Bartlett Camp within the next week. He jumped back onboard without saying good-bye, slammed the cockpit door shut, and after the most cavalier of takeoffs, he disappeared into the polar sky. The chances of seeing our final resupply again are suddenly in serious jeopardy.

8. On Thin Ice

DAY 23: 11 APRIL
−22°C, Fifty-eight Miles Ahead of Peary,
209 Miles to Go

WE WERE KEPT UP MOST OF THE NIGHT BY a fierce wind that started building not long after Rod's departure. The gale, gusting at fifty knots, whistled around us relentlessly, causing the tent walls to flap furiously and the guy ropes to hum like electricity cables.

At 6:00 A.M., a bleary-eyed Hugh peeled back the tent door to see if the situation outside was as bad as it sounded in the tent. Sure enough, he reported the sky was thick with snow and the sleds were already half buried by drifts. Not a nice day to be tackling leads and pressure ridges. There was zero enthusiasm amongst the group for heading into the storm, and after twenty-two consecutive days of travel, we decided to take the day off and disappeared back into our sleeping bags.

We dozed until well after 10:00 A.M., with not even the faintest twinge of guilt. Peary had been held up by the weather, in his case by unseasonably mild temperatures at the Big Lead, and it was inevitable that sooner or later, we, too, would be caught out. A combination of fatigue, the cold, the punishing terrain, and the day-to-day stresses of a long expedition had eroded team morale and left us all in desperate need of a rest. The same went for the dogs, who seemed grateful for the opportunity to bury their heads back into their tails and let the snows drift over them.

We spent the morning sipping tea, making repairs, repacking our new supplies, drying kit, tending to injuries, writing in diaries, and munching through another cake which Ozzie's wife had sneaked into our resupply before it left Resolute Bay.

With only limited fuel supplies, the stoves were used sparingly, and as soon as they were switched off after lunch, the temperature plummeted.

The tent shook violently all day, covering our faces with cold feathers of hoarfrost. All we could do was retreat into our sleeping bags and either chat between the gusts or try to get some shuteye. We fantasized about the things we're most looking forward to when we get home. "No question," said Andrew, "a bacon double cheeseburger from the Texas Lone Star on Gloucester Road. With a side order of spare ribs and barbeque sauce."

Food is definitely occupying our thoughts more and more as the days go by. There's a place that serves great fish and chips round the corner from Mary's apartment and I can't wait to take her there when the expedition is over. Brady's may not be the most romantic dinner venue in South London, but the fish is wonderfully fresh and the mushy peas are pure heaven. Hugh's counting down the days until he's back in Thunder Bay with Amy and their two-year-old daughter Wynne, while Matty is looking forward to seeing her children and spending the summer at her mother's house in Pennsylvania. "Definitely a bath," was George's number one wish, "ideally with Annie T. in there, too. I absolutely reek. It's also going to be a joy to be able to sit down and take my time over a number two for a change, maybe even read the paper while I'm at it. Taking a crap in a blizzard is not my idea of a good time."

A replacement satellite phone came in with the resupply, so we could all call loved ones for the first time in nearly two weeks. Everyone back home had been worried by the radio silence, so it was great to be able to reassure them that we were still just about in one piece. I resumed typing my daily dispatches for the expedition website and managed to upload a few photos and a short video clip of the tent being rattled by the storm.

We also spent much of the afternoon berating Rod's efforts to drop our final cache of provisions at Bartlett Camp. Andrew did some rough calculations and worked out that there was no way Rod could have got anywhere near the 87th Parallel, let alone all the way to our prearranged drop-off point at 87°47N. Because we knew Rod was still on the ground at Eureka at midday and he reached us at 3:30 P.M., he could have only been in the air for a maximum three and a half hours. Twin Otters cruise at a speed of around 140 knots, but as Rod said himself, he had been slowed down by strong headwinds. "We're nearly 450 miles away from Eureka right now," protested Andrew. "The guy basically couldn't be bothered to go up to Bartlett and thought he could palm us off with some bullshit about the weather."

I spoke to Mickey at Kenn Borek to explain how angry and let down we felt by Rod's slapdash approach towards our resupplies, but there was nothing he could do. "I'm really sorry, Tom," he kept repeating, "we've got to take the pilot's word on this." Mickey told me that they hope to have a plane free around four days from now, but it was going to cost us a horrifically expensive $29,000. With the expedition coffers completely empty, I had no option but to make a groveling phone call to the Barclays Capital marketing department and beg them to pick up the tab. The expedition's fortunes were now totally dependent on our being resupplied at Bartlett Camp. To our immense relief and eternal gratitude, they agreed. It made me realize just how fortunate we were to have such generous backers, and I'm now more determined than ever to get the job done. It's the only way that I can pay them back.

Orchestrating these wretched resupplies from the air is much more of a logistical headache than they would have been back in 1909. On Day 25 of the expedition, at a latitude of 86°38N, it was time for Peary's penultimate support division to offload the majority of their supplies and return to base. The 133 dogs, nineteen sleds, and twenty-four men that had originally set out from Cape Columbia had now been whittled down to a unit of just fifty-six dogs, seven sleds, and nine men, just as Peary had planned. As the tall, softly spoken Ross Marvin and his two Inuit dog drivers bid the remaining men farewell, Peary warned Marvin, "Be careful of the leads, my boy." It would be the last time that the two would speak. As Peary would discover many weeks later, while returning to Cape Columbia the young professor fell through an area of treacherous young ice and drowned. While some have suggested that Marvin was in fact killed by one of his Inuit dog drivers, most historians seem to agree that it was simply a tragic accident.

Before dinner, I made some time to have a wash and a shave. Using the mirror on my compass and with a ziplock bag of tepid soapy water doubling up as a washbasin, I hacked away at my three-and-a-half-week-old beard with a disposable razor. I should point out that being someone who didn't start shaving until he was nineteen and last got asked for ID six months ago, my "beard" was a pretty token effort and only really consisted of a patchy moustache and a few blond whiskers on my chin. Being the hairiest amongst us, Andrew has been shaving regularly, but I've been putting it off until today. Hugh and George began cultivating their beards long before we even arrived in Iqaluit, and while George's stopped growing some time ago, Hugh's has blossomed to such an extent that he already resembles an Afghan warlord. At least with Matty around, I know there's no chance of my coming in last in the expedition beard award.

While facial hair acts as a natural windbreak and does provide cheeks and chin with some insulation, it's also a constant nuisance. In the bitterly cold air, water droplets from our breath collect and freeze amongst our stubble. The frost builds up throughout the day, and one of our first chores in the evening is to remove these giant hailstones from our faces. It's not an enjoyable experience. On windy days when we have to pull our neck gaiters over noses and faces, our facial icicles bind the fleecy fabric to our chins like Velcro. Prying them apart at the end of a long day is excruciatingly painful, and it's not uncommon for a small clump of stubble to come away with the mask. My shave this evening revealed a nasty frostbite wound under my lip that stings like crazy. Hopefully, now that I'm clean-shaven again, it will have a better chance to heal.

While our day of inaction has helped us relax for the first time in weeks and recharge our batteries for the next leg of the expedition, the clock has never stopped ticking. By nightfall, the GPS revealed that the storm had carried us a full 5.5 miles southwest, stealing 3.7 miles of our hard-fought northerly miles from under our noses. Depressingly, the Pole is now farther away than it was more than two days ago, and Commander Peary and his band of merry men are looming large in the rearview mirror. There are times when this expedition feels like we're trying to run up the down escalator.

Our lead has been slashed to less than forty miles and the first doubts are starting to creep into my mind that we might not make it to the Pole, let alone beat Peary. Maybe Wally Herbert was right after all. Maybe it really is impossible to get to the Pole in thirty-seven days. We're attempting something that nobody's ever done before, but if we think things have been tough thus far, the expedition is about to get a whole lot more challenging with open water posing an increasingly hazardous threat to our northerly progress.

The maths is completely against us. We've used up almost two-thirds of our allotted time, but we haven't even covered half the distance. Having averaged just 8.7 miles a day for the first twenty-three days, we need a daily average of 15.2 miles from here on in to beat Peary to the Pole, a mileage we've managed just three times since Cape Columbia. In theory, the farther away we get from the land, the better the conditions, and the faster we should go, but the Arctic is so unpredictable that we have no idea what might be lurking round the corner. It could be flat pans one day, towering pressure ridges the next, followed by endless tracks of open water. Luck is going to play a huge factor in determining whether we pull it off. I know that everyone's going to give it their all, but all my early optimism is gradually ebbing away.

−22°C, Thirty-nine Miles Ahead of Peary, 212 Miles to Go

We emerged into the bright light of a new day to find great banks of snow piled up against the walls of the tent. The drifts were so deep in places that some of the dogs were totally buried, and it wasn't until we called out to them that we could tell where they lay. It was like a scene from Peary's expedition: "Any one seeing our camp at the end of one of these storms would believe us buried alive, the only signs of our presence being the snow-mounds covering us and the dogs."

The surface cracked like an eggshell before a string of drowsy dog faces hatched from the snow. They yawned and stretched their legs, the signs of a good night's sleep. Zorro was particularly groggy this morning and so reluctant to get up, despite Matty's encouragement, that it was like trying to wake the dead.

Our routine had been completely thrown by the rest day. We had forgotten to untangle the dog lines when we originally camped, which had now frozen together in a knotted mass. Both sled bags had been left wide open and were overflowing with windblown snow that needed digging out. Incredibly, it appeared that nothing had actually blown away.

It took us longer than normal to break camp, and we hit the trail under clear skies with a keen wind in our faces. Having been cooped up in the tent for thirty-six hours, it felt fantastic to be on the move again, and the dogs had a real spring in their step. The storm had deposited three inches of fresh snow, which had accumulated in deep drifts between the ice boulders. The pans had been largely scoured clear of snow by the strong winds, providing a much more compacted surface on which to travel. It was a stop-start sort of a morning with twenty minutes of rapid progress across a pan, immediately followed by an unwelcome forty-foot pressure ridge and its accompanying snowdrifts.

Matty complained of stomach cramps for much of the day and several times had to disappear behind a ridge to relieve herself. Having diarrhea when the windchill is in the minus-forties is no fun at all, and I really felt for her. But she didn't let it get her down and kept battling on.

As the day wore on, the giant walls of ice gradually thinned out, and we spent the early afternoon weaving our way through rubble fields. Shortly before the third break, we came to a pan whose whole surface was slashed with leads. These fault lines within the ice pack pose the greatest threat to our progress, and with the onset of spring, we're expecting to see more and more of them. The first two cracks were no more than three feet across, narrow enough for the dogs to jump and for sleds and skis to span.

We were then stopped in our tracks by an eight-foot gap. George removed his skis and left me to keep an eye on the dogs while he went ahead to help Matty look for a crossing point. Thinking that the far side of the lead might offer easier terrain for his search, George peered over the edge to see if the near bank would give him a firm enough base from which to jump across. And then all of a sudden, he vanished.

Not realizing that he was standing on an overhang, the ledge gave way and George was promptly dunked up to his neck into the icy waters of the Arctic Ocean. The first that we knew about it was the high-pitched shriek we heard coming from inside the lead. The temperature of the polar sea is a constant −1.8°C, the freezing point of seawater, and a human being's survival time would be no more than a couple of minutes.

We rushed over to find George already hauling himself out. After bobbing about for a second or two, and with nearly two miles of water beneath him, he had managed to hook his leg over a natural platform of ice and pull himself up onto dry land. But he was now on the opposite side of the lead to us. He was coherent but shivering uncontrollably. We needed to get him dry as quickly as possible. "Don't just stand there, you idiot!" I screamed. "Roll around in the snow like the dogs do when they fall in."

My panicked voice spurred him into action and he dutifully followed my instructions, the theory being that the snow acts like a giant sponge and soaks up much of the water before it freezes. George was soon back on his feet again, windmilling his arms around and running on the spot. He looked vulnerable and very scared. While Hugh frantically pulled everything out of the front sled to locate the one set of spare clothes we had amongst us, Matty came dashing over with a ski pole. "Here, grab this," she said as she thrust it out over the lead towards George.

Weighed down by iced-up trousers, and with his legs stiffening up with cold, it would have been impossible for him to jump the crack without Matty's help. George grasped the ski pole with both hands and lunged towards Matty, very nearly falling back into the water again. Andrew's attempts to record George's struggles on the video camera almost ended in the same fate when he slipped into the lead himself and got a wet leg for his troubles.

The great blessing was that by now the wind had completely died and the temperature was −23°C, almost the mildest of the trip so far. But hypothermia and frostbite were still a major concern and we had to get George into dry socks, thermals, and fleeces as quickly as possible. Rather than setting up camp and using the stoves to get George warm again, we decided to continue travelling. Fresh from his freezing plunge, the adrenaline would be pumping in his body for some time yet, and vigorous exercise would help him regenerate lost body warmth.

Immediately, we were underway again, and it wasn't long before we had found a straightforward place to cross the lead. I kept a close eye on George throughout the final two hours of the day and talked to him relentlessly. Although he contributed nothing to the conversation and probably found my inane chatter incredibly irritating, I hoped that it would at least help keep his mind engaged. The delayed effects of shock could easily have triggered hypothermia, but George stayed amazingly calm and focused throughout. We kept up a fast pace, helping to keep his body temperature up and keep the evils of frostbite and hypothermia at bay.

We're now in the warmth of the tent and George is back to his normal chirpy self again, seemingly none the worse for wear. Every item of clothing he had been wearing when he fell in was sodden and frozen solid, and much of this evening has been spent drying it out over the stoves. The main thing is that George is now OK and there is no need to call for an evacuation.

Sometime during the morning we passed halfway, the point of no return. At about the same time, we also overtook the Italians, who, under the command of the Duke of Abruzzi, held the farthest north record from 1900 until 1906. Peary paid close attention to the farthest north records held by his predecessors and just like us, saw them as short-term goals to focus his energies on. I can see how it would have given him a real boost each time he overtook one of his great rivals.

Abruzzi was one of Europe's wealthiest men and had already proven himself a distinguished mountaineer with a string of notable first ascents in the Alps and Alaska.* While the majority of polar attempts at that time had used Ellesmere Island as their launching pad, the Italians began their assault on the Pole from Franz Josef Land on the Russian side of the Arctic.

Unfortunately for Abruzzi, he lost two fingers to frostbite during the winter, forcing him to hand over command to his deputy, Captain Umberto Cagni. Using dog teams, Cagni and three others reached a new record northing of 86°34N, twenty-one miles beyond Nansen's best but still over 200 miles from the Pole. The drifting ice eventually got the better of them, and they were barely making any northerly progress. A despondent Cagni gazed forlornly to the north and wrote, "The air was limpid and the wind ranged between north east and north west. Innumerable were the points – dark blue, white, sharp and blunt, often of the most curious forms – of the great blocks of ice which the pressure had raised. Further away on the clear horizon, in the form of a crown from east to west, was a bluish wall, which from afar appeared insurmountable. It was for us *Terra Ultima Thule*," literally, "the last place on Earth."

DAY 25: 13 APRIL
−17°C, Thirty-seven Miles Ahead of Peary, 200 Miles to Go

Winter's grip is weakening by the day, and thanks to the twenty-four-hour daylight, the temperature inside the tent last night was a stifling

---

*Abruzzi would later go on to climb most of the prominent peaks in Uganda's Ruwenzori Mountains, and in 1909 he reached an altitude of 22,000 feet on the treacherous K2 in the Karakoram Range. His route up the mountain is still called the Abruzzi Spur today.

−6°C. Sleeping in unbroken sunshine is not easy, and we've all brought along airline eye patches to reduce the glare. Despite the warmth, George endured a pretty rough night by all accounts, curled up in the foetal position and struggling to keep warm. It seems those few seconds in the freezing water were enough to chill him right to the bone.

I turned on the satellite phone for our breakfast-time text-message fix. We usually receive a handful every morning, a mixture of messages of support from friends and members of the public, sweet nothings from loved ones, and the latest soccer scores from my sports-mad brother, Leo. This morning, however, the phone greeted us with dozens and dozens of "bleep bleeps." At first I thought someone might have accidentally sent the same message a hundred times, but it quickly became clear that the website dispatch I had compiled last night had triggered a constant stream of messages of concern for George from family and friends.

I had deliberately written a brief, toned-down version of yesterday's drama, so as not to cause any undue alarm, but it seems to have had the opposite effect. The story has got so out of hand that Barclays Capital's marketing team has apparently been bombarded by journalists' requests for more news on George's condition. George is quietly loving all the attention, but our shock at the level of the reaction back home is a measure of how our daily run-ins with the Arctic Ocean have simply become part of our everyday routine. For us, confronting leads, thin ice, and pressure ridges, however dangerous they might be, just feels like another day at the office.

Going to the bathroom in the cold is one of the most traumatic parts of these expeditions. Armed with a shovel, we dig a pit well away from the dogs, downwind, and out of earshot of the tent. Then it's time to squat. Using the shovel for support, and with back to the wind, the key is to be done as quickly as possible, a lesson I learned all too painfully in the early stages of our South Pole expedition when I managed to frostnip my backside. We take turns carrying out our morning ablutions after breakfast, making sure we re-cover our individual pits once we've finished.

The frustrating business of motivating the dogs to hit the trail in the mornings has taken on a new twist. Not only do they waste precious time forensically sniffing out the patch of snow where the tent had been in the hope of finding any leftover food scraps, but they're now so hungry that they've added another course to their breakfast menu – our feces. While Matty skis farther and farther off into the distance, it's not uncommon for the rest of us to take ten minutes to get under way. The foraging animals dig up the entire campsite, dragging us and the sleds around with them, our stern and exasperated protestations falling on deaf ears.

After the excitement of yesterday's encounter with the lead, today turned out to be a steady, unspectacular day. We saw almost no open water, just a succession of small pans interspersed with the occasional rubble field. With not a breath of wind and the sun shining brightly throughout the day, it almost felt hot and I repeatedly had to vent my jacket just to keep cool. Given how intense the cold had been for the first three weeks of the expedition, it felt very odd to be wearing sunglasses and sunscreen today. The holiday to Sardinia that Mary and I are booked to go on once the expedition is over, and which has been filling my daydreams, no longer feels that far away.

Day 26: 14 April
−17°C, Thirty-six Miles Ahead of Peary, 186 Miles to Go

The day began as a real pea-souper. Thick clouds and light snowfall made for almost impossible travel conditions as we stumbled our way through the murk, unable to gauge whether the ground ahead was rising, flat, or about to drop away into a hollow. Angular shards of blue ice lurked beneath a fresh layer of snow, causing painful falls and a string of expletives when they successfully managed to trip us up. So often have these Arctic banana skins swept us off our skis that at times it feels like learning to walk again.

I put my hand out to break one of many falls this morning, only to land on another submerged block of ice. My right thumb bore most of the impact, and despite removing my glove and burying it in the snow, it quickly began to swell up like a golf ball. The pain was excruciating and for the rest of the day, maintaining any grip on the sled's handlebars was almost impossible. George didn't fare much better and was left winded by a particularly awkward landing. This expedition has left us black-and-blue, and the day that the torture ends cannot come soon enough.

The flat light and undulating surface made route-finding unbelievably taxing, and with Matty feeling disoriented and still not fully recovered from her stomach bug, she decided to ski along with George and my sled. Now it was Raven's job to lead us north. With Andrew and Hugh yelling out directions from behind, Raven responded to the challenge admirably, sticking to a straight course as if he had known exactly where the Pole was all along. He was clearly relishing the extra responsibility thrust upon him, and to our great surprise the speed of the dogs picked up dramatically.

Around midday, the clouds melted away and we were bathed in watery sunlight, with tiny ice crystals being picked up by the freshening wind and twinkling in the air like magic dust. Just occasionally, this godforsaken place reveals a softer side to its character, and when it does, it leaves you totally entranced.

To try to eke out whatever extra mileage we can, the dogs are rotated almost continuously. Up on the front sled, Denali has been distracted from her sledging duties for days, thanks to some serious flirting with Odin, so the decision was made to separate them, swapping Denali for Apu, who's been on our sled since Day 1. It was a shame to part company with the stoical old campaigner, but having the bubbly character of Denali on the team seemed to give the rest of our dogs a real lift.

Baffin continues to keep us amused. At the first break, he came out of the closet, showing what can only be described as openly gay tendencies towards Axel. The poor dog looked absolutely terrified at Baffin's advances and sprinted off as far away from the sexual predator as the length of his trace would allow. Baffin merely looked on, licking his lips suggestively.

It clearly did Matty the power good to take a break from scouting and navigating, but while it was great to have her company on the sled today, having an extra person with us disrupted the team's natural balance. The dogs, who have grown so accustomed to seeing Matty skiing ahead in the distance, seemed confused as to why she was now behind them, and sometimes when she called "Hike, hike!" or "Kimmik, gee over," they turned around to look at us and ground to a halt.

The improvement in the surface conditions continued, and I only had to take my skis off twice all day. Some of the pans we crossed this afternoon were over a mile across, and despite being a balmy −17°C, we didn't come across a single open lead.

Peary and his men are hot on our heels, and our lead has now been whittled down to just two days. We have to make the most of the calm conditions when we can, so we decided to tag another half hour to the day's sledging.

Further problems are brewing over the horizon. For the past few days we've been crossing a broad swathe of ice, influenced by an ocean current called the Transpolar Gyre, which flows across the top of the world from eastern Siberia to the Greenland Sea. In just the same way as the least turbulent water in a river channel can be found farthest from the shore, so the flow in the centre of the Transpolar Gyre, where we currently find ourselves, is the most consistent and the ice less likely to be churned up.

Much of our understanding of these polar currents can be attributed to a sea container holding some 30,000 rubber ducks, beavers, and frogs that fell from a cargo ship in the North Pacific in 1992. Over the next few years, this floating menagerie circled the oceans, travelling thousands of miles. A few dozen of the more intrepid critters found their way through the Bering Strait before becoming trapped in the pack ice. The Transpolar Drift carried them directly over the Pole and into the North Atlantic before their journey came to an end on a stretch of Scottish coastline.

Two miles beneath our feet, the ocean floor is about to undergo a major upheaval as we begin our approach towards the 1,200-mile-long Lomonosov Ridge. From its current depth of nearly 10,000 feet below sea level, the ocean floor will rise 5,000 feet during the coming days as we near the crest of the ridge. As the current sweeps over the peaks and valleys of the Lomonosov Ridge, it produces colossal backwater eddies, which play havoc with the ice pack, ripping the pans apart or buckling them against one another. If luck is against us, the place can resemble a war zone, and many expeditions have met their end in this unpredictable section of the route. We can wave good-bye to the giant pans, at least for now. Only when we clear the last of the seamounts and the ocean floor plunges again to a depth of 15,000 feet, can we hope for calmer conditions. To make the current situation worse, the increased strength of the wind suggests that the next storm system may be gathering force.

It's been a long day. Though we can all feel it in our legs, we have the satisfaction of having chalked up a further 18.3 miles. This new daily record is essentially due to Raven's phenomenal efforts at breaking the trail, and it's a unanimous choice to crown him Dog of the Day. He also helped us tick off another important milestone, the first of Peary's farthest north records of 87°06N, set in 1906.

On these long polar expeditions, chafing comes with the territory, and my backside is now so raw and tender that sitting down in the tent is not much fun. The only treatment we have is Johnson's Baby Powder. Hugh is suffering from the same affliction, and we both come in for a fair amount of ridicule from the others for suffering from nappy rash. I also raided the medical kit for some anti-inflammatories for my thumb, Matty took some Imodium for her upset tummy, and Andrew tended to his frostbitten nose, which has become so disgusting that it looks as though it may well fall off. Most of us have blisters that need to be drained and patched up daily. At this rate, our battered bodies are going to struggle to hold out much longer.

DAY 27: 11 APRIL
−20°C, *Thirty-five Miles Ahead of Peary, 167 Miles to Go*

The wind has picked up again, contributing to more than 1.5 miles of southwesterly overnight drift. Odin kept us awake most of the night, whining continuously like some lovesick Romeo after being moved to the end of the chain, far away from Denali. The object of his affections is a total tease and appears to have already found herself a new squeeze, the dashing white-and-ginger Seegloo. The two of them have been flirting like a pair of soppy teenagers ever since being put next to one another yesterday evening.

Today's strong headwinds and relatively mild temperatures (only −20°C) reminded me a lot of our time manhauling to the South Pole in 2002, where the wind never let up. For the first few hours of the day, the terrain was so flat that we could easily have been in Antarctica. Sadly, it didn't last long. In the middle of the day we were held up by a series of awkward pressure ridges. Much of the afternoon was then spent criss-crossing a combination of open and unfrozen leads which cost us a lot of time.

Up here on the Arctic Ocean, you have to take each day as it comes and deal with each obstacle as and when the goddess Sedna throws them in your path. We're so physically and emotionally drained right now that the constantly changing terrain is making our mood swings all the more volatile. One minute, it's total elation when the route ahead opens up into a giant, unbroken pan, the next it's utter despair when a gaping lead or monstrous pressure ridge blocks our path. It makes planning our itinerary particularly difficult as we have no idea how far we're going to travel each day, a job made all the more challenging by the vagaries of the ocean currents. The only way of measuring our progress is to make direct comparisons with Peary's. He's been taking a mile or two out of our lead for the past four days now, and when we set off this morning our advantage was down to less than thirty-five miles for the first time in twelve days. We may still be ahead for the time being, but Peary is definitely inching closer.

Odin has not taken his breakup from Denali well, and spent most of the morning squabbling with Seegloo. Odin's punishment was an afternoon in what we call the "dungeon,". Hugh shortened his trace and retied it so that rather than being attached to the pituk like all the other dogs, Odin found himself tied directly to one of the sled runners and only five feet away from being run over by the sled. A terrified Odin had no option but to keep his line taut, and he pulled like crazy for the rest of the day. Due to his cocky demeanor, Odin is already despised by the rest of the pack, but getting into scraps does little to restore any of his popularity. It doesn't seem to bother him one bit, and I can guarantee that it won't be long before he's picking a fight with someone else.

Odin wasn't the only dog testing our patience. Ernie was another whose line was almost constantly slack, the only time he decided to put in a spurt being whenever George and I had stopped the sled. Like sheep, the rest of the team all decided it would be fun to mimic the troublemaker, and before we knew it, eight dogs would be stampeding towards Hugh and Andrew. The dogs took no notice of our repeated calls to stop, and the only way to prevent the sled from careering into the back of the team in front was for us to use all our strength to pull the handlebars to one side and capsize the sled. Ernie received some severe talking-tos, but they did little to dissuade him from doing it again. It drives me nuts that he blatantly has it in him to pull the sled, but only when he chooses to do so. It's pure exhibitionism and extremely irritating.

Amundsen was right when he said that "driving dogs is the best way I know to make a man angry," but it can also be the most rewarding. They may get on our nerves most days, but our dogs have been the most loyal of companions, and nothing can beat that feeling of man and dog resolutely striving for the horizon as one. That common bond and shared spirit is unbreakable. In fact, it's the driving force that has helped us get so far. I know there will be a large void in my life when the expedition is over.

By the time we made camp, it was so blustery that we felt it necessary to construct a six-foot-high wall around the tent, to shelter it from the gale. Quarrying blocks of snow from the ground with axes and shovels at the end of another long day was just about the last thing I felt like doing. Nevertheless, we'd find ourselves in dire straits were our bottomless wigwam tent to blow away in the middle of the night, so it's a necessary precaution.

Fuel rations are running low, so we're down from using four stoves to two. It makes the tent much colder than we've been used to, but it gets us into our sleeping bags early, which is a bonus as we're all pretty tired right now. At least it's still sunny and relatively mild. All being well, we should have just enough fuel to keep us going until the Twin Otter's next visit in a day or two.

The wind has blown from the northeast for more than a week now, carrying us not just backwards but also to the west, by a full five degrees of longitude in fact. While it's deeply demoralizing to be losing mileage to the elements, we're counting our lucky stars that we're being transported west not east. Every year, the Arctic Ocean sheds more than three-quarters of its pack ice down the narrow channel between the east coast of Greenland and Spitsbergen, where the Transpolar Gyre is at its strongest. It's the Arctic basin's plughole. If we had drifted too far east, we could find ourselves being flushed out into the North Atlantic at a rate of twenty miles a day, as so nearly happened to Peary in 1906.

Our sights are set firmly on Bartlett Camp, now less than twenty miles to the north of us. With favourable conditions and the sleds now super-light, we might even be able to get there in a single day. It's only when we pick up our final resupply that our focus will turn to the remaining 130 or so miles separating us from the end of the earth. It's starting to feel a whole lot closer.

DAY 28: 12 APRIL ·
−24°C, *Thirty-four Miles Ahead of Peary, 154 Miles to Go*

By morning, all of last night's optimism had evaporated. The day would turn out to be one of the hardest and most frightening days of my expedition life. The winds had buffeted us throughout the night, the rhythmical flapping of the tent porch driving me crazy, and making sleep almost impossible. But it was only when we peered outside before breakfast that the storm's true ferocity became apparent. Half of the snow wall we had erected the previous evening had now collapsed, and with a large drift banked up against the side of the tent, one of its walls appeared to be on the point of caving in. Rivers of windblown snow snaked and curled their way around the tent and any obstruction on the surface, like some sort of supernatural spirit. The dogs were almost totally submerged by snow.

The only blessing was that the sun was still out, although the ground blizzard meant that its rays were partially obscured, particularly during the more violent gusts. We should probably have sat out the gale in the tent, in the hope that tomorrow would herald better conditions, but with supplies running low and another three miles lost to the drift overnight, time is very much against us. We just can't afford any more delays. Our only feasible option is to keep on pushing.

Matty's shoulder was still causing her problems, so I volunteered to swap places with her and take on the route-finding responsibilities myself. I took a bearing, drew my hood tight around my face, and set off into the teeth of the wind. No longer being joined at the hip to a creaky timber sled was unbelievably liberating, and it took me a few minutes to get used to the sensation of skiing with a ski pole in each hand again. It was so refreshing not to be faced with the view of the backsides of eight dogs, and I was totally consumed by the new job of scouting the trail. This was the first time that I had actually led my team from the front. Looking back at the two teams battling against the blinding wind behind me made me realize just how far we had come.

On we pushed. Streams of white powder hissed around my boots. I could feel the moisture from my breath freezing onto my eyelashes and the hairs in my nose. It hadn't felt this cold in days, and the windchill cut right through my clothing. Exposed flesh can freeze in minutes in these conditions, and with the wind increasing, I decided to put on my goggles and face mask. The downside of this is that it would restrict my vision and make the job of finding a route even more demanding. The gusts were now more than thirty knots and the snow was being whipped up into such a frenzy that the surface appeared to be boiling. It was a wild and dramatic scene.

Visibility soon dropped to one hundred yards. I was acutely aware of the importance of not getting too far ahead of the others. Skiing in front of the dogs is like being the hare at a greyhound track. I had to stay close enough to Raven and the front team to make them believe they could chase me down, but far enough ahead so I didn't keep getting overtaken. It was a fine balancing act, all designed to keep the dogs motivated and to get the maximum possible speed out of the whole caravan. But headwinds are the Eskimo dog's worst nightmare, and I could tell from the haggard look on their faces that they weren't enjoying it one bit.

An hour after the first break, a cloud bank drifted in from the north, reducing visibility and wiping out the sun's shadow altogether. Up until then, I had been navigating by shadow, so I was now completely reliant on my compass. The snow was coming at me horizontally, and my fur hood was totally encrusted with a mixture of frozen breath and wind-blown snow. I had tunnel vision. Looking back to see how the others were getting on, I could just make out the dark, silhouetted figures of Hugh and Andrew, standing at the crest of the pressure ridge I had just crossed. Acutely aware of the perils of becoming separated, I decided to wait until they caught up with me. I waited and I waited. Occasionally they disappeared from view, only to return again when the latest gust of wind subsided. But they were clearly having difficulties, so I headed back to investigate and lend a hand.

As I approached, it gradually dawned on me that the two objects I had been training my eyes on for the past five minutes were in fact two six-foot ice pinnacles on the crest of the ridge. My heart sank. What the hell do I do now? I knew that my survival was dependent on finding my teammates. I clambered up the ridge in the hope that they would be wait-ing for me the other side. But they weren't. I called out but my voice was lost on the wind.

My breathing became heavier as the adrenaline flooded through my veins. I was starting to panic. I had no radio with me. No GPS. No tent. No stove. No food. Nothing. It was just me, my skis, my compass, and the clothes I was wearing. And it had all been my fault. I was furious with myself. Thanks to a momentary lapse in concentration, I had put my life in danger. Only luck could save me now.

"Pull yourself together," I shouted. I had to stay focused. I reminded myself that these kinds of emergency situations have a habit of spiraling out of control very quickly. The next few minutes would determine whether I survived, or whether I just became the Arctic Ocean's latest grisly statistic.

I hoped that by this stage the others would have at least noticed that I was missing, and rather than blindly plowing on northwards, they would be in the vicinity somewhere, searching for me amongst the crumpled walls of ice.

The cold spurred me into action. I wanted to retrace my steps, but my ski tracks and the holes where my ski poles had punctured the surface had already drifted in. As I started skiing and my stress levels increased, so my goggles began fogging up, the condensation quickly turning to ice as it cooled. Everywhere was white. Fearful of leading myself even farther astray, I decided to ski back and forth over the same stretch of snow for one hundred paces, in the hope of a chance meeting with the others. With the compass frosted over, I figured that I would be better off navigating by the wind. It had been blowing consistently from the northeast for more than a week, causing all the sastrugi (windblown ridges of snow) to be aligned in the same direction. By keeping the sastrugi and the wrist-loop on my outer mitt, which was streaming off to the side in the wind, at the same angle to my skis, I knew that I would at least be travelling in a straight line.

I had only gone a few yards when I skied straight into a wall of ice and fell awkwardly on my side. My heart rate went up yet another notch. Cold and disoriented, I picked myself up and continued the search. But still nothing. I was seriously worried. I had now gone back over the same ground four times and had almost lost my voice from so much shouting. It was very difficult, but I tried to block Mary and my family from my thoughts entirely and concentrate purely on the present. There was still hope.

After accidentally stumbling on a giant snowdrift in the lee of a pressure ridge, I came up with a plan. Why not hollow out some sort of snow cave in the drift in which to hunker down for a few hours until the storm blew itself out? If I placed my skis in a cross on top of the ridge, they would show the others exactly where I was. However appalling the prospect of shivering away in an emergency shelter in only my thin microfiber jacket, the cold was really getting to me, and I was desperate to get out of the remorseless wind.

I took off my skis and dropped to my knees. I was about to start scraping away at the snow with a ski when Raven's frosted face suddenly appeared from behind an ice boulder. Showing affection towards the dogs while on the trail is a big no-no, but I was so overcome with relief that I instinctively enveloped him in a great bear hug. Whether we had been reunited by providence, or by the sixth sense of a dog, I have no idea, but I would like to think that Raven had somehow managed to track me down.

After swapping brief pleasantries with the team, we were on our way again and normal service was resumed. The whole drama was over less than half an hour after it had begun, but the awe in which I held the Arctic Ocean had risen to a new plane. I cannot think of anywhere else on earth where nature is so in total command. We are nothing out here, mere pinpricks in a tempestuous cauldron of snow, water, and ice. Today's little crisis has given us our strongest warning yet that this place can snuff us out in the blink of an eye.

I had never fully appreciated just how draining it must be for Matty to find the best route through this labyrinth of ice. Keeping a steady course for hours on end requires total concentration. The day has also made me more appreciative of the daily scouting job Matty does. She may not get involved in the heavy lifting and shoving work with the sleds, or the stresses of driving dogs, but skiing along, hundreds of yards out in front, she is all alone. It would be so easy for her to become cut off from the rest of us, whether by the elements, open water, or rough ice, and at fifty-three, Matty is a year older than Peary was in 1909. In one fell swoop, she's also dispelled the notion that Peary was too old to cope with the rigours of a North Pole expedition. She's an inspiration.

Wrapped up in our down jackets, we groped around in the whiteout for a short while, but we were barely making any progress. With visibility now non-existent and Hugh bent over double and complaining of stomach cramps, the only sensible option was to call it a day. We had made six miles in five long, grueling hours. A pressure ridge provided just enough of a wind break to make camp, and its rock-solid blue ice gave us a secure foundation to which we could securely fix the tent guy lines with ice screws. Pitching the tent was still a nightmare, and it needed all hands on deck to prevent it from blowing away.

The storm had left us mentally and physically drained, and the last thing we felt like doing was faffing around with tie-out chains. Instead, we just let the dogs go loose, safe in the knowledge that they would quickly find a nearby depression in the snow in which to make their bed. Or so we thought.

We're worried about our fuel reserves, which are now very low. Did we just not ration enough for this leg of the journey, or has there been another leak in one of the canisters? Either way, we need to save what precious fuel we have, just in case the bad weather adds further delays to our final resupply, originally scheduled for today. So the stoves remained off all afternoon, and we retreated into our sleeping bags to keep warm. We're also starting to run out of food, so after munching on a couple of cheese crackers, we decided to stockpile the leftovers from lunch and save them for another day.

I was just nodding off to sleep when George announced, "I'm just going outside to see a man about a horse." It was our standard code word for going to the bathroom. With a roll of toilet paper under his arm, George opened the tent door and headed out into the maelstrom. Talk about bad timing.

He hadn't been gone long when above the din of the wind, we heard George's voice. "Marvin, piss off! Marvin! Oy, that's my bog roll!"

For the next few minutes, all we could hear was a series of high-pitched squeals. "Everything alright out there?" called Andrew.

There was no answer, only more squealing.

A few minutes later, George, minus the toilet paper, burst back into the tent, cloaked in windblown snow and panting heavily.

"What the hell happened to you out there?" I asked.

George paused for a moment and replied, "I'm so traumatized by the whole experience, right now I just can't face talking about it. Give me an hour to pull myself together and I'll give you the full lowdown." He looked as though he had seen a ghost.

Ten minutes later Hugh couldn't take the suspense any longer. "Come on man, just tell us what happened!" he demanded.

"Where do I start? I found myself a nice sheltered corner, dug a hole and dropped my trousers," explained George. "I hadn't been in the squat position for very long, when I suddenly found myself surrounded by at least ten dogs, all licking their lips and looking at me, but I had got to the point of no return so I couldn't really move. Then Marvin jumped in and ran off with the toilet paper I had stupidly left on the ground. No idea what he did with it because he promptly disappeared into the whiteout. This only seemed to spur the other dogs into action and before I knew it they were all sniffing around my backside. I tried shooing them away but it didn't work."

"How close were they?" asked Andrew.

"Put it this way, it didn't touch the ground." Our mouths dropped.

"And the fact that I no longer had any bog roll didn't actually matter because Denali and Gloria cleaned me up afterwards."

There was a short silence as it all sunk in. "Are you honestly saying that you let those dogs lick your backside?" I asked incredulously.

"I didn't let them!" protested George. "It just . . . sort of . . . happened."

"Fucking hell!" I chuckled, shaking my head. "That's a seriously disturbing story. Never heard anything like it in my life. Mate, you're never going to live this down!"

It was the first time the five of us had all laughed together for several days, and that provided a light relief from our current difficulties.

Later, as the tent flapped about in the gale, a ski pole became detached from Andrew's and my side of the tent, and the tent wall collapsed in on itself, right by our heads. It needed fixing, but we were so snug in our sleeping bags that neither of us wanted to move. The other three were fast asleep, so Andrew and I decided that the fairest way of deciding who should head outside to repair it was to play a best-of-three game of papers, scissors, rock. To my great satisfaction, I won, and it was hard not to be smug as Andrew stepped out into the blizzard, cursing his bad luck.

During the evening, we heard a growl and what sounded like a ripping noise outside. Our worst fears were realized when we looked outside to see a gang of bickering dogs, ravaging our supplies.

Hugh and Matty were too ill to leave their sleeping bags, so George, Andrew, and I pulled on our tent booties and rushed out of the tent door, still only half-dressed. It was a scene of total chaos. The dogs had some-how managed to unzip one of the sled bags and had quietly devoured all that remained of the dog food, almost an entire forty-pound sack. They had scavenged an assortment of other items, too. One of our daily ration bags had been emptied and Raven was wandering around camp with an empty plastic salami packet in his mouth. Denali was chewing her way through one of Hugh's thermal tops, while Bert and Ernie were trying to have Odin for dessert.

It took us a good twenty minutes to bring the dogs under control and secure them to the tie-out chains. My hands went numb. Sifting through the contents of the sleds, we surveyed the damage. Our supplies had been totally decimated. There was no more dog food left and only enough human food to last a couple of days, to say nothing of our fuel ration problems. We had completely underestimated just how hungry these dogs have become. If we've learned one painful lesson, it's that we'll never make the mistake of letting them wander freely around camp again.

Although the dogs won't need feeding for a while, their afternoon feast has put the expedition in serious jeopardy. We need that resupply to come in as quickly as possible, but having spoken to Tim Moffatt this evening, the Kenn Borek guys are very reluctant to fly until the winds subside and there's an improvement in the visibility. Even if the plane does manage to come in on time, with 150 miles still separating us from the Pole, and just nine days to get there, it's going to be a desperately hard slog to reach it in time.

Peary is now just twenty-five miles, or twelve hours sledging, behind us. We need to average nearly seventeen miles a day from here on in if we're going to beat him to the Pole. Days like today are most unhelpful and just reduce our chances further.

Day 29: 13 April
−24°C, *Twenty-five Miles Ahead of Peary, 150 Miles to Go*

We lost yet more distance to the backdrift overnight, resulting in more than half of yesterday's six-mile effort being wiped out. But the good news is that the storm blew itself out overnight and we woke to a calm and beautifully clear morning. We stepped out into the new day and discovered that, by a complete stroke of luck, the pressure ridge that we pitched the tent behind yesterday, turned out to be a solitary ice mound in the centre of a vast pan. At the height of the blizzard, we might as well have been travelling with our eyes closed, yet somehow we had managed to locate the only bit of shelter for miles around. It had to be a good omen.

After our extended rest, we were up much earlier than usual and on the trail by 6:30 A.M. With no more dog food, their breakfast consisted of a mixture of beef and pilau rice (which I had managed to burn), mixed in with some granola cereal chunks and a slice of salami. It didn't amount to very much, but after gorging themselves silly last night, we thought it would be enough to get them through the day. As it was, the dogs were revitalized from having only put in a half-day's work yesterday, and with the sleds carrying next to nothing, they sprinted north with energy levels we hadn't seen since Cape Columbia.

For most of the day we cruised through undulating pans, dotted with polished ice boulders and weathered old pressure ridges. So soft was the thin layer of fresh snow that the dogs' paw prints took on an aquamarine tinge in the bright sunlight. One of the floes looked like a vast Arctic graveyard, with individual tombstones of ice dotted about haphazardly, supported by flying buttresses of windblown snow. The ice sculptures were so spectacular that Michaelangelo and his chisel couldn't have done a more impressive job. Some contained a horizontal, rather striking green seam of seaweed – the first sign of life we had seen in nearly a month on the Arctic Ocean.

I still find it difficult to get my head around the fact that we're at sea, and that in three months' time, much of the surface we've been travelling across will be open water. Peary's description of life up here is very apt: "What contrast this country affords. Yesterday hell, today comparative heaven, yet not such a heaven as most would voluntarily choose."

Matty seemed back to full health today and kept us all amused by etching smiley faces on the ice towers with a ski pole to mark out the trail. I wish the same could be said for Hugh who, despite starting a course of antibiotics last night, had another tough time of it today. He's completely lost his appetite, hardly says a word now, and is in such pain that every ten minutes or so, we looked up to see the front team parked and Hugh either clutching his stomach, or collapsed on the sled, or dashing off behind a ridge to relieve himself.

It's heartbreaking to see Hugh like this. With his infectious laugh, he's entertained us with his storytelling and formed a close bond with every one of us. Even though it's been less than two months since we first met, I feel like I've known him for years. Whether using his knot-tying skills to repair damaged sleds or simply lifting the sleds out of tight corners with his brute strength, Hugh has been the unsung hero of the expedition, and has stuck to the task with incredible stoicism. He never complains, never has a bad word to say about anyone, and I'm so glad that we asked him to step in at the eleventh hour as the fifth member of our expedition. I just hope his debilitating condition is over very soon.

After eight hours, we pulled the GPS out to find that we had covered a whopping eighteen miles. Then, just as we began contemplating a really big mileage day, possibly our first twenty-five-miler, we spotted a thin, dark stain on the horizon, the telltale sign of a large expanse of open water ahead. I'll let Peary explain the bizarre phenomenon called "water blink" in his own words: "There is always fog in the neighborhood of leads. The open water supplies the evaporation, the cold air acts as a condenser, and when the wind is blowing at just the right angle, this forms a fog so dense that at times it looks as black as the smoke of a prairie fire."

Our hearts sank. As we approached, the true enormity of the lead became apparent. 300 yards across, it appeared to stretch from east to west as far as we could see. With clouds of cold steam rising from the stagnant surface, the water couldn't have looked less inviting. After such great progress, it was a shattering blow. We haven't seen much open water for several days now, in part because the northeasterly winds have carried the ice pack steadily southwards, closing up many of the leads as the ice becomes trapped against Ellesmere Island. This great lead could be due to the fact that we're now directly over the Lomonosov Ridge, where the ocean currents are particularly erratic and turbulent.

Banks of sea mist occasionally wafted over us, sending the temperature plummeting and chilling us to the core like the Dementors in the Harry

Potter books. We had only just arrived at the lead when the black heads of three seals popped up out of the water, glaring at us suspiciously with large mirror-ball eyes. We stared back in wonderment that animals should choose to make this frozen hell their home. Moments later, they disappeared back beneath the surface, a trail of bubbles indicating which direction they were swimming in.

Peary had spotted a seal in almost exactly the same location in 1909, so I took this as a positive sign. Leaving the dogs with the others, Andrew and I followed the lead in the same direction as the seals in the hope that they might bring us good luck. After a couple of minutes skiing to the east, we reached a two-story-high pressure ridge. The wall of crumpled ice formed the perfect watchtower, and after climbing it, we were given an excellent view of the surrounding terrain. After pointing due east for a quarter of a mile, the lead, and its accompanying water cloud, appeared to curve around to a more northerly direction before splintering off into a series of much smaller leads.

We returned with the positive news, only to find Matty scouting the area for a possible campsite. "It's been a long day," she said. "Let's get the tent up and hopefully this thing will close up overnight."

George, Andrew, and I were eager to get moving, not least because the presence of seals often indicates there are polar bears in the neighborhood, lying in ambush, ready for their next meal. "And what if we get the call that our resupply is on its way?" I added. "There's no way a plane can land here. Let's keep going, at least for a bit, and if we haven't found a suitable runway by seven o'clock, we'll call it a day. The dogs are running great, but I guess it all depends on Hugh."

With his head in his hands, the big man was slumped on one of the sled runners, a shadow of his former self. I was fully expecting him to want to turn in for the night, so it came as a complete surprise when he raised his head and groaned, "Let's do it." I put my hand on his shoulder and returned to my sled.

On we went. With the long cloud bank as our guide, we followed the lead in an easterly direction, veering gradually northeastwards. However, we soon found ourselves in a total mess of open leads, most of which were flanked with towering ridges. Some of the cracks proved straightforward enough to cross, but others were far too wide to bridge with the sleds. Some imaginative bridge-building was called for. Cue Andrew, who decided to clamber up one particular pressure ridge so steep that it was almost overhanging the thirty-foot lead we were trying to cross. There's no way we would have got this far had it not been for his limitless energy reserves. "Watch out!" he yelled as he began kicking away at the top of the ridge, sending enormous ice cubes crashing down into the water and showering us with icy spray.

This spurred the rest of us into action, and with Matty coordinating the whole construction process from the bank and helping Andrew with his aim, a revitalized Hugh, George, and I shoveled vast quantities of snow into the chasm. I thought back to Peary's famous motto, "Find a way or make one," and smiled. The old commander would have been proud of us. It was tough work but also great fun and a wonderfully bonding way to spend an afternoon. It was a flashback to my childhood, mucking about in the woods after school. This was pure, unadulterated adventure and a welcome release from the day-to-day travails of driving sleds.

After half an hour's hard labour, the bridge looked solid enough. As the dogs edged nervously towards the edge of our makeshift pontoon, we all held our breaths. Would it hold their weight? The dogs could sense the danger, and when the command was given, they sprinted across, two of us pushing hard from the rear. A couple of dog paws slipped through the flotsam of ice and snow, but everyone made it safely to the other side and we were able to continue on our way.

The remainder of the day was spent trying to get as far away as possible from the countless black tributaries. It was slow progress, but shortly before 7 P.M., after more than twelve hours on the trail, we reached a pan easily large enough to land a Twin Otter. We were just one mile closer to the Pole than we had been four hours earlier, but it was still a record day. Shattered but pleased with our day's efforts, we pitched the tent at almost exactly the same latitude where Peary had sent back his fourth and final support party. This would be our Bartlett Camp.

Peary's close friend and captain of the *Roosevelt*, Bob Bartlett, had broken trail almost the entire way from Cape Columbia and must have felt that he deserved to be a part of the polar party. I can only imagine how devastated he must have been when at a latitude of 87°47N, just 133 miles from the Pole, Peary told him that there was no room in the final party for him. Instead, Peary would be making his polar dash with Matthew Henson and his four best Inuit: Seegloo, Ooqueah, Egingwah, and Ootah. "It's all in the game," Peary told Bartlett, "and you've been in it long enough to know how hard a game it is."

Unbeknown to Peary, his decision to discard his top ice navigator would be the chief catalyst to the controversy that would erupt on their return home. Accusations came in from far and wide that Peary had surreptitiously chosen not to bring any "reliable witnesses" with him to the Pole who could verify his claims.

It's interesting to get Bartlett's take: "The American public has held it against Peary for not taking me. They say that he should have taken me instead of Henson . . . I don't deny that it would have been a great thrill to have stood at the peak of our globe. But don't forget that Henson was a better dog driver than I. So I think Peary's reasoning was sound; and I have never held it against him."

No sooner had we crawled into the tent than I called Tim to tell him that we had found a runway. But the news from Kenn Borek was not what we expected. "Tom, according to the satellite imagery, you guys are sat right in the centre of a giant low pressure system, so we're going to have to postpone the flight."

"But that's ridiculous," I protested. "The storm passed through yesterday. We've had clear skies all day, with very light winds from the southeast."

"That's the problem. We need the winds to pick up to blow this storm well away from you before we'll be prepared to fly."

Aggravated that he didn't believe me, I pleaded, "But Tim, the weather here is perfect. I'm begging you. We've almost run out of food here."

But it made no difference. "The weather reports say that it's about to turn nasty again where you are. Sit tight and we'll talk tomorrow. Don't worry, we're not going to forget about you."

It was hardly reassuring. The more immediate concern is that we need to make what meager fuel and rations we still have to stretch out as long as possible. Tonight's menu consisted of a handful of meatballs in a tepid tomato sauce. The dogs ate nothing. What we would all give for a big fat steak right now.

9. On Top of the World

WE WOKE TO A SPECTACULAR, DEEP BLUE SKY and hardly a breath of wind – perfect conditions for flying, just as they had been yesterday. So much for us being in the centre of a low pressure system. It's incredibly frustrating that the pilots seem to put all their faith in the Canadian meteorology office satellite images instead of in the eyes of those of us on the ground.

As soon as I was out of my sleeping bag, I phoned the Kenn Borek team with the news that their phantom storm had failed to materialize, only to be told that the weather front had now tracked southwards and Eureka (where the Twin Otter is parked) was in the midst of a blizzard. All flights would be grounded until further notice.

The situation is growing bleaker by the hour. We reluctantly agreed to Matty's suggestion of giving each of the dogs two buttered crackers and a thin slice of cheddar for their breakfast. Our stomachs feel permanently empty, and having to part with some of our last remaining rations was the ultimate sacrifice, particularly for the permanently famished Andrew. Still, however hungry we are, there's no question that the dogs must come first. We shouldn't be complaining that we're on half rations – for the dogs, it would be their only meal for the day.

Late last night, I sent a brief update to the website. Following George's fall through the ice, I've learned the lesson of limiting bad news on my dispatches to the absolute minimum. The last thing I want to do is cause further alarm to already worried family and friends, so I kept it short and sweet and made no mention of the fact that if the plane couldn't take off, we could very feasibly be facing starvation in a few days.

With Matty back in the lead again, we trudged away from camp with our energy levels as low as I can remember. Throughout the day, my mind was all over the place. After our encounter with the seals, I was convinced that we were being stalked by hungry polar bears and kept turning around just in case one was about to pounce. The nagging anxiety about the grounded aircraft gnawed away at both mind and stomach. All afternoon I fantasized about blueberry cheesecake. The worries about the resupply were never far away: What if Eureka is gripped by this blizzard for a whole week? How much farther can we travel on half rations? What happens when we run out of food altogether?

The giant lead we ran into yesterday turned out to be part of a much more complex system of shattered ice, with countless tributaries branching off in all directions. We had hoped that by heading in a more northeasterly direction, we might get away from this extremely treacherous area. As the morning unfolded, however, we encountered increasing numbers of these narrower leads. While some had already frozen over, the majority had not, and again much time was wasted making detours in the hope of finding some means of getting across. We had to build three separate bridges of floating snow and ice in the day's first session alone.

Having fallen in the water twice yesterday, Ernie managed to go for yet another swim today. This time, as I went to drag him out of the narrow crack, the snow ledge I was standing on gave way, and my left leg slipped into the water. I pulled it out as fast as I could, but the water had already seeped in, and I spent the rest of the afternoon squelching with every step. Fortunately it was a still, relatively mild day, and as long as we kept moving quickly, frostbite was less of a threat than it easily could have been. As for Ernie, he just shook himself dry, rolled around in the snow, and carried on pulling, seemingly none the worse for wear.

Hugh is still suffering from diarrhea and all day long kept having to disappear behind blocks of ice to relieve himself. It did at least mean that snacks were regularly available for the ravenous dogs, disgusting spectacle though it was. On one occasion, our dogs spotted the sorry figure of Hugh, midsquat, one hundred yards in the distance. They knew exactly what it signified, and despite George's and my best efforts to stop them, they stampeded across the rubble towards Hugh. He had barely pulled his trousers up before the dogs were by his feet, fighting over whatever scraps they could get their paws on.

Leaving the pitiful state of our food supplies aside, it was a fantastic day to be driving dogs across the Arctic Ocean. Not only were the weather conditions ideal, but once we had finally got away from the complex lattice of leads, we were blessed with a series of large pans, some stretching all the way to the horizon. Many were littered with giant pepperpots of ice, which held the dogs' attention in the way that a large open pan could not. It was a constant game of hide-and-seek as we weaved our way between the frozen monoliths, dogs and people disappearing and reappearing all the time.

With light sleds and the first signs of some helpful northerly drift, today's eighteen miles was better than expected. Peary was held up by open water today, so his decision to take a rest day has caused our advantage to jump to fifty-seven miles. We're now over the 88th Parallel, with only two more of them to go. But we're being seriously weakened by lack of food, the dogs especially, and unless that plane comes in soon, our daily mileages are going to plummet. Having come so close, and with Peary's record there for the taking, it would be a bitter pill to swallow were this final resupply to rob us of our chance to rewrite the history books.

The evening call to Kenn Borek confirmed our worst fears – that the blizzard at Eureka was still raging. Things have now become so desperate that we've started looking at getting resupplied from the Russian side of the Arctic. For two months every spring, the Russian authorities set up a floating camp called Ice Station Barneo at 89°N, sixty miles from the North Pole and 170 miles northeast of our current position. It caters to a mixture of scientists and people skiing the last degree to the Pole. I spoke to the camp manager at Barneo, Christian de Marliave, on the satellite phone this evening, who said that if needed, a helicopter could be scrambled to drop us some emergency supplies. The quote was $100,000. We don't exactly have many alternatives, but this one would bankrupt us. I told them we'd get back to them tomorrow.

The past few days have given us an insight into the horrors faced by the hundreds of Arctic pioneers who starved to death in the Far North. All we talk about now is food. During dinner, George came up with the imaginative idea of launching a hunting mission back to the lead where we had seen the three seals. The plan was quickly put to rest by Hugh who interrupted, "Nice idea, George, but assuming you don't miss, what are you going to do with the seals once you've shot them? They'll sink like stones to the bottom of the ocean and I'm sure as hell not going to go swim down there to get them for you."

We all howled with laughter. Having felt lousy for so long, it's great to see our bearded companion back to his former self again. Rather than making us more divisive, the difficulties of the last few days have actually cemented our little unit together and made us even more determined to keep pushing.

That said, we're all deeply worried about the food situation. Matty even raised the previously unmentionable option of slaughtering one of the dogs. The fact that it came from Matty, and these were her own dogs, made us realize how desperate things have become. A single dog would keep us and the fifteen surviving animals going for two days, and I suppose we could at least console ourselves that Peary, Amundsen, and Scott had sacrificed their dogs to prolong their polar quests.

Having put in the least effort since Cape Columbia, it was unanimously agreed that, should the need arise, Axel would be the first to be culled, with Baffin a close second, for the simple reason that they haven't pulled as hard as the others. Still, the welfare of these amazing creatures matters deeply to us, and we've grown so close to them over the past year and a bit. Shooting one of our Eskimo dogs would be as bad as killing a member of the family. We're completely indebted to these dogs, and ending any of their lives so that we can keep ours would feel like the ultimate betrayal. It's so horrific that I don't want to think about it.

We're living on borrowed time.

Day 31: 19 April
−24°C, Fifty-five Miles Ahead of Peary, 113 Miles to Go

I woke at 2:00 AM with chronic stomach cramps and shivering with cold. It was a sign of just how much we were wasting away. To make up for the 4,000-calorie shortfall in our diets, our bodies are effectively digesting themselves by drawing on our precious fat reserves for energy, which also drastically reduces our tolerance to the cold. It's a godsend that the temperatures are no longer in the minus-thirties or forties because I don't think we'd be able to cope.

To everyone's great relief, the news from Eureka was that the storm had blown itself out and the Twin Otter would be taking off imminently. We all shrieked and cheered with delight. We would eat again. Axel had no idea how lucky he was. There was just the small problem that our campsite was surrounded by leads and pressure ridges, and the wind was gusting up to twenty knots. Luckily, the sky was clear. Rod anticipated being with us around 12:30 P.M., leaving us less than four hours to break camp, find a runway, and set up the tent again. "I don't want to tempt fate here. I'll only start celebrating when I see that plane on the ground," announced Andrew.

Chaos ensued as we hastily dismantled camp, throwing all expedition protocol out the window by stuffing everything into the sleds haphazardly. We sped off with great excitement, but on empty stomachs and feeling a little faint, it was hard going for everyone. The dogs were panting heavily, their tongues flopped out of the sides of their mouths, only just above the snow. True to form, Baffin wasn't going to let the chance of a free meal go begging and spent most of the morning licking the other dogs' poo-coated traces like iced lollies.

Driving these incredible animals is such a fine balance. The Eskimo dog was bred by the Inuit to go for days without food and still put in a heavy workload. But this expedition is far more grueling than the two-week hunting forays for which they were designed. We need to keep doing the miles, but the harder we push our dogs, the greater the risk that they'll burn out altogether. We're all putting in an extra effort to keep them motivated by constantly encouraging them on the trail and taking the time to sit and talk to them in the evenings. They, too, have visibly lost a lot of weight on this long journey, but they remain in good spirits. Maybe they can sense the Pole is drawing closer.

The unstable zone of rough ice and open water lasted more than two hours, and despair was creeping in that we'd never find a suitable runway. Just as I was beginning to calculate the astronomical size of the Kenn Borek bill for sending the plane back, we were greeted with the incredible sight of an enormous, completely flat, multiyear pan. With no time to lose, I called in the coordinates to Tim back in Resolute Bay, so he could relay them on to Rod.

Barely half an hour later the Twin Otter was on the ground, the dogs all howling excitedly as Rod taxied towards us. After all the stress of the last few days, I felt a huge weight lift off my shoulders. The only thing to prevent us from making the Pole from now on is going to be the state of the ice.

Rod didn't seem as pleased to see us as we were to see him. "There's a much better runway a mile to the north of here you should have used. You're very lucky I didn't decide to dump your crap over there," were his first words to us.

"But you could land a 747 on this thing," I replied. "It's one of the biggest pans we've seen on the expedition."

"It's way too short for my liking. And not nearly smooth enough."

"Well if it was that bad, why didn't you bother making a pass before landing?" asked Andrew, the disbelief and resentment etched across his face. "You just cruised straight in."

Rod merely shrugged his shoulders and kept passing our resupply bags out of the plane. Once the last sack of dog food was on the snow, he said, "And I haven't forgotten that bottle of whiskey you owe me."

Andrew had had enough of Rod's terseness and snarled, "Whatever," before returning to the tent. It was probably just as well, because I was half expecting Rod to deck him. He departed without saying good-bye, the skis of his Twin Otter narrowly missing the top of the tent as he took to the skies. I guess he was trying to make some kind of a statement.

The time had come to feast, the moment we had been yearning for throughout our four-day famine. The dogs were fed first, an entire forty-pound sack of kibble being gobbled up within seconds. Then it was our turn. My mouth was watering as we emptied the contents of one of the resupply bags inside the tent. "Ready, steady, go!" announced Matty. It was then every man and woman for themselves as we dived into the bonanza of chocolates, cookies, crackers, fudge, and other goodies. Andrew ate so quickly that he didn't say a word for ten minutes. It wasn't long before we started to feel sick, our tiny stomachs unable to cope with such a high volume of food.

Stowed away inside one of the bags was a card from Mary, which she had scented with some of her perfume, no doubt because she knew I'd get my leg pulled – and I did. "Mate, that's the kind of shit that schoolkids get up to," mocked Andrew. Mary had also included a topless photo of herself, "to keep you warm." Frustratingly, two cone-shaped party hats had been strategically placed over the important parts. God, I can't wait to be with her again.

It would have been so tempting to take an afternoon siesta, but with the skies still clear and our goal drawing ever closer, we grasped the opportunity to bank some more miles before the day's end. After a stock-check of our new supplies, melting snow for water bottles, and repacking the sleds, we headed north at 7:00 P.M.

The going was excellent for the next five hours. Despite the heavy loads, it felt wonderful to be cruising along on full bellies, the dogs with a real spring in their step, a keen southerly wind blowing us along, and the warmth of the midnight sun on our faces. The Arctic looked like a different world at this early hour, with a sharper, more dramatic contrast between shadow and sunlight than when the sun had been behind us. Who would want to be anywhere else?

Yet, the final session was no walk in the park, with lots of awkward ice and more than a dozen open leads. It was a nightmare. Some leads were narrow enough to span with the sleds, but others involved time-consuming detours. One particular pressure ridge, made up of perfectly symmetrical turquoise ice bricks, really took its toll on the dogs, so we decided to call it a day at 5:30 A.M. Given everyone's physical state, the greatly increased sled weights after the resupply, and the difficulties of the final two hours, we were ecstatic to record our first mileage in the twenties. In less than ten hours of travel, we had managed 21.8 miles of northerly progress.

Our supplies for Bartlett Camp may have been a little late in reaching us, but now that we've been resupplied, it feels as though we're finally on the homeward run. Our chances of success now lie solely in the hands of the elements. Beyond the northern horizon, the Pole lies a tantalizing ninety-one miles away. There are just over six days left on the clock and the pressure is starting to build. We're utterly exhausted and are going to need a fair slice of luck if we're to make it to the Pole before Peary, but the struggles of the last few days seem to have galvanized us as a group and we're more determined than ever to finish the job we set out to do two long years ago.

The big push for the Pole is under way.

Day 32: 20 April
−20°C, Sixty-two Miles Ahead of Peary, Ninety-one Miles to Go

For the time being, the drift is on our side, and it carried us another mile farther north overnight. Regardless, life on the open ocean is so unpredictable that it could all be taken back tomorrow. Not only are we in a race against the rising thermometer, but to make matters worse, the next full moon is just around the corner. It all means one thing: more open water and drift, and still having to clear the Lomonosov Ridge only complicates things further. Just last night we heard that a team attempting to ski the sixty miles from the Russian Camp Barneo to the Pole had to be helicoptered off the ice two days ago after becoming encircled by open water.

The Arctic Ocean was in an extremely agitated state during the day's first session. Pressure ridges were collapsing before our eyes, and the mechanical creaking and groaning of the disintegrating ice pack filled the air. The southerly winds of the past few days are a mixed blessing – they may be carrying us closer to our goal, but they also have the power to tear the ice pack apart.

We had only been going for an hour when we heard what sounded like an almighty thunderclap. Everything shuddered. The startled dogs immediately stopped in their tracks. Some of them whimpered and both Axel and Baffin crapped themselves.

"Bloody hell!" George exclaimed, "We need to move!"

To our utter horror, the pan across which we were travelling was splitting in half. About 150 yards ahead, we could see a fresh fault line spanning the full width of the pan, no doubt triggered by the force of the front team careering across it. We yelled at them to stop, but they never heard us and just carried on, completely oblivious to the drama unfolding in their wake.

There was not a moment to lose. The dogs were clearly jittery, so I skied out in front of them, encouraging them forwards as best I could while George pushed the sled from the rear. By the time we arrived at the great gash in the ice, it was already three feet wide and expanding rapidly. Chunks of baby blue ice bobbed about and water bubbled out over the edges of the pan, flooding the white surface like an oil slick.

I didn't have much time to think so I skied at full pace across the crack and made it safely to the other side. George then shunted the sled forwards to give the dogs some slack. "Come on, Kimmik, you can do it," I beckoned, but Kimmik, and the other dogs, just recoiled and barked back at me.

The situation was becoming desperate. I had visions of George and eight dogs being cast adrift, never to be heard from again. The lead was now five feet wide. I recalled Peary's advice: "For a polar-sea explorer these leads are an omnipresent nightmare . . . To make dogs leap across a widening crack is work which requires an expert dog-driver. Some can do it without any trouble by use of the whip and voice, others have to go ahead of the dogs and coax them to make the jump by holding their hand low and making a pretence of shaking a morsel of food."

We could hardly call ourselves experts, but I thought it was worth a try. To my amazement, no sooner had I put my hand out when suddenly Kimmik decided to go. A huge great leap of faith and he was over. The others all followed like lemmings, their momentum pulling the sled across the great divide. Only Axel fell in, but I was able to fish him out easily.

George, however, was still stranded on the other side. The malevolent lane of black water was now over eight feet wide, and mounting fear was etched across his face. A fresh tributary then splintered off at right angles to the main lead, water gushing over the ice with the force of a burst water main. In the blink of an eye, the serenity of the Arctic Ocean had been shattered by a cacophony of barks, frantic shouting, and the chilling sounds of fracturing ice and gushing seawater.

Time was of the essence. A running jump was all that could save George now. He tore off both skis and threw them like javelins to my side before breaking into a sprint. His cumbersome boots and the slushy surface slowed him down, but his speed was just enough to carry him over with only one soggy boot for his troubles. A minute later and the consequences could have been catastrophic.

The rest of the day passed without major incident. The ubiquitous rumbling of the ice was a sign that the spring breakup of the pack was very much under way. I lost count of the number of leads we crossed, but it must have been well over fifty. Most were small enough for us to fly straight over, but others involved taking off skis and bridging the gap with either sled or snow pontoon. These fissures come in all shapes and sizes and there's no way of telling where they might be. I'm so fed up with them that I can't face writing about them anymore.

Fortune was at least on our side when it came to the weather, and the sun shone throughout the night, casting long, purple shadows over the ice. With the temperature only −20°C and the rays of the midnight sun warming our faces, it felt positively springlike. For several hours the sun was encircled by the spectacular halo of a sun dog, and the sky was filled with weightless silver crystals that flickered in the sunlight. I hope it brings us luck.

DAY 33: 21 APRIL
−20°C, Sixty-one Miles Ahead of Peary, Seventy-two Miles to Go

A full degree to the south of us, Peary spent the thirty-third day of his expedition resting at Bartlett Camp at 87°47N, preparing for his final sprint to the Pole. Having the previous day sent the last of his support divisions back to the ship, Peary wrote, "Pacing back and forth in the lee of the pressure ridge near which our igloos were built, I made out my program. Every nerve must be strained to make five marches in such a way as to bring us to the end of the fifth march by noon, to permit an immediate latitude observation* . . . This was the time for which I had reserved all my energies, the time for which I had worked for twenty-two years, for which I had lived the simple life and trained myself as for a race."

Peary may have been approaching his fifty-third birthday, but "In spite of my years, I felt fit for the demands of the coming days and was eager to be on the trail. As for my party, my equipment, and my supplies, they were perfect beyond my most sanguine dreams of earlier years."

Peary held a distinct advantage over us because up until Bartlett Camp, he had saved his polar party (namely himself, Matthew Henson, and the four Inuit Ootah, Seegloo, Egingwah, and Ooqueah) from the arduous work of being in the lead groups. "I had thrown the brunt of the dragging on the poorest dogs, those that I judged were going to fail, so as to keep the best dogs fresh for the final spurt . . . and those men who I expected from the beginning would form the main party at the last had things

*When navigating by sextant, latitude observations are best taken at local midday, when the sun is at its maximum altitude.

made easy for them all the way up. It was part of a deliberate plan . . . to keep the main party fresh up to the farthest possible point."

His plan was ruthlessly effective, and just five days later they had supposedly covered the remaining 133 miles to the Pole. Peary's "final spurt" is the most contentious part of his expedition, because having averaged less than thirteen miles per march since Cape Columbia, his five marches from Bartlett Camp to the Pole averaged twice that distance.

We may have a sixty-one-mile cushion over Peary, but no one's feeling complacent. Despite being in a much weaker physical state than Peary's polar party, we're going to need to put our foot on the throttle if we're to stand any chance of making it to the Pole ahead of Peary. Consequently, we've decided to adopt a technique of his and "roll the clock."

With the sun now above the horizon both night and day, the twenty-four-hour clock has essentially become redundant. Rolling the clock simply involves manipulating the length of our "day" to boost the amount of time we spend on the trail. In the words of the great commander, "As the daylight was now continuous we could travel as long as we pleased and sleep as little as we must."

From Bartlett Camp to the Pole, Peary still travelled ten hours a day, but by sleeping for only five hours a night, he was able to shorten the length of his travel day to twenty-one or twenty-two hours, thereby enabling him to spend a greater proportion of his time on the trail. Crowding his marches into a shorter time period also enabled him to complete his fifth and final march in time to make his midday sun shot in the vicinity of the Pole.

Due to the modern wonders of the GPS, there's no need for us to be at the Pole at a specific time to confirm our position with a sun shot. The dogs are now definitely flagging. Since leaving Marvin Camp ten days ago, their performance has been dropping off significantly in the final hours of the day, and any more ten-hour marches could easily burn them out altogether. Having said that, Axel has suddenly mutated from team wimp into this bionic animal with extraordinary supernatural strength. George and I have nicknamed him "the Torpedo" because all day yesterday he was starting the sled on his own, his bloodshot eyes bulging and sinews strained as he threw his slender body against his harness. They say that every dog has its day, but if Axel carries on at this rate he's going to explode.

In order to get the most out of the whole team, we've decided to break the day up into two shorter marches of six and a half hours each, making our days an insanely annoying twenty-nine and a half hours long. This breaks down as follows:

2½ hours for breakfast and breaking camp
6½ hours travel (includes 2 × 15-minute breaks)
4 hours to set up camp, rest the dogs, have lunch, and break camp
6½ hours travel (includes 2 × 15-minute breaks)
3 hours to set up camp and have dinner
7 hours sleep

To give an idea of how topsy-turvy our world has become, we had breakfast at 5:30 P.M. today. Our body clocks are all over the place, and when checking the time on my wristwatch, I have to really rack my brain to decipher whether it's night or day.

We emerged from the tent to discover that the wind had shifted to the east and brought with it a pall of low, dark clouds. It made life on the trail decidedly unpleasant all night long. We did manage a respectable 11.2 miles during our six-and-a-half-hour session, but the flat light caused us all to trip and fall repeatedly. One of my tumbles sent me into such a rage that I took aim at the offending blue ice chunk with a ski pole and whacked it repeatedly like some demented golfer. There are times when I love this place, others when it drives me mad.

We're currently camped a few dozen footsteps short of the 89th Parallel. Only one more degree to go. My fingers are cracked and sore, and everyone's suffering from split lips that bleed whenever we open our mouths. I'm feeling pathetically weak. I dread to think how much weight I've lost. Our bodies are desperately craving rest but we simply can't stop now. We're running on sheer willpower alone.

DAY 34: 22 APRIL

−20°C, Seventy-three Miles Ahead of Peary, Sixty Miles to Go

There was so much to do during our four-hour "lunch break" (namely erecting the tent, then dismantling it again, unpacking and repacking the sleds, unharnessing and reharnessing the dogs, melting water, having lunch, and sending a short website dispatch) that I only managed a twelve-minute nap.

When the time came to hit the trail again at 5:30 A.M., we were all semi-comatose and questioning the benefits of our clock-rolling experiment. But our new strategy was designed to maximize the dogs' performance, and to our great surprise they emerged from their brief slumber with the same energy levels as if they'd been asleep for ten hours straight.

Many of our polar predecessors, including Peary, talk about a dramatic improvement in the conditions in the closing stages to the Pole, with endless pans and very little open water. The strength of the Transpolar Gyre diminishes in the vicinity of the Pole, and the most stable weather on the Arctic Ocean is usually found there, too. If only the same could be said for our own journey. Today was a total nightmare. For the first two hours we had to deal with the sort of enormous pressure ridges that we hadn't seen since we left Canadian coastal waters. Chopping a route through a mass of ice boulders with blunt axes in our totally exhausted state is no fun at all.

More flat light today, with light snow flurries and a freshening breeze from the east. Both ground and sky were a ghostly, chalky white. It may have only been −20°C, but combined with the high humidity, it felt much colder and uncomfortably clammy. It's hard to believe that the Arctic Ocean is one of the most humid environments on earth.

A build-up of frost on the windward (left) side of the dogs' bodies was a sure sign that there was more open water nearby. Right on cue, a twenty-foot-wide crack soon appeared right across our path. It was the first of many, and we spent the remainder of the day making frustrating detours around these black gashes in the ice.

Six dogs had to be pulled from the water at various points during the day. Ernie went in on three separate occasions. I'm sure he goes swimming just so he can shower us with icy water when he gets out. I also ended up soaking a boot, as did Andrew. One positive aspect of the leads was that they provided some contrast against the monochrome surroundings, and we spent far less time on our backsides than yesterday.

We'd only just begun the day's final two-hour stint when we came to a thirty-foot lead, stretching from east to west as far as we could see. It was too wide to cross, and with little enthusiasm for wasting hours on a wild goose chase looking for a way around, we decided to make an early camp and pray that the gap would close by morning.

Frustrated by the holdup, but excited about the prospect of a longer sleep, we started untying the sled lashings when, in the centre of the lead, away to our left, Hugh spotted a large slab of ice drifting our way. Transfixed, we stared in silence at the mini iceberg as it came steadily closer. Beneath the waters, it had an emerald-green root, in stark contrast to the black and white icescape around us. Not far from where we were standing, the lead narrowed and with a great crash, the berg wedged itself against the two shores. We all looked at each other in disbelief before Matty yelled, "Quick! It won't last long!"

In fact, no sooner had we sped across our temporary drawbridge than it began disintegrating under the pressure of the millions of tones of ice on its flanks. The deafening roar of grumbling ice floes echoed all around. Seeing Mother Nature at work on this scale is an awesome, frightening sight.

Our stroke of good fortune enabled us to travel for a further two hours, although it did take us a while to find a safe place to camp. George and I were so physically worn out by the end of our long march that several times we actually managed to drift to sleep while skiing, waking with a start moments later with the same panic as if we'd nodded off behind the wheel.

As soon as the tent was up, we collapsed in a heap inside. Unless these leads miraculously disappear, it's going to be impossible for us to get to the Pole before the clock runs out. As I write this, George has just reported seeing steam clouds on the northern horizon – the telltale sign that there's more open water ahead. The ice pack is giving us one hell of a fight. I don't know what it is, but whether I'm climbing a mountain or sledging to a Pole, the final stretch always seems the hardest.

On his thirty-fourth day, Peary wrote in his journal, "Going the best and most equable of any day yet. Have no doubt we covered thirty miles, but will be conservative and call it twenty-five." Today we only managed seven. There are fifty-three more to go and just over three days to get there. It's going to be a close, nerve-jangling finish.

Too tired to write anymore. These are difficult days.

DAY 35: 23–24 APRIL
−21°C, Forty-nine Miles Ahead of Peary, Fifty-four Miles to Go

We were ten minutes late leaving camp after I managed to snap not one, but two of my shoelaces after pulling on them too hard. I managed to repair them with some spare cord but it was a cold, time-consuming job and by the end my frost-damaged fingers were in agony. While much of our equipment has held up well to the rigours of a North Pole expedition, some has not, and much of our tent time in the last couple of weeks has been spent making repairs. Matty has restitched the seams of our canvas sled bags countless times already, and all of us have an assortment of multicoloured patches on the palms of our mitts where they've worn through. Our insulated overgaiters are also on their last legs. The zips no longer work on mine, and I've ripped the fabric so many times with poorly directed skis that almost all the stuffing has fallen out. But there are only a few days to go now so who cares!

Blessed with cold, clear weather, frozen leads, and almost no rough ice, Peary pushed his team hard on Day 35 and chalked up another twenty miles. They would no doubt have travelled farther, had both Peary and Henson not fallen through the ice. Peary went in up to his waist, while Henson suffered a near identical dunking to the one George had received almost two weeks ago. Henson was very fortunate that he wasn't alone when he broke through, commenting, "I tore my hood from my head and struggled frantically. My hands were gloved and I could not take hold of the ice, but before I could give the 'Grand Hailing Sigh of Distress,' faithful old Ootah had grabbed me by the nape of the neck, the same as he would have grabbed a dog, and with one hand he pulled me out of the water . . . He had saved my life, but I did not tell him so, for such occurrences are taken as part of the day's work."

Because our clock rolling is so out of sync with Peary's and our days are eight hours longer than his, he's effectively gained a day's travel on us. On 4 April 1909, Peary scribbled in his diary, "Hit the trail again before midnight after a short sleep. Something over ten hours on a direct course, dogs often on the trot, occasionally on the run. Twenty-five miles. Give me three more days of this weather." Four weeks earlier, he had been cursing his misfortune, having been stranded at the Big Lead for days, but now his luck had changed for his sprint to the Pole.

As for us, well, we had it all today. After leaving camp just after midnight, our day involved countless open leads, tricky pressure ridges, and lots of rubble. The one blessing was that the clouds have finally dispersed and the sunny conditions made it much easier for Matty to navigate. Much of the turmoil in the ice pack over the past forty-eight hours can be attributed to tonight's full moon. We lost another 1.6 miles to the drift overnight. I'm as amazed by at the gravitational pull it exerts as Peary was almost a century ago when he wrote, "The approaching full moon was evidently getting in its work. Looking at its pallid and spectral face . . . it seemed hard to realize that its presence had power to stir the great icefields around us . . . The moon had been our friend during the long winter, giving us light to hunt by for a week or two each month. Now it seemed no longer a friend but a dangerous presence to be regarded with fear."

We were well into the day's second six and a half hour session when we came to the most enormous lead. Our hearts sank. It was impossible to gauge just how wide the stagnant expanse of water was, but it must have been nearly a mile. It was as if the goddess Sedna had slammed the door to the Pole firmly in our faces.

There was nothing we could do but follow its shore in the hope that it might close. The views to the east and west looked equally depressing, so we took a vote on it and decided to head east. We might as well have flipped a coin.

After two soul-destroying hours Matty came to a hundred-foot-wide peninsula of new ice, jutting out onto the lead. The only way to find out if the thin film stretched all the way to the far side was by trial and error. Matty seemed to have more confidence in the strength of the ice than the rest of us; it flexed under our feet like a giant waterbed. Her standard strength test was to drive a ski pole into the ice as far as the pole's basket. If no water bubbled up through the hole, the ice was deemed to be at least three inches thick and safe enough to cross. After a dozen or so dry prods, she announced, "It's strong. I think we should give it a go."

"What if the ice thins the farther out we go?" queried Andrew, as unconvinced as the rest of us.

"Well, we'll just have to turn back again and find another place to cross," she chirped.

Peary's words rung out loud in my ears, "A man who should wait for the ice to be really safe would stand small chance of getting far in these latitudes. Travelling on the polar ice, one takes all kinds of chances. Often a man has the choice between the possibility of drowning by going on or starving to death by standing still." For his own peace of mind, Hugh then pulled out an axe and, with a loud grunt, swung it deep into the ice. It wasn't until the fourth blow that he struck water. Hardly what you would call safe. But Matty's enthusiasm won us over, and with no Plan B up our sleeves, we decided to take our chances and cross.

The sleds were carefully lowered down a steep bank and onto the slippery surface. With sickening apprehension, we began tentatively making our way across. Nobody spoke. The only sound was the panting of the dogs and the gentle glide of the sled runners as they floated on a thin layer of frost flowers. I tried to ignore the bow wave rippling away in front of the sled, but it was hard not to. Our bridge appeared to be narrowing. On either side of us was inky black water, as flat as a millpond. The dogs tiptoed along nervously, their tails more upright than usual.

Five long minutes passed. We were beyond halfway when it became clear that there was a good chance that the bridge did in fact stretch all the way across. There would be no turning back. Whenever one of the runners began slicing through a thinner bit of ice, George and I had to be on our toes and yank the handlebars of the sled either to the left or to the right to prevent the sled from going through. We were getting cramp, having been skiing with our legs wide apart to spread our weight. Any slight stumble and the ice could give way, leaving us all in dire straits. We had to keep concentrating. I locked my eyes onto the far bank.

We were almost across. Seeing Matty, and then the front sled, climb safely across onto "dry land," our dogs panicked and charged towards them. George and I clung to the handlebars for dear life as we hurtled towards the shore. Fortunately, a natural ramp made it an easy hop up. We were soon all on solid ice, gazing back at the sled tracks and puddles from where we had come. Everyone was overcome with relief. I think I had been holding my breath most of the way across. As Matty had said, "That could easily have been an 'expedition over' lead." A week ago, there would have been no way we would have even considered crossing something so precarious, but so desperate are we to get to the Pole now, we're throwing caution to the wind.

Reaching the northern shore of that great lead felt as though we had reached the Promised Land. We had arrived in a different world, a succession of flat, unbroken pans stretching all the way to the horizon. At last, we had hit the highway to the Pole. Another three hours of effortless sledging brought us seven miles closer to our goal. We had made more than twenty miles in the day, although thanks to our detour along the banks of the lead, only 18.6 of these were in the right direction. The vertical degrees of longitude, which circle the planet in giant rings, are now drawing so close together that our hunt for a way across the lead carried us the width of an entire time zone. By the time we reach the Pole, the zones will be separated by inches.

There are just thirty-five miles to go now and the Pole suddenly feels within reach. I'm filled with a mixture of excitement and impatience. Much of today has been spent fantasizing about what it will be like to be there, what the North Pole will look like, how we will celebrate, and what will it feel like to have achieved what we set out to do. Nevertheless past experience has taught me that the elation that comes with the successful completion of an expedition is always tinged with a degree of sorrow. In an instant, the common bond that has held us together, not only during the expedition but over the course of the two long years of planning, will be broken. I could not have wished for a better team to share this expedition with. This would all have been impossible without them.

I'm looking forward to the end, but I know that I shall miss this wickedly cruel, breathtakingly beautiful wilderness. A few days from now, thoughts will turn to going home, and each of us will set new goals in our lives. Over time, this unique, magical experience that has brought us together will gradually fade in memory until all that remains will be our photographs and the rough notes in our journals. Our adventure is almost over.

Day 36: 24–25 April
−19°C, Twenty-three Miles Ahead of Peary, Thirty-seven Miles to Go

Yesterday was the first time I felt that, barring any unforeseen disasters, we would make it to the Pole. Not even a mile-wide lead had halted our progress, and with flat conditions ahead and enough provisions to see us through, it looked like clear sailing from here on in. But reaching the Pole was one thing; getting there before Peary was another matter altogether.

Having felt so positive about our chances when we had camped yesterday, we received a nasty reality check this morning when we discovered that the drift had stolen more than two miles from us overnight. Peary was just twenty-three miles behind us, and speeding up. It was a lesson in not counting one's chickens before they hatch – particularly out here on the despairingly fickle Arctic Ocean. I was annoyed with myself for being so complacent yesterday.

The frustration at our lost mileage propelled us into action. Our morning routine is now so slick that it takes us little more than two hours to get ready, with everyone carrying out their preassigned tasks with ruthless Swiss efficiency. Today we even managed to get under way a full ten minutes early. Day 36 of Peary's expedition journal reveals a man who was becoming increasingly confident of success; "Over the 89th!! Ten hours, twenty-five miles or more." We needed to put in a big day to maintain our advantage.

As it was, the conditions all day were as perfect as you could wish to hope for on the frozen sea. We didn't see any open water and the sun shone night and day. The surface was smooth and hard-packed, and we only had to take our skis off once to cross an area of rafted ice. The few pressure ridges we encountered were so small that the sleds just trundled right over the top of them without us even having to slow down. Throughout the day, the sleds bounced along the surface, often skidding from side to side when we crossed a frozen meltwater pool from the previous summer. These were just the conditions Peary described during his final push to the Pole when he wrote, "The going was the best we had had since leaving the land. The floes were large and old, hard and level, with patches of sapphire blue ice . . . I had not dared hope for such progress as we were making."

Nevertheless, the polar party's impressive daily distances to the Pole can't be put down to the improving conditions alone. As Henson explains, Peary was pushing them harder than at any stage of the expedition: "The memory of those last five marches, from the Farthest North of Captain Bartlett to the arrival of our party at the Pole, is a memory of toil, fatigue, and exhaustion, but we were urged on and encouraged by our relentless commander, who was himself scourged by the final lashings of the dominating influence that had controlled his life."

Axel's brief stint as chief-sled starter fizzled out some time ago. In fact, most of the sixteen dogs are so totally spent that on our sled, only Kimmik, Ernie, and Bert seem to have the will to pull anymore. They've worked themselves into the ground for our benefit alone, and I just don't have the heart to get cross with them anymore. In sharp contrast to us, Peary's carefully selected dogs were still in prime condition, Peary noting that, "The dogs were so active . . . that I was frequently obliged to sit on a sled for a few minutes or else run to keep up with them . . . Some of them even tossed their heads and barked and yelped as they travelled."

The weakened state of our dogs meant that we progressed at a steady if unspectacular pace. What I wouldn't have given to have been able to rest my aching legs on the sled as Peary had done, even for just a few minutes, but the sled would have come to an abrupt halt.

The uniformity of the surroundings and the lack of anything to do, apart from sliding one ski in front of the other thousands of times, caused my mind to wander. I thought of Mary, my parents, my brother and sister, and my friends. I miss them all terribly, but it won't be long before we're back home again.

I thought of the long, meandering journey that has brought me to this otherworldly place. Captain Scott was my childhood hero, and I always dreamed of one day being a polar explorer like him. Unfortunately, polar exploration is not on the school curriculum. Instead, I played rugby. I tried my hardest, but being five-foot-nothing until I was sixteen (to my great relief a late spurt eventually took me to six-foot-two) inevitably led to me being flattened by a burly prop forward twice my size. I didn't stand a chance.

I soon discovered that there was a school-climbing club, called the Marmots, which organised weekends away to the crags and mountains of Britain. Run by the enthusiastic Mr. Greenstock, it sounded like a fantastic excuse to escape the rugby field. I signed up immediately. Even though they were alarmed that I had suddenly found such a dangerous new pastime, my parents encouraged me wholeheartedly, and bought me my first pair of climbing boots.

Until that moment, I had spent my school career trying to fit in with the crowd, because being "different" made you a target for the school mob. But I had never felt comfortable conforming to the masses and felt that climbing might be an opportunity for me to prove myself to my peers. It would be a decision that would change my life forever.

The Marmots took me all over the country: to Snowdonia, the Lake District, and the Scottish Highlands. Not only did I find that I had some natural talent for getting up a rockface or a snow-clad mountain, but I actually enjoyed it. It was the excitement of being surrounded by wild, dramatic landscapes, and the thrill of a challenge. The sense of achievement of reaching a seemingly insurmountable summit with a close-knit team was an incredibly bonding, powerful experience. Climbing seemed the purest way of discovering my true potential. It was a way to test myself, to find out what I was made of. For the first time in my life, I felt free.

The Marmots was a springboard for me to start organising and raising the necessary sponsorship for my own expeditions. Since leaving school, I've been fortunate enough to climb, ski, and pull my sled all over the world, with people who would become my closest friends. This expedition is a continuation of that escapism – an escape from everyday life, from traffic jams, credit card bills, double glazing salesmen, and reality TV. Part of me is still not ready to go back, and probably never will be.

I'm often asked why I do these expeditions. I go on expeditions for the simple reason that I enjoy them. There's something about polar and mountain landscapes that I find totally addictive. It's a combination of the awe-inspiring scenery, the deafening silence, the clarity of the air, the connection with the explorers of yesteryear, and the power of seeing Mother Nature at her most raw. This expedition has been undeniably difficult, the hardest thing I've ever done, but like some sort of sadistic pleasure, I've absolutely loved it. I cannot put it more eloquently than Peary, who wrote, "The charm of the Arctic is the appeal of the primeval world to the primeval man, stirring the last drops of the blood of the caveman in our veins. It is the physical lust of struggling with, and over-coming, the sternest natural obstacles on the face of the globe."

We camped at 11:00 P.M. after another very long day. The one big difference between the conditions we had today and those Peary had experienced during his final dash to the Pole were the strong headwinds that have been blowing incessantly since we crossed the giant lead. Not only have our poor noses, cheeks, and lips taken yet another hammering, but the northerly blast is carrying us wherever it pleases. These cruel winds accounted for our lost miles last night, so when the time came for us to make our estimates for today's mileage, everyone verged on the side of caution. The average of our guesses came to a very conservative 21.5 miles.

When the GPS revealed that in fact we were only 18.6 miles north of our last campsite, there was a collective intake of breath. We were stunned. This milage still represents a good, solid march, but given that we had almost no obstacles in our path, and no detours to make, it should have been so much farther. The GPS also told us that even just sitting in the tent doing nothing, we were speeding back towards Canada at a rate of 0.3 knots. We've effectively lost a full nine miles to the drift in one twenty-nine and a half hour day. It was a devastating blow.

Had it not been for the northerly drift, we'd be talking about a mileage for the day of more like twenty-eight miles – just the sort of daily distances Peary achieved as he neared the Pole, the ones Sir Wally Herbert said that "no explorer, before or since, has claimed to have covered." As well as providing the perfect riposte to Peary's critics, a twenty-eight-mile day would have also put us within spitting distance of the Pole, and we would probably have just added another two or three hours on to the day and got there in one hit.

As it stands, the Pole is still sixteen miles away and our lead over Peary has been whittled down to just nineteen miles. If the drift keeps up, those numbers will look even more depressing come morning. This is all part and parcel of travelling in the Arctic, but to happen now, so close to the end, feels like daylight robbery.

Whether we beat Peary to the Pole or not, today has at least made us realize how he managed the seemingly impossible daily mileages he claimed. If we, in our debilitated state, could have travelled so far over the ice in one day, then surely Peary's fresh, supertalented team of dog drivers could have done the same.

It's been a real emotional roller coaster of a day; we couldn't have dreamed for a better surface on which to travel, but to be drifting south so rapidly is truly gut-wrenching. We're all much more tired than is good for us and are longing for the end now. Nothing is going to stop us from reaching the Pole – it's just a question of whether we'll get there before the clock runs out. Having come this close, the thought of failing is too terrible even to contemplate.

DAY 37: 25–26 APRIL
–21°C, Sixteen Miles Ahead of Peary, Nineteen Miles to Go

The drift gobbled up another three miles while we slept, giving us an increased target of nineteen miles in the remaining twenty-four hours. Still, everyone was in an upbeat mood as we prepared another bland, albeit filling breakfast of muesli and hot chocolate for what we hoped would be the last time. We figured the lack of any leads over the previous day and a half was because they had been closed by the northerly wind as it swept the ice floes back against the Canadian coast. As long as yesterday's near-perfect travelling surface continued, and the leads stayed away, we knew we still had every chance of making it.

If only the dogs knew that the end was in sight. When the order was given for the front team to leave camp and pick up Matty's ski tracks, the dogs merely glanced back at Hugh and Andrew with a look of utter dejection. Most of them then sat back down again, prompting Hugh to storm up to lead dog Raven. He bent down, lifted the 125-pound furball back to his feet, and pleaded, "Now listen here, buddy. This is the last day I'm gonna ask you to do this. Please, for the love of God, will you just pull that damn sled."

Hugh then snapped the dogs' traces, calling, "Easy, ready, hike!" as Andrew shunted the sled from the rear. This time the sled did move, and the dogs reluctantly broke into a gentle trot. There was just a minor problem; they had turned around and were heading for home, back along yesterday's trail towards Canada. As George and I giggled at the blatant display of disobedience, the others screamed, "Raven, wohhh!" The sled duly stopped. The normally phlegmatic Hugh suddenly became angry and ran out ahead of the dogs. Pointing to the north, he barked, "Raven, I think you'll find the North Pole is that way!"

Eventually we all got going, shortly after midday. The weather remained clear and relatively mild (–21°C) throughout the day, with the biting north wind now reduced to a light breeze. Even better news was the lack of pressure ridges and leads. All seemed well.

After an incident-free first session, we camped at 7:30 P.M. to rest the dogs, take an early dinner/lunch, and melt snow for the water bottles. According to the GPS, the ice pack was still drifting at a steady 0.3 knots, but there were only 7.4 miles to go. For the first time on the expedition, we had the luxury of knowing that we had more than enough provisions to last until the end, so we could afford to indulge ourselves as much as we pleased. Long after the rest of us had had our fill, Andrew then decided to consume half a stick of salami, an entire bag of nuts, and about twenty dried apricots. I've never met anyone with such an appetite, and the poor guy only received unsympathetic laughter from everyone when he later started complaining of stomach cramps and dizziness.

I found it impossible to unwind during our brief stop. I was fidgety, irritable, and eager to hit the trail as soon as possible, lest some last-minute obstacle should lie in our path. There was no time to sleep. We were under way again at 10:45 P.M., by which time the distance remaining had crept back up to 8.5 miles. To beat Peary, we had to reach the Pole before midday the following day. The race was by no means won.

Peary began his final march at almost exactly the same time as we did, only from a more southerly latitude. He jotted in his journal, "Weather thick . . . a dense lifeless pall of gray overhead, almost black at the horizon, in striking contrast to the glittering sunlit fields over which we have been travelling for four days." The ice surface conditions, however, were ideal: "The going better than ever, hardly any snow on the hard granular surface of the old floes, the blue lakes larger . . . Not a sign of a lead in this march."

Twelve hours and thirty miles later, Peary and his men made camp, barely three miles shy of the Pole. The date was 6 April 1909. As Henson explains, Peary "fastened the flag to a staff and planted it firmly on the top of his igloo" before turning to the loyal servant who had served as his right-hand man on almost all of his polar journeys and announcing, "This my boy, is to be Camp Jesup,* the last and most northerly camp on Earth."

---

* Named after the late Morris Jesup, founder of the Peary Arctic Club and Peary's chief benefactor.

Peary was satisfied that he had got as close to the North Pole as it was possible to get with the navigation tools of the day. "The Pole at last!!!" he wrote in his journal, "The prize of 3 centuries, my dream and ambition for 23 years. *Mine* at last. I cannot bring myself to realize it. It all seems so simple and common place . . . I wish Jo could be here with me to share my feelings. I have drunk her health and that of the kids from the Benedictine flask she sent me."

As our night march wore on, both George and I needed matchsticks to keep our eyes open. Each stride was heavy work, and we were falling over all the time. It would have been so easy for one of us to badly injure ourselves. The huge effort we've put in since Bartlett Camp and our self-imposed sleep depravation have left us so drained of energy that it was a miracle we could keep going at all. We even tried belting out tuneless Monty Python songs at one point, just to keep our brains alert.

By 2:00 A.M. we were a tantalizing 2.9 miles from the Pole. Then just at the very moment that the end appeared to be in sight, the clouds rolled in – just as they had done in the closing stages of Peary's expedition. To the north, three dark ribbons hovered ominously above the horizon. Open water wasn't far away. "Not more bloody leads," moaned George.

The flat pans we had almost taken for granted in recent days vanished, and we soon came to an extremely active area, with twenty-foot pressure ridges and our first leads in days. The first of these was 400 yards across, but at nearly four inches thick, the ice was just strong enough to support our weight, and we crossed without a hitch.

That said, the goddess Sedna had one final trick up her sleeve. We had safely negotiated another four freshly frozen leads before coming to one that remained open in the centre. It was no more than fifty yards wide, but it stretched from east to west as far as the eye could see, completely blocking our path to the Pole. Growing excitement had by now been replaced with despair.

Matty led us east but came to a dead end after twenty minutes when the lead splintered off into multiple cracks. We then backtracked and headed west, wondering if we would ever find a way to the Pole at all. There seemed to be almost more water than there was ice. We were less than a mile away, but the drift was now carrying us away from the Pole at a faster rate than we could travel north. The Pole was slipping from our grasp. Serious doubts began creeping in. I figured we must be cursed, destined never to reach our goal.

Almost an hour later, Matty found what she hoped would be a possible crossing point. She slowly skied across to the far bank, testing the strength of the ice all the way with her ski poles. The lead flexed under her slender frame. It was still open in the centre, but the gap was only a couple of feet wide, narrow enough for dogs, sleds, and skiers to cross, provided they had enough momentum. Or so we thought.

Things almost ended in disaster when Raven's team broke through the thin ice bordering the narrow split. All eight dogs ended up in the water, although incredibly, the sled remained on solid ice. With the four of us desperately beckoning the dogs from the near bank, they eventually managed to haul themselves out and return to the safety of the pan. It was a heart-stopping moment. Had the sled gone in, too, it could easily have sunk, dragging the dogs down with it. The dogs were a little shaken up, as were we, but after drying themselves off in the snow, they were ready to carry on. Matty rejoined us, and the search continued.

As we followed the shore of the lead ever westwards, a cloud of utter despondency hung over the group. I kept checking my watch. Throughout the expedition, the hours and days had dragged on interminably. All of a sudden, at the very moment when I wanted the clock to slow down, time was flying. I was racked with worry. I had always hoped that our arrival at the Pole would be an enjoyable, liberating experience, but it was turning into my worst nightmare. There was no time to fantasize about the lavish meals, warm baths, clean beds, and that first pint that awaited our return to civilization. All thoughts were focused on trying to find a safe way across and getting to the Pole in time. There were only six hours to go. The stumbles and falls continued. We were beyond exhaustion, our bodies running on pure adrenaline.

Finally, after what seemed like hours, we reached a section of the lead that had totally frozen over. For a fleeting moment, the sun came out, too. Again, the ice was desperately thin, and we had to be on our guard as first the sleds and then the four of us cautiously made our way across to the far bank where Matty was waiting. A couple of paws punctured the sticky surface and one of the sled runners started to cut in, but we managed to get everyone safely over. It would be the last lead we crossed.

Pinpointing the exact position of the North Pole, armed with a sextant and a wristwatch alone, is pretty much impossible. This is due to the lines of longitude all converging together on the Pole, making it increasingly difficult to judge exactly in which direction the North Pole lies. Matters are complicated further by the drift, which unless you have a GPS, is very difficult to monitor accurately. In 1969, during his epic crossing of the Arctic Ocean, Sir Wally Herbert spent a whole day going around in circles, trying to reach 90°N. He compared the challenge of finding the Pole to "trying to step on the shadow of a bird that was circling overhead."

In the end, Herbert had to settle for a final latitude 89°59N – one mile short of the Pole, but near enough amongst the exploration fraternity to say he had got there. How close Peary came has been the source of fervent speculation for almost a century. What we do know is that after claiming to have made camp at 89°57N, he spent another thirty hours sledging back and forth in four different directions to "box the Pole in." He made a total of thirteen separate sun observations during this time and concluded that "at some moment during these marches and counter-marches, I had passed over or very near the point where north and south and east and west blend into one."

Matty navigated by compass and dead reckoning until we were within a couple of miles of the Pole. After that, it was up to the GPS, which as well as being able to locate the Pole to an accuracy of just six feet, could also point us in the right direction. Nearly an hour after crossing the final lead, and after much meandering as she took instructions from the GPS, Matty stopped in her tracks, making her customary cross above her head with her ski poles to indicate it was time to stop. "We're really, really close!" she shrieked, with a giant grin plastered across her face. "The Pole is in there somewhere."

We had stopped at the entrance to a cul-de-sac, a tiny ice floe no bigger than a tennis court, bordered on all sides by pressure ridges. The GPS gave our latitude as 89°59.989N. The Pole was just sixty-four feet away, but the drift was still steady at 0.3 knots.

There was no time to lose. The dogs were sat down and skis removed in super-quick time. What a bizarre sight we must have made, huddled around the small device, aimlessly wandering around the pan. The GPS read 89°59.994N – thirty-five feet to go. Navigation was now down to trial and error, like searching a field for a bunch of keys with a metal detector. Hysteria was taking over, with George hollering repeatedly like a wild man. We walked on air.

The GPS read 89°59.997N, then 89°59.998N, and finally 89°59.999N, the most northerly coordinate a GPS can register. "We've done it!" I yelped at the top of my voice. The time was exactly 7:32 A.M. We had beaten Peary to the North Pole with barely four hours to spare. The whole world was spinning around our feet. We were standing at the timeless place where the sun rises and sets just once a year, the centre of the planet's axis. Every direction we looked was due south. We hugged, laughed, and cried with joy. We had reached the end of the earth.

10. True North

THE NORTH POLE IS A PRETTY UNREMARK-
able place. There is no vertical beam of light
emanating from the earth's core to mark the centre of
its axis. Unlike its polar opposite, there is no science
base there, no United Nations-style crescent of national flags, and no red-and-white barber's pole to tell you
that you have reached the end of the earth. There is
no giant column of basalt as speculated by nineteenth
century academics and no opening to John Cleeve
Symmes's great inner universe. We even scanned the
horizon for a bearded old man in a red coat, but alas,
he and his team of elves and reindeer were nowhere to
be seen.

The North Pole looks just like every other piece of
ice we had encountered during our 413-mile journey.
Even if a monument had been erected at ninety degrees
north, due to the drifting ice pack it wouldn't have
remained there for long. As for the glass bottle which
Peary left at the Pole, containing a brief note of his
triumph and a strip from his American flag, it now
probably rests on the Arctic seabed, many miles from
the spot where he originally left it.

By the time we had finished our group hug and wiped away the tears, we were no longer at the North Pole. We had drifted thirty-four feet in the space of a minute. That golden moment we had been striving towards for more than two years was over before it had even had a chance to sink in. With our final steps behind us, we were now being carried by wind and current like driftwood on the high seas. When the time eventually came for us to leave some thirty hours later, the drift had transported us over six miles from the Pole.

An hour after reaching our destination, we witnessed the most bizarre moment of the expedition when the hulking mass of a bright orange Russian helicopter descended from the clouds, landing on a small ice floe one hundred yards from the tent. We were totally bewildered – I had only just got off the phone to Kenn Borek Air who had told me that two Twin Otters would be with us the next day to take us home. With mouths wide open, we then watched in disbelief as a six-foot blonde climbed down the steps of the helicopter, clutching a bottle of champagne and a tray of flute glasses. George, salivating at the vision of totty and alcohol ahead of him, said, "Please tell me I'm not dreaming."

We dropped what we were doing and headed towards her. A dozen people eventually emerged from the helicopter, each being given a glass of champagne when they stepped onto the snow. We shook hands, both parties as confused as the other. We must have smelled quite awful because not only did the group step back from us, we weren't even offered any champagne.

Adriana, the blond siren, then explained all in a thick Russian accent: "We fly from Ice Station Barneo. I am tour guide. I take group from Portugal to North Pole. You that team who come from Canada? My crew see your tent from sky and come say hello. It's OK if we take pictures?"

It was all very surreal. I had once seen an advertisement in a travel magazine offering sightseeing trips to the North Pole for the small matter of sixteen thousand dollars, but the last thing I ever expected to see at the top of the World was a group of champagne-swilling Portuguese tourists. As it turned out, they were far more interested in taking photos of the dogs than they were of us, and before we knew it they were gone.

Other than sleeping, eating, and calling loved ones on the satellite phone, we didn't do much at our polar camp. I was overcome with a profound feeling of release, not just from our struggle against the elements and the strict regime of expedition life, but also from the long, challenging years of planning and preparation that had totally consumed my life. I was ready to go home, but there was also a great sense of sadness and loss that our time in this ethereal wilderness of ice and snow had finally come to an end.

I phoned our expedition patron, the Prince of Wales, to report that the trip had been an unqualified success. He told me how proud he was of us, asked me to pass on his congratulations to the team, and wished us a safe passage home. "And I want to hear all about it when you get back!" were his parting words.

We had dozens of calls to field from TV, newspaper, and radio journalists from both sides of the Atlantic, all wanting to conduct live interviews from the Arctic. Absolutely exhausted, it was the last thing we felt up to at that precise moment, but we knew it was a small price to pay to get the world talking about Peary and Henson again. It was ironic that Peary, who had spent his life seeking fame, had to wait five months before getting the chance to announce his conquest of the Pole to the media, whereas our story had already hit the twenty-four-hour news channels before we had barely pitched our tent.

With a fairly sizeable pan close by, we didn't have to look far to find a decent landing strip. A brief weather delay meant the Twin Otters didn't arrive until the afternoon of the day after we reached the Pole. It gave us time to flatten the surface with axes and shovels and mark out a runway.

After touching down, Dave and Jim, the two pilots, told us that a fast-moving weather front was heading our way and that unless the planes were loaded immediately, we could be stranded for days.

Three months before the expedition had left the U.K., I was asked to be an ambassador for London's bid to be host city for the 2012 Olympic Games. Dog sledging seemed a long way from becoming an Olympic sport, but it was a huge honour to be asked to support the bid. What with London being my home city, I accepted with great pride. Lord Coe, the bid chairman, lent me the Olympic torch that he had paraded through the streets of London the previous summer during the torch relay for the 2004 Athens Games. "Tom, it would be incredible for the bid if you could take the Olympic torch to the Pole," Lord Coe told me with all his customary enthusiasm. "What a fantastic way to take the Olympic spirit to the furthest corners of the globe."

For thirty-seven days the torch had sat in the bottom of our sled, surviving 413 miles of broken pack ice before being paraded at the Pole for publicity photographs. I tell this story because during all the panic of dismantling camp, loading the dogs and all our clothing and gear onto the two planes, the Olympic torch somehow got left behind on the ice. To my immense relief, I would later learn that there was more than one Olympic torch. Although the one entrusted to us didn't make it home, at least we had fulfilled our duty of getting the torch to the farthest corner of the globe.

AS WE GAZED DOWN AT THE PATCHWORK OF ICE AND LEADS during the long flight south, it was clear that to attempt a return journey would have been suicidal. We were horrified by the amount of water we could see. The frozen ocean marks the frontline of the battle against climate change, and the speed of the melt is accelerating year after year. Satellite imagery has shown that the three million square miles of Arctic Ocean still covered by summer sea ice in 1980 had halved in size by the time I wrote this postscript in 2008. That represents a loss of area the size of India. While most of the open water refreezes again in the winter, the new ice floes are much thinner than multiyear pans and therefore much more likely to fracture.

The Arctic Oceans of 1909 and 2005 were by no means level playing fields when it came to dogsledging. Peary may have been delayed by the Big Lead early on, but for the rest of his journey he came across far fewer leads than we did, which of course would have saved him huge amounts of time. In addition, with fewer leads around, he would have experienced less drift, because the extent to which the ice pack shifts about is largely governed by the size and number of gaps there are to close up.

Peary also held an advantage over us when it came to the surface of the ice. Because multiyear pans are thicker than newly formed ice floes, they can withstand greater amounts of sustained pressure, which also makes them less susceptible to buckling. This would explain why Peary regularly travelled for hours without having to negotiate a single pressure ridge, particularly as he neared the Pole.

Nevertheless, the benefits of a more consistent surface were counterbalanced by the fact that Peary's pressure ridges, when they did form, would probably have been larger than ours, and therefore more time-consuming to cross. The size of some of the pressure ridges in his photographs is quite staggering. There was a simple reason for this – the ice pack of 1909 had an average thickness of twelve feet, compared to just eight feet today, and so a greater volume of ice was being compressed together.

NASA's dire forecast that the Arctic Ocean could have ice-free summers as early as 2013 was recently backed up by the National Snow and Ice Data Centre in Colourado. It warned that the Arctic is at a climatic tipping point and that the speed of melting was set to increase dramatically. I hope I'll be proved wrong, but I'd be very surprised if people were still attempting to make the journey over the ice pack from the shores of the Arctic Ocean to the North Pole in 2013. Arctic explorers may soon be an endangered species.

And it's not just the ice pack that's disintegrating. The ice shelves fringing Ellesmere Island's coast are shrinking at an alarming rate. In 2008 alone, some twenty-three per cent of the total mass of the island's ice shelves vanished, including the entire Markham Ice Shelf. Located just ten miles to the west of Cape Columbia, this floating ice shelf was once the same size as Manhattan Island and had been attached to the land for nearly five thousand years.

Sadly, this unique ecosystem, which Peary and his men would have crossed countless times, has now been lost forever. Aside from leading to severe repercussions for local fauna and drastically altering the coastal landscape, its disappearance has also caused huge volumes of freshwater to be drained from Markham Fjord, as the ice shelf is no longer there to hold it back.

The catastrophic loss of so much ice should be a wake-up call to governments around the world that urgent action is required to combat climate change. This book is not the place for a discussion on what needs to be done, but having seen for myself just how sensitive the Arctic Ocean is to an increase in global temperatures, I sincerely hope that those with the power and influence to reduce humankind's contribution to global warming will turn their rhetoric into action.

It's tragic enough that the unique frozen wilderness at the top of the world is being decimated, but even more so for the Inuit and polar bears who rely on the ice to reach their traditional hunting grounds. A recent study by the U.S. Geological Survey predicted that two thirds of the world's polar bears will have disappeared by 2050.

It may sound odd, but were all the ice in the Arctic Ocean to melt, there would be zero impact on global sea levels because, just like ice cubes in a gin-and-tonic, the ice is already floating. When the ice melts, the water merely fills the voids where the ice used to be. It's the melting of ice on land that causes sea levels to rise, as new water is being added to the oceans.

Why the Arctic Ocean is so important in the fight against climate change is that this vast white blanket acts like a giant mirror, shielding three per cent of the earth's surface from solar radiation and reflecting it straight back into space. Remove it, and the sun's rays will instead be absorbed by the dark waters beneath, heating the oceans and creating further global warming.

The warming of the polar seas is also producing a new, possibly even more serious threat. Scientists have recently found evidence that millions of tons of methane, a greenhouse gas twenty times more potent than carbon dioxide, are being released into the atmosphere from beneath the seabed. Vast underground reservoirs of the gas, locked up in the sediments beneath the Arctic Ocean for thousands of years by a layer of permafrost, are now rising from the ocean floor as the permafrost thaws. The fear is that the escaping methane will cause global warming to accelerate even faster in a giant positive feedback loop, where more methane in the atmosphere causes temperatures to increase, which in turn leads to further melting of the Arctic ice pack, increased thawing of the permafrost and yet more methane released into the atmosphere.

In the U.K., compared to many other countries, most of us are fairly blasé when it comes to global warming. Yes, we'll eventually be affected by rising sea levels, but in the meantime, thanks to our temperate climate, a bit of extra warmth would actually go down well in many quarters – a longer growing season for farmers; snow and ice would be less likely to bring our transport systems to a standstill; and hot summers would make St. Ives feel more like St. Tropez.

The reality is that the impacts of climate change are already being felt around the world, be it flooding in low-lying countries like Bangladesh, the "Big Dry" drought in Australia, or increased hurricane activity in the Caribbean. If climate change continues at the rates scientists predict, it won't be long before similar natural catastrophes start affecting us in Britain. In time, the vanishing polar ice cap will be felt by everyone on the planet.

One of the most alarming developments of the thawing ice cap has been to raise geopolitical tensions in the High Arctic. The U.S. Geological Survey estimates that a quarter of the earth's untapped oil and gas reserves lies beneath the Arctic seabed, and the melting ice is opening up previously inaccessible areas for exploitation. As commodity prices continue to rise, Arctic nations are becoming increasingly territorial about which part of the Arctic belongs to them. And it's not all about oil and gas – vast new fishing grounds are also being disputed. The Arctic has suddenly become more than just an inhospitable wilderness of snow and ice – it's a potential gold mine.

In 2007, a Russian submarine planted its national flag on the seabed at the North Pole more than two miles beneath the ice pack, staking a claim on all the natural resources between the Pole and the Russian coast. Even though international law limits coastal nations to territorial claims within two hundred miles from their coastline, Russia argued that because the Lomonosov Ridge is part of the Russian landmass (which has yet to be geologically proven), its territory actually extends all the way to the Pole.

I had always assumed that the Arctic Ocean was protected from commercial and military activity by a United Nations treaty, as is Antarctica. Clearly I was mistaken. "This is our responsibility and our direct duty to our descendents," said Russia's president Medvedev recently. "For the long-term future of the state, we must secure Russia's interests in the Arctic."

The Russian move provoked outrage from the other four circumpolar nations (Canada, the United States, Denmark, and Norway) as it was seen as direct aggression from Moscow to further its claim on Arctic territory. Denmark promptly dispatched a research ship to try to prove that the ocean floor beneath the Pole was in fact geologically linked to Greenland, which has been Danish territory since 1536.

The response from Canada's prime minister Stephen Harper was to fly immediately to the previously insignificant Arctic hamlet of Resolute Bay (which we had passed through on our way north) to announce that the Canadian government would be building a military installation there. Another will be built at Nanisivik on Baffin Island, all part of Canada's moves to assert its sovereignty over the hotly contested Northwest Passage.

The mythical shipping route linking the West to the Orient is shedding its cloak of ice even faster than the Arctic Ocean. It won't be long before tankers will be able to sail straight through, shaving four thousand miles off the current route between the Atlantic and Pacific through the Panama Canal. Who knows, one day it might even be possible to sail directly over the North Pole itself, just as Edward Parry and his reindeer had tried to do all those years ago.

During her acceptance speech for her nomination as the Republican vice presidential candidate, the governor of Alaska, Sarah Palin, declared her intention to open up the state's vast untapped offshore oil and gas reserves. "Take it from a gal who knows the North Slope of Alaska – we've got plenty of both," she boasted.

The Arctic gold rush has become even more frenzied because the UN Convention on the Law of the Sea stipulates that unless circumpolar nations agree their maritime boundaries by May 2009, any unclaimed area will be designated as international waters.

Tensions in the region are now so great that Rear Admiral Gene Brooks, commander of the U.S. Coast Guard in Alaska, warned that unless these territorial disputes were resolved soon, conflict in the Arctic was a distinct possibility. He said, "The potential is there with undetermined boundaries and great wealth for conflict, or competition. There's always a risk of conflict [especially] where you do not have established, delineated, agreed-upon borders." Sobering words indeed.

Climate change is transforming the Far North. Because the ice cap is disappearing, short-term economic greed is now endangering the fragile Arctic ecosystem and the well-being of the planet as a whole. Not only will the plundering of all this extra oil and gas warm the planet even further, but a major oil spill would be catastrophic for the entire region. I don't dare to imagine what the silent frozen wilderness, which was our home for those thirty-seven awe-inspiring days, will look like in another one hundred years. I just pray that the day when there's an oil rig at the North Pole doesn't occur during my lifetime.

FROM THE WINDOW OF OUR LITTLE PLANE, THE SLED TRACKS AND dog prints we had left behind were nowhere to be seen amongst the great leads and pressure ridges of the Arctic Ocean. They had been covered by the drifting snows just as quickly as Peary's had nearly a century earlier. But it soon became clear that we had still left our mark. Before we had even returned to warmer climes, storm clouds were brewing far to the south that would prove as tough to negotiate as the worst blizzard we had encountered on the frozen sea.

Our expedition was always going to be controversial. It was intended to challenge the beliefs of a small but influential group within the polar community about the integrity of Commander Robert E. Peary's claims. Ever since his nemesis, Frederick Cook, had been shown to be a fraud, the knives had been out for Peary, too. Why? There are several reasons, but the simplest of these is that character assassination sells. Books, television documentaries, and magazine articles that set out to discredit the achievements of the famous have a far better chance of becoming ratings successes than conventional biographies do.

The polar world seems to be a hotbed for these literary hitmen. Following its publication in 1979, Roland Huntford's *The Last Place on Earth,* in which Captain Scott was portrayed as an incompetent, bungling fool, became *the* Scott reference book. It wasn't until 2003, when Sir Ranulph Fiennes exposed the author as a "debunker" who had played with the facts to paint a highly inaccurate and defamatory picture of the great polar hero, that the record was finally set straight.

Us Brits are particularly good at it, but we're not the only ones to denigrate our national heroes. Successive generations of American historians and journalists poured scorn on Peary's claims, using his character flaws and second-hand accounts of conversations he might or might not have had as evidence against his claims. Some of their arguments were imaginative speculation, others outrageous lies.

As I would learn during the aftermath of our own expedition, many of Peary's biographers had egos even larger than the commander's himself and hit back in self-defence the moment someone posed a threat to their theories. Some of these academics had dedicated their entire careers to staking out a position in the long-running North Pole debate. Their views had become so entrenched that to convince them otherwise would have been impossible. They either flatly ignored those who dared disagree with them or launched personal attacks in order to weaken their arguments.

By reopening the controversy and telling the media and the exploration community at large that we believed that Peary had made it to the Pole, we laid ourselves open to attack. We were expecting it, but the ferocity really took us by surprise. It quickly became clear that some people were deeply offended by the news that five people, sixteen dogs, and a couple of timber sleds had reached the Pole in under thirty-seven days. They had no idea who we were or understand our motives. We were unwelcome outsiders in an already crowded academic battlefield.

By and large, the press in Britain reported positively about our expedition, but a flippant jibe from naïve journalists that I repeatedly had to fend off was, "Of course it's not the same as it was back then, what with all the technology nowadays." That remark used to really get under my skin. The major hazards Arctic explorers face are open water, unstable pressure ridges, polar bears, and blizzards, and they are just as prevalent and dangerous today as they were in 1909. Dialing international rescue on a satellite phone isn't going to be much use when you're flailing around in a lead, about to be eaten by a polar bear, or lost and disoriented in a whiteout. It could take days for a Twin Otter to be scrambled, whereas the chief dangers in the far north are likely to finish you off within minutes. All the GPS would be able to do is record to the nearest six feet the precise location where you met your death.

Individuals began crawling out of the woodwork to protest that the two journeys simply couldn't be compared because we held a "psychological advantage" over Peary, whatever that meant, or that we had used satellite imagery to help us avoid leads and bad weather (which of course was complete nonsense). The reality was that even if we had had access to the latest meteorological reports, we wouldn't have paid any attention to them as we always tried to head due north, irrespective of the weather or surface conditions.

Our detractors said that modern maps and GPSs make the North Pole far easier to reach today than it was in 1909. The route map for the Pole is essentially a blank piece of paper, with the coast of Canada at the bottom and the Pole at the top. There's nothing in between but hundreds of miles of ocean, so to take a map with us would have been completely pointless. As for the GPS, while it was a much more straightforward and accurate way of pinpointing our position than Peary's sextant, not once did it warn us of impending open water, help us find a way through rubble fields or recommend safe places to camp. While on the trail, we navigated just as Peary had – by sun, compass, watch, and wind, only calling on the GPS once a day to compare the average guestimates for our mileage to the actual distance we had travelled and to confirm our position.

Some of our critics said we weren't even qualified to set foot on the Arctic Ocean, accusing us of not even knowing how to tie our shoelaces. Others lambasted us for hiring Matty, as if having someone on the team with greater Arctic experience than the rest of us somehow made our expedition null and void. I chose Matty because I wanted the best possible team, as did Peary when he selected four Inuit guides to join him and Matthew Henson for his final dash to the Pole. The same held true in 1953 when a paid Sherpa, Tenzing Norgay, was chosen to accompany Edmund Hillary to the summit of Everest. Besides, as Matty herself acknowledged, all her accumulated miles in the Arctic still fell way short of even the most inexperienced member of Peary's polar party.

The most telling aspect of the past three years has been that not one of the people questioning our achievement seemed interested in hearing about the practicalities of driving dogs across the frozen pack with light-weight sleds. To them, it seemed completely irrelevant. In their eyes, Sir Wally Herbert had already produced the silver bullet by alledging that Peary's speeds were impossible. Distinguished historians and academics though they may have been, it quickly became evident that almost all of Peary's biographers had never even ventured beyond the Arctic Circle, let alone driven dog teams. The only one who had was Sir Wally Herbert, and it was Herbert himself who was amongst the first to fire a shot across our bows.

Two days after our return to the U.K. Sir Wally e-mailed me a tongue-in-cheek congratulatory note, saying that we had merely "triumphed at the half way point." He then asked me to send him, "a copy of the daily log for the entire trip, with 'confirmation' of course that you had no airlifts."

In reply, I explained, "It would have been great to make the return journey but global warming has made the Arctic Ocean a very different place from how it was in 1909 . . . After we were picked up from the Pole on April 27, the Kenn Borek Air pilots told us that the ice pack was as fractured as it normally was in late May. A Korean team arrived at the Pole two days after us in temperatures of just −4°C." I also said that I had yet to type up the expedition log and sought clarification for the term "airlifts."

Shortly afterwards, a reply from Herbert entitled "Daily log missing" arrived in my inbox; "The daily log of a journey to the North Pole is an essential part of any historical claim – it should show in brief the position of the camp, the main features of the weather during the day in question, and whether or not any obstacle encountered on that day was big enough to justify accepting an airlift in order to cross it."

I was completely taken aback. Before the expedition began, Herbert had unequivocally written off our chances of making it to the Pole at all. In his eyes we were a group of total amateurs, attempting the impossible. Despite his reservations, Sir Wally was a man I had unbridled respect for, whose own polar CV was more impressive than any other British ice traveller since the days of Scott and Shackleton.

Our expedition was never going to change Herbert's long-held views on Peary, but the last thing I expected was for him to demand proof that we hadn't cheated by being airlifted over tricky obstacles. I had just assumed that we would be taken at our word, but here we were, being subjected to the same kind of scepticism that had greeted Peary on his return to America ninety-six years earlier. Having my integrity called into question by a journalist was one thing, but for it to come from one of this country's polar heroes really stung.

Were I to send Sir Wally our expedition log, I knew very well that he would have gone through every figure and coordinate with a fine-toothed comb, just as he had done with Peary's, searching for the slightest inconsistency to build an argument around. We had nothing to hide, but the last thing I wanted was for our expedition to be dragged through the gutter. Consequently, I sent him a short reply, confirming that the only airlift we received was the one that picked us up from the Pole. My e-mail also contained the phone numbers of the handful of Twin Otter and helicopter businesses currently flying over the Arctic Ocean, and a polite suggestion that he should contact them about any requests they may have received to carry out clandestine sorties over tricky terrain.

In all the media interviews I gave on our return, not once did I say that our expedition had proven once and for all that Peary had discovered the North Pole. In the case of a disputed ascent of a mountain, the surrounding terrain in summit photographs can be analyzed to help pinpoint exactly where the climber was standing when the photograph was taken. This is impossible at the North Pole, which, to quote British explorer Pen Hadow, is "a pinprick of nothingness in the middle of nowhere."

The shadows in Peary's polar photographs have been scrutinized in forensic detail for clues as to his whereabouts, but the results have proved inconclusive. Even if the glass bottle that Peary left on a pressure ridge at the Pole were eventually to be discovered on the seabed directly beneath the Pole, the anti-Peary camp would merely argue that a drifting ice floe could have carried it there from some other spot on the Arctic pack before it sank to the ocean floor.

Therefore, we will never know for sure who was the first to the Pole. It's a matter for people to form their own opinion, based on the evidence available. But as I said at the press conference on our return to the U.K. and in all the interviews I have given since, I believe that we have shown that Peary *could* have done it.

Some of our critics made the case that had it not been for Peary's six-day delay at the Big Lead, we would never have beaten his record. However, this argument fails to take into account that Peary had some clear advantages over us. To start with, Peary's divisions set off from Cape Columbia with sleds only half the weight of ours. Only later were the loads increased as divisions returned to land to pick up extra supplies. In addition to the benefit of superlight sleds, the constant shuttling back and forth of dogs, sleds, and men would have bulldozed a clear, wide trail through the worst of the coastal pack ice, helping Peary reach the Big Lead in just four days. It took us eight days to reach the same latitude.

The section of the route where the two expeditions most closely resembled one another was between the Big Lead and Bartlett Camp, a distance we both covered in twenty-one days. Our four resupplies were made during this period, as were Peary's, so our sled weights were broadly the same. The effects of climate change, however, gave us a much more challenging surface to travel across. Endless detours around open water cost us valuable time, wiping out whatever remaining advantage we would have had by the absent Big Lead.

It's also worth mentioning that the dog-driving skills of Peary's Inuit were far superior to our own. They were able to get far better results from their dogs than we were. Whereas our attempts to use the whip often ended with us accidentally hitting ourselves on the backside, motivating the dogs by cracking the whip mere inches over their backs would have come as second nature to the Inuit. Furthermore, while we regularly had to stop to untangle the dogs' traces, the Inuit were so nimble on their feet that they could sort out the tangles by jumping between the lines while still on the move. Driving a dog team came as naturally to Peary's Inuit as driving a car does to us.

Be that as it may, the first month of Peary's journey is not where the controversy lies. Even Peary's fiercest critics agree that Bartlett probably turned back at about 87°47N, just as he had always maintained. It's the 133 miles from Bartlett Camp to the Pole, and Peary's subsequent return to Cape Columbia, which lie at the heart of the debate. As Peary acknowledged, "Many laymen have wondered why we were able to travel faster after the sending back of each of the supporting parties."

Having averaged thirteen miles per march until Bartlett Camp, Peary's average daily mileage promptly doubled to twenty-six miles during the five days from Bartlett Camp to the Pole, so it's hardly surprising that people have their doubts. Still, we found that, just like Peary, the length of our marches increased dramatically as we neared the Pole, with twenty-mile days not uncommon. This could largely be attributed to fewer pressure ridges and more large pans – all because of a weakening of the Transpolar Gyre. Had it not been for the negative drift in our final few days, and an abundance of open leads brought on by the milder temperatures of late April, our daily distances would have been similar to Peary's.

Almost every North Pole expedition in history has experienced favourable ice conditions in the vicinity of the Pole. Approaching the 88th Parallel in 1969, Herbert himself observed that "the surface was improving too . . . we were constantly travelling across hard wind-packed snow and seeing 'sastrugi' from time to time . . . The sastrugi, while not as regular as a ploughed field, nevertheless was a perfect surface across which to sled – in fact sleds hardly left a track at all." Herbert also discovered that "From latitude 89° to the Pole was really invigorating . . . Conditions got better and better all of the time. The surface was so good that once or twice the dogs actually broke into a gallop, the first time they had done so during the whole journey." And all this, despite the fact that Herbert's 1,200-pound sleds were twice the weight of ours and Peary's, and it required twice the effort to get them moving.

In terms of pure speed, Peary averaged 2.48 knots from Bartlett Camp to the Pole. We were not as skilled at driving dog teams as Peary's Inuit, nor were we as fresh and nor did we have the unbroken surface they had, but we still managed to average 2.24 knots on our best day. In fact, analysis of our expedition video footage back in the U.K. revealed that when crossing unbroken pans or frozen leads, our speeds regularly exceeded five knots over short stretches.

It took Peary just three days to return from the Pole to Bartlett Camp, an average of forty-three miles a day. Two weeks later he was back on dry land. In *The Noose of Laurels,* Sir Wally Herbert's critical judgment of Peary's claims, Herbert scoffs at these huge distances. However, he overlooked the major factor in Peary's rapid acceleration, which was that he had simply increased the length of his travel day. One of those marches was an eye-watering twenty hours long, during which he made fifty miles, a daily mileage Herbert said was impossible. Peary was able to put in such long days because, unlike our weakened state after thirty-seven days, the dogs and men in Peary's polar party were still relatively fresh, having been spared the hard work of breaking trail for the first month of the journey from Cape Columbia.

From the Pole to Bartlett Camp, Peary's average speed was 2.74 knots, an easily explained increase of 10 per cent from the outward leg. During our many sledging excursions while training in Baffin Island, we often had to return along the same route as our outward trail. Even though the trail was sometimes over a week old and tracks had long blown over, we were astonished at the dogs' ability to find the trail from the old scent of their urine. It was as if they had an in built homing device and motivated by the promise of food and rest, their speeds increased accordingly – often by as much as twenty-five per cent.

Peary's own motive to get home at top speed was simply because his life and those of his five companions depended on it. They would have been driven on by the fear of being cut off by the advancing spring, as so nearly happened in 1906. He also had the benefit of a freshening north wind that would have driven him southwards as the leads ahead of him closed up.

Time also would have been saved by the fact that they had a well-marked trail all the way back to Cape Columbia as well as igloo camps already built during the outward journey. Their sleds were becoming lighter as food supplies diminished and the mild mid-April temperatures would have replaced the abrasive sandpaper texture of the snow with a much smoother surface.

In fact, all of Peary's returning divisions (except for Marvin's after he drowned in a lead) made equally fast homeward journeys after turning back from their respective farthest norths. MacMillan returned in four marches after making seven outward marches, Borup returned in seven marches after twelve outward marches, Bartlett returned in thirteen marches after twenty-two outward marches, and Peary returned in sixteen marches after twenty-seven outward marches.

Had Captain Scott not found Roald Amundsen's tent at the South Pole in 1912 and verified that the Norwegian had beaten him to it, it is highly likely that Amundsen would have faced the same cynicism as Peary did on his return home because Amundsen's travel speeds were even more impressive. After covering the 900 miles to the South Pole in fifty-six days, he returned in forty, covering as many as sixty miles in one single march.

Over the years, much has been written about Peary's seemingly lackadaisical approach to finding his way across hundreds of miles of shifting pack ice. Peary's navigation techniques have become almost as important in the case against him as his travel speeds, so it's worth going through the arguments.

The Noose of Laurels is a highly forensic investigation of Peary's supposed route, with Herbert producing detailed hypotheses of how far off course the winds and currents might have carried him. He accused Peary of navigating like a rank amateur, making errors that "can only be described as astonishing." The crux of Herbert's case was that Peary didn't make enough observations to know where the ice floes were carrying him. "What then gave him the crazy idea," asks Herbert, "that he could strike out across the drifting pack ice, and without any observations for longitude or any checks on the variation of the compass, could aim for and hit the Pole?"

I believe that all of Herbert's complex assumptions about Peary's attempts to get back on his intended route are totally irrelevant because Peary never tried to stick to a straight course. In theory, the fact that all lines of longitude converge on the North and South Poles should make them the two simplest places on the planet to navigate to, armed only with a compass and wristwatch. Wherever you are in the world, as long as you keep correcting your bearing to due north, you will eventually come to the North Pole. Peary's strategy would have been identical to our own; every morning, no matter how far east or west the currents had taken him during the previous day's march, he would work out where due north was, adjust his compass accordingly, and try to head straight towards it, using the angle of his shadow as a guide.

The key question is, how did Peary know where north was? In order to identify True North, one needs to know what time local noon is. Local noon is the exact time at which the sun crosses the line of longitude (also known as a meridian) on which you are standing. At almost exactly local noon, not only is the sun due south, but that is also when it reaches the summit of its daily arc across the sky. Walk on your shadow at local noon, and wherever you are in the Northern Hemisphere, you'll be heading straight for the North Pole. An hour after local noon, your shadow will need to be fifteen degrees to the right to maintain a northerly heading because that's the distance the sun travels in an hour. Using a sextant to measure the altitude of the sun at local noon will also establish one's latitude and the number of remaining miles to the Pole.

Peary's starting point at Cape Columbia is about a longitude of 70°W, the 70th Meridian, where local noon is at 12:40 P.M. every day. On his outward journey to the Pole, Peary used the 70th Meridian as a guide to help him work out his longitude. Because the sun completes a full 360-degree circle of the earth in one twenty-four-hour day, one degree of longitude equates to four minutes' time. For example, if Peary found that local noon had slipped to 12:52 P.M. one day, he knew that he was now close to the 73rd Meridian and so would adjust his bearings accordingly.

So how did Peary determine the time of local noon? For the first forty or so miles of the route, he would not have bothered, relying instead on a compass bearing off the twin peaks of Mount Cooper Key, the mountain directly behind Cape Columbia.

In the Arctic, because the transit of the sun during the course of a day remains so low above the horizon, it's almost impossible to gauge with the naked eye when it has reached its maximum altitude in the sky. This could only be done on the days when the sextant was used to measure the sun's culmination for a latitude sight. But Peary had other solar aids at his disposal. On 5 March the sun returned to the Arctic Ocean for the first time since the previous October. The sun was visible for only a fleeting moment, but the time had to be local noon because the sun was at the top of its arc.

As the days grew longer, Peary would have made a simple calculation to work out the midpoint between sunrise and sunset, and that would have given him his local noon. For instance, if one day the sun rose at 9:32 A.M. and set at 3:32 P.M., local noon would have occurred at approximately 12:32 P.M., placing them near the 68th Meridian. The reason there are no longitude computations in Peary's journal is that he could do it all in his head with some simple mental arithmetic. It was very similar to the way we adjusted our bearings and used our shadows and a compass to help us steer north. Of course, the technique would have been impossible in overcast conditions, but for the majority of the time, the frozen desert of the Arctic Ocean is blessed with clear skies.

"Sun did not set last night" were the closing words in Peary's diary for 27 March 1909. It marked the beginning of twenty-four-hour daylight. However many miles east or west he had drifted since leaving land, the point at which the sun just skimmed the horizon that night would have told him where due north was. From late March onward, with the sun no longer rising or setting, accurately determining local noon, and therefore longitude, became increasingly more challenging.

As it turned out, the rapid convergence of all 360 meridians on the Pole would have made judging longitude impossible. As Peary said, "In the neighborhood of the Pole it is generally recognized that longitude observations are not practicable with any degree of accuracy." All he could do was make a beeline for the Pole along the same meridian as his final sun shot and hope that the wind and currents didn't carry him too far off course. Even if they did, Peary's plan to box his target in by carrying out sledging forays at the Pole at right angles to his original trail gave him a margin of "approximately ten miles for possible errors in my observations."

Fortunately, the elements were on Peary's side, and those final days to the Pole were clear, calm and bitterly cold, holding the pack ice in frigid suspension. He saw almost no leads or pressure ridges beyond 88°N, meaning very few detours to throw him off course. "Give me three days more of this weather," begged Peary in his journal on 4 April. The weather duly held, and a few days later Peary reached the Pole.

Because of the difficulties of working out local noon as one nears the Pole, and determining whether the sun is rising or falling becomes much harder to judge, Peary knew it would become increasingly challenging to calculate his latitude accurately. From Bartlett Camp to the Pole, he navigated by watch, shadow, and compass, taking one rough sextant sight at 89°25N. The frequent adjusting of his bearings to local noon during the first month of the expedition would have given him some indication of how much to fine-tune his compass for magnetic variation in the final days to the Pole.

Further help would have been provided by the sastrugi, which, because of the relatively uniform nature of the ice beyond 88°N, would have been parallel to one another, as Herbert himself had witnessed in 1969. As I had found for myself when lost in the blizzard on Day 22, sastrugi can be an invaluable navigation tool. By keeping the angle at which the sleds crossed these hard-packed ridges of windblown snow constant, Peary would have known he was travelling in a straight line.

Peary's way of establishing that he had reached his goal was to add up the estimates for his daily mileages until they totaled the 133 miles separating Bartlett Camp and the Pole. Henson wrote, "With my proven ability in gauging distances, Commander Peary was ready to take the reckoning as I made it and he did not resort to solar observations until we were within a hand's grasp of the Pole . . . Commander Peary took his sights from the time our watches gave, and I, knowing that we had kept on going in practically a straight line, was sure that we had more than covered the necessary distance to ensure our arrival at the top of the earth."

This seemingly slapdash technique has been criticized by many of Peary's biographers, but before the days of the GPS, there was no alternative. Writing about his own 1968–1969 expedition to the North Pole, Sir Wally Herbert wrote, "Our final approach to the Pole was made on dead-reckoning using a very hazy sun for a general direction."

We found for ourselves the practice of dead reckoning to be surprisingly accurate during our own expedition. Before turning on our GPS in the evenings to find out our mileage, we compared each other's estimates of the distance travelled for the day. We were nothing like as well versed in dead reckoning as Peary, Henson, and the others, but it was very rare that the average of our guesses was more than a mile from the actual figure. In fact, the sum of our average guesses for daily mileage over the course of our 413-mile journey was accurate to within two per cent, shedding new light on the value of dead reckoning to Peary's navigation.

Trying to keep a course on the shifting ice floes of the Arctic Ocean may appear complex to those unfamiliar with celestial navigation. To Peary and his men, however, with all their experience of travelling in the far north, it would have come as second nature. Not only did Peary have experienced mariners on his team, but Peary himself was a highly qualified surveyor who understood the scientific principals of celestial navigation better than anyone.

My great frustration is that Peary didn't go to greater depths to explain his methods, particularly as his ambiguity on the matter has fueled many of the deep suspicions against him. Had he been more open, history might have judged him in a much kinder light.

It's interesting to note that not one of Peary's teammates, both the ones who accompanied him to the Pole and those who had the disappointment of being sent back to the ship before the Pole had been reached, ever questioned Peary's claim that he had triumphed, not even John Goodsell, the one member of the expedition who Peary fell out with. George Borup wrote that Peary was "always kind, considerate, giving us fellows good advice, going out of his way to help us. Had the Commander been the grim, military martinet or despot his enemies make him out to be, he would never have got the work out of either the Eskimos or us fellows, and it was due to his great determination, his never knowing when he was kicked, and his ability to encourage and hold all of us together, to hold every man to the main purpose of the Expedition, that the American Flag is where it now is – at the North Pole."

Sir Wally Herbert's *The Noose of Laurels* is written in a way that implies that Peary had something to hide. Irrelevant scribbles, assumptions, and omissions in Peary's personal journal form a large part of Herbert's evidence that this was a man who lied about reaching the Pole. But I believe the picture of Peary as a man who couldn't be trusted is without any justification.

Throughout his expedition career, not once did Peary deliberately set out to exaggerate his achievements or claim to have accomplished something he hadn't. His mistaken sightings of Crocker Land and Independence Channel have since been shown to be mirages caused by ice blink. With literally hundreds of other geographical discoveries already to his name, Peary hardly needed to fabricate two more. And no one has ever claimed he chickened out of a challenge. His record for pushing on until the last possible turning point is undisputed.

Peary was a high-ranking figure within the U.S. Navy. He prided himself on being military through and through, a man of honour and a man of his word. No wonder his team all looked up to him. Roald Amundsen, first to reach the South Pole in 1911, once wrote, "I know Peary reached the Pole. The reason I know it is I know Peary."

Sir Wally also makes much of the fact that once Peary had sent Bartlett back to the *Roosevelt*, "his last reliable witness [was] gone," implying that Peary was free to fake his North Pole observations and that his five supposedly unqualified polar companions would have been none the wiser. This is simply not true, as Henson had been taught the art of celestial navigation by Marvin the previous winter and even helped Peary compile the sun shot at the Pole. Henson was also an expert at dead reckoning distances. Peary chose Henson because this time he wanted to make sure that he reached the Pole. He could never have envisaged the controversy would flare up as it did on his return and having been taken at his word throughout his expedition life, the last thing on his mind was ensuring that he was accompanied to the Pole by a "credible witness."

The rest of his team was unanimous that Peary had made the right decision in selecting Henson over Bartlett. Borup wrote, "Matt Henson, a jack-of-all-trades . . . a dandy sled maker, good shot, and as good a dog driver as the best Eskimos. Many have been the criticism of the Commander for having taken Matt with him in the final dash, but we who knew his merits felt that Matt, from his long training in the North, thoroughly deserved to go."

Donald MacMillan wrote, "The rest of us were tenderfeet compared with the Negro, Matt Henson . . . Henson is probably the best dog driver in the world to-day. He could talk the Eskimo language like a native. He could get along better with the natives than any of us; the Eskimos all liked him. He was the only man in the party who could build a snow house. He made every sled and every cookstove used on the route to the Pole. Henson was altogether the most efficient man with Peary."

In 1988, Matthew Henson's coffin was moved from an obscure grave in New York to Arlington National Cemetery where it now lies alongside Peary's grave. It was a fitting tribute for a man who sacrificed so much to help Peary raise the Stars and Stripes at the North Pole. I believe that it is hugely symbolic that Peary chose to share the honour of discovering the Pole, not only with an African American, but also with four Inuit, the original people of the North.

OUR JOURNEY REVEALED AS MUCH TO US ABOUT PEARY'S CLAIMS AS they did those of his great nemesis, Frederick Cook, who claimed to have reached the Pole the year before him. Before our departure, I had read much about Cook's apparent inability to tell a straight story and had just taken it as read that he was a habitual liar whose claims could not be taken seriously. A group of two hundred diehard fanatics, calling themselves the Frederick A. Cook Society, seemed to be the only ones who still believed that Cook had made it to the Pole.

Nevertheless, the vast majority of what I had read focused on Cook's character as opposed to the practicalities of his 1908 expedition. Now that I have seen what manpower and equipment is required to tackle the Arctic Ocean, I am left with no doubt that, irrespective of the numerous inconsistencies in his claims, Cook got nowhere near the Pole.

First, Cook's flimsy hickory sleds would have been no match for the endless rows of towering pressure ridges that are so abundant in the first hundred miles of the route to the Pole. Our replicas of Peary sleds took a daily battering during those early weeks. Chunks of timber regularly splintered from the sides, the lashings were always coming loose, and one of the crosspieces even snapped off altogether. Peary's own sleds took even more punishment in 1909, several being damaged beyond repair. Nevertheless, the Peary sled was still incredibly robust, weighing double that of Cook's fifty-five-pound hickory models, with reinforced runners shaped in such a way as to withstand the most brutal collisions with the ice. Cook boasted that he had managed to "eliminate useless weight," but the contorted pack ice of the Arctic Ocean is not the place to compromise on the strength of one's sleds.

However, the main reason I believe that Cook's claims don't stack up is that he had no external support. It was just him, his two Inuit companions, two sleds, and twenty-six dogs. Cook claimed that the 1,200 pounds of provisions he set out with were more than sufficient for the eighty-six days he spent on the frozen sea. Even allowing for the extra food that would have been provided by the slaughtering of dogs during the return leg, his supplies would have been woefully inadequate for the journey. We had far fewer mouths to feed than Cook and were only on the ice for thirty-seven days, but we still consumed over 1,700 pounds of provisions. And like Peary, we used resupplies to spread this weight over the length of the journey, reducing our sled weights considerably. As Peary explained, "Supporting parties are essential to success because, a single party, comprising either a small or a large number of men and dogs, could not possibly drag all the way to the Pole and back . . . as much food and liquid fuel as the men and dogs of that party would consume on the journey."

NOT LONG AFTER RETURNING HOME FROM THE ARCTIC, I ESCAPED to Sardinia for a wonderfully relaxing two weeks with Mary. I was going through the post on our return when I was jolted out of my post-holiday haze by an envelope containing a 1,500-word report written by Sir Wally Herbert entitled, "Earning the Applause: Modern-day Pole-Seekers Fail to Vindicate Peary's Claim." Also included in the envelope was a copy of a cover letter that Sir Wally had sent to various magazine editors. He didn't hold back in his views on our expedition, and in particular on me, writing, "The arrogance of the man thoroughly disgusts me."

The article itself was published in various exploration journals and was apparently the summer's hot topic of conversation in the Royal Geographical Society's dining room. The main cornerstone of Herbert's argument was that I was in no position to form an opinion on Peary's expedition because I had spent just thirty-seven days on the Arctic Ocean, compared to Herbert's 477 days. He concluded that "all you have to do to become famous in these times, it would seem, is to beat the record of one of the great pioneers and to tell the world on your mobile phone that you have done so."

But Sir Wally did not stop there. He lobbied the Council at the Royal Geographical Society to drum up support for his campaign against us and circulated his paper far and wide. Writing an article about his old friend in the Royal Geographical Society's monthly magazine *Geographical,* Robin Hanbury-Tenison, an experienced jungle explorer and anthropologist, said of Sir Wally, "This year the old lion, now resting in his remote lair in Scotland has had to raise his head and speak up for the truth again. Young polar traveller Tom Avery has claimed to have demonstrated that Peary could have done it after all by following the same route to the Pole in the same time . . . Avery who by all accounts is a charming and truthful fellow, incurred the wrath of the master by failing to consult him prior to announcing his intention to recreate Peary's journey and has had his knuckles well and truly rapped." Hanbury-Tenison also said that Herbert was "intolerant of what he calls 'glory seekers' and dismissive of those who go in search of short, 'extreme' adventures."

Things were beginning to get out of hand. Herbert's attack was both aggressive and personal. Much of it was also untrue, starting with the fact that I had failed to consult him before our plans become public. I had done so, and his immediate response had been to swear at me down the telephone. Sir Wally said my motivations for doing the expedition were simply to "earn the applause" and that we were no more than novice, paid-up "clients" on a commercially organised North Pole expedition.

He also accused me of deliberately misleading the press and said that I was in no position to speculate on Peary's return march from the Pole because I "had no personal experience of trying to follow an 'outward trail' that was several days or weeks old." None of this was true.

In his article, Herbert was equally disparaging of Peary, directly comparing his expedition to the ground-breaking exploits of the Canadian Richard Weber and the Russian Misha Malakhov, who in 1995 made the only confirmed return journey to the Pole and back since Peary. Theirs was one of the greatest feats in the history of Arctic exploration. Herbert used their journey as evidence against Peary's claim, writing, "Their round trip journey of 121 days, however, had convinced them that Peary could not have covered the same distance in only 53 days regardless of how many marches he had made in that time." What Herbert failed to mention was that not only were Weber and Malakhov manhauling their own sleds, but, unlike Peary, they had no resupplies. He may as well have compared the speed of a Formula one car to a horse and cart.

The last thing I wanted was a major confrontation, particularly as Sir Wally was someone whose polar achievements we had the utmost admiration and respect for, but I felt I needed to make some sort of public defence of both our expedition and Peary's. I set up a series of meetings with senior figures at the RGS to see what I could do to prevent my name, and those of my teammates, becoming mud in the tight-knit exploration community. That is, if I wasn't too late already.

My meetings revealed that the row seemed to stem from a combination of two things. To start with, some of the "old guard" at the RGS were not surprisingly growing irritated at the seemingly infinite flow of press coverage and sponsorship generated by some of the current crop of mountaineers and polar travellers, whose expeditions they felt paled into insignificance compared to what they had achieved in their heyday. However, I also learned that much of the controversy was motivated by Sir Wally Herbert's apparent desire to be recognized as the first person to reach the North Pole on foot. And the problem for us was that he still carried huge influence at the RGS.

I was shocked by what I was told. Why, almost forty years after making the herculean first crossing of the Arctic Ocean, was Sir Wally suddenly being so fervent in his claims for the less cherished prize of "first to the North Pole on foot"? Particularly when for years he had never made a big deal about the fact that he had passed through the Pole. The emphasis had always been that his expedition had completed the first traverse of the Arctic Ocean.

During the intervening sixty years between Peary and Herbert's expeditions, the North Pole was reached a number of times by mechanized transport. The first confirmed sighting of the Pole was by Roald Amundsen, who, along with four others, flew an airship right across the Arctic Ocean from Spitsbergen to Alaska in 1926. It took them just two days.

In 1948, three Russian planes, carrying seven crew, touched down at ninety degrees north, the first men on record to set foot at the Pole. The U.S. submarine USS *Nautilus* passed directly under the Pole in 1958 and the following year, another nuclear submarine, USS *Skate,* surfaced through the ice there.

The first undisputed surface crossing to the Pole was made in 1968 by the Minnesotan insurance salesman, Ralph Plaisted, whose four-man, heavily resupplied team reached the North Pole on skidoos forty-three days after setting out from Ward Hunt Island. None of these expeditions however, had travelled by the traditional methods of manhauling or dog sledging.

Sir Wally, like Peary, was clearly a man who yearned for public recognition for his achievements. There's nothing wrong with that – I have always sought media coverage for my expeditions because it's the best way of pleasing sponsors. If sponsors are kept happy, they're more likely to support future expeditions. Besides, the greater one's public profile, the easier it becomes to secure book deals and lecture tours – which help pay the bills in between expeditions. As I later discovered, when Herbert embarked on his epic journey across the Arctic Ocean in 1968–1969, he had almost no PR plan whatsoever.

Herbert often referred to Sir Vivian Fuchs as his mentor and inspiration. For years, they had worked together at the British Antarctic Survey before Fuchs went on to make the first successful crossing of Antarctica, via the South Pole, with Sir Edmund Hillary in 1957–1958. Following his historic achievement, Fuchs became a household name in Britain, was knighted and showered with medals and awards.

Herbert was twenty years Fuchs's junior but no less ambitious. In 1968 he set out to mirror Fuchs's Antarctic conquest and compete the first crossing of the Arctic Ocean, a far sterner challenge, particularly as he chose the longest possible route. If successful, Sir Wally no doubt expected to achieve the same acclaim as Fuchs, and richly deserved it would have been too. In a television interview a few years ago, he confessed, "I was looking for the real big one . . . It was the *Guinness Book of Records* Syndrome all over again. I wasn't interested in getting in the *Guinness Book of Records* unless I was going to be there for a long time."

After more than four hundred days on the Arctic Ocean, Herbert and his three companions made landfall on 29 May 1969. Their epic 3,720-mile journey from Alaska to Spitsbergen via the North Pole was an extraordinary feat of endurance and bravery and has never been repeated. But a series of unfortunate events meant that the expedition barely made the headlines.

Halfway through the expedition, disaster struck when one of the team, Allan Gill, badly injured his back. The expedition committee back in London wanted him evacuated immediately. Herbert felt he was best placed to make the decision and insisted that Gill stay put and be given a chance to recover. I'm sure I would have acted in exactly the same way. Unfortunately for Herbert, the radio connection to London was still live when he blurted out, "They don't know what the bloody hell they're talking about." To make matters worse, the correspondent from the *Sunday Times* was also on the line. The committee was furious that its authority had been undermined so publicly, and once the expedition was over, some commitee members went out of their way to make sure that Herbert didn't receive the public recognition that he might otherwise have achieved.

By the time Sir Wally and his team sailed back into Britain aboard HMS *Endurance,* the market for pioneering adventurers was already saturated. Shortly before the expedition began, Francis Chichester had become the first person to sail solo around the world, receiving a knighthood for his achievement and gaining such iconic status that his face was printed on postage stamps throughout the land. And then, only weeks before Herbert's homecoming, Robin Knox-Johnston became an overnight celebrity for winning the inaugural Round the World Yacht Race, completing the first nonstop solo voyage around the world in the process. But the most serious dent to all his PR hopes occurred when Neil Armstrong and Buzz Aldrin made the first lunar landing, just as HMS *Endurance* was pulling into port. What with glamoros yachtsmen aplenty and astronauts walking on the moon, the attention of the world was elsewhere.

During my various meetings at the Royal Geographical Society, it seemed to be widely known that Wally Herbert had been offered a CBE for his leadership of the Trans-Arctic Expedition but, clearly expecting higher recognition, he had turned it down. It wasn't until 1999, after a long campaign by key figures within the RGS, that he finally received the knighthood he so richly deserved.

The reasons why our expedition had so rankled Sir Wally were now falling into place. During the 1970s and 1980s he had watched on as the expeditions of the much more commercially-savvy Sir Ranulph Fiennes and Robert Swan gained worldwide attention. *The Noose of Laurels* was his final shot at receiving lasting immortality. If he could show that Peary had been a fraud who never got anywhere near the Pole, that would make Herbert himself the first person to reach the North Pole on foot – a feat of human endeavor far easier for the man in the street to understand than "the first to traverse the Arctic Ocean." After logging on to Sir Wally's personal website, I found it revealing that the caption beneath the main image on his home page did not commemorate his historic crossing of the Arctic Ocean, but stated "The first team to reach the North Pole on foot (6th April 1969)."

In his article for the Royal Geographical Society's magazine, Robin Hanbury-Tension wrote that Herbert's *The Noose of Laurels* was "meticulously researched by the man best qualified to do so." Although Herbert didn't make the connection directly in his book, by alleging that Peary had missed the Pole by at least sixty miles, he was effectively crowning himself as the conqueror of the North Pole by default. It's therefore hard to agree with the notion that Sir Wally was the man best qualified to comment on Peary's expedition. It would be like expecting Sir Edmund Hillary to produce an impartial account of George Mallory's possible ascent of Everest three decades before he and Tenzing Norgay reached the top in 1953.

Why all this matters so much, and why I have gone to such great lengths to fight in Peary's corner, is that *The Noose of Laurels* has become the authoritative judgemnt on the discovery of the North Pole. Because of his unmatched polar pedigree, Herbert is regarded as the most reliable narrator, and in most quarters his book is now accepted as gospel. Yet one cannot ignore the simple fact that Herbert had so much to gain by dismissing Peary's claims. He has acted as both judge and jury in the great debate. That is why I have felt duty bound to speak out on the old commander's behalf to try to put right what in my opinion is one of the great injustices in polar history.

AS THE STORM RUMBLED ON OVER THE SUMMER, I RECEIVED A letter of support from a most unexpected source. Dr. Geoffrey Hattersley-Smith was not a name that rang any bells but I learned that after World War II he had been an explorer of some repute, working for the British Antarctic Survey and carrying out a series of detailed geological studies of the north coast of Ellesmere Island in the 1950s. He returned in 1967 to make the first ascent of the 8,583-foot Barbeau Peak, Ellesmere Island's highest mountain. This was someone I just had to meet.

By an extraordinary coincidence, Dr. Hattersley-Smith happened to live in the next village to my parents, just across the border in Kent. One weekend George and I drove over to pay him a visit. "Lads, I think what you did up there was quite brilliant," he enthused in a soft Kentish accent as he welcomed us in, "you've shown as close as dammit that Peary could have reached the Pole."

Geoffrey's own story blew us away. His had been the first expedition to northern Ellesmere Island since 1909 and he told us how he had come across many of Peary's discarded stores and equipment caches while travelling with dog teams along the coast. He had stopped at Peary's signpost at Cape Columbia and climbed Mount Cooper Key, the twin-headed peak we had still been able to see from sixty miles out to sea. Geoffrey then produced a small ceramic urn that he had found beside a stone cairn on the summit in 1953. Inside the urn, Peary had left a handwritten note, dated 8 June 1906. George and I had goose bumps as Geoffrey read, "In April of this year, I reached the highest northerly attained, going north along the meridian of this Cape and returning from the Greenland coast a little east of 50°W.Long. I build this monument and leave this record with a portion of my U.S. flag as a permanent mark of my visit. R. E. Peary U.S.N."

On his homeward journey, Geoffrey had stopped off in Portland, Maine, to visit Peary's ninety-year-old widow, Jo. After presenting her with the scrap of Stars and Stripes he had found in the urn, Geoffrey watched the old lady totter upstairs and return with the cornerless sledging flag she had made for her husband, which had never left his side during all his expeditions. Mrs. Peary then sat down on a sofa draped in an old musk ox skin, and with a tear in her eye, began stitching the segment back into its rightful place. The flag is now on display in the main hall at the Museum of National History in New York. It was spine-tingling stuff.

The stories kept on coming. During a separate visit to Greenland in 1954, Geoffrey had met the eighty-year-old Ootah, the strongest of the four Inuit who had accompanied Peary and Henson to the Pole. Ootah was unequivocal in his praise for the old commander and said that when they turned for home, Peary appeared satisfied that he had got what he had come for. He also confirmed that they had had excellent travel conditions on the last stretch to the Pole.

During his time in Ellesmere Island, Geoffrey had found one of Peary's discarded sleds not far from Cape Columbia and used it for a sixty-mile journey along the coast. "All it needed was a couple of new lashings and it was good as new," he reminisced. "She went like a dream."

He also found various food caches along the north coast of Ellesmere Island, just in case Peary's returning parties should be carried off course on the way back to the coast. One of these caches contained a note dated 21 March 1909 from Donald MacMillan, who had returned with the first support division after reaching a farthest north of 84°29N. It read, "At the request of Commander R E Peary, who is now out on the Polar Sea at about Lat 85, I am leaving this cache as a possible aid to someone landing near here by a westerly drift." The note had emphasized to Geoffrey that Peary was a man who planned every aspect of his expedition with a military eye for detail. Absolutely nothing had been left to chance.

The same cache contained an old stove, but it was unclear whether the fuel inside was alcohol or methylated spirits. Morale amongst Geoffrey's team was quite low at the time, so he ordered for the stove to be emptied and its contents consumed, irrespective of what they might be. "Thankfully it turned out to be alcohol, and a riotous party then ensued under the midnight sun," he chuckled. Two fruit puddings from 1909 were also discovered, completely preserved by the cold and untouched by scavenging animals. One was eaten on the spot "and absolutely sublime it was, too," while the other was brought back to England where Geoffrey and his young bride Maria served it on their wedding day.

It also transpired that Geoffrey and his team had stumbled upon Crane City, Peary's base camp just along the coast from Cape Columbia. He, too, had uncovered rusty fuel cans, wooden boxes, and sled runners amongst the snowdrifts, quite probably the exact same relics we had held in our hands on that bitter March afternoon some half a century later.

I didn't mind one bit that this now meant that we hadn't "discovered" Crane City after all, because it placed Geoffrey, this great character who had suddenly come into our lives, as the intrinsic link between our own expedition and Peary's. And the fact that the final piece in the polar jigsaw happened to fall into place, just a few miles from home, made it all the more extraordinary.

We stayed for hours. It was like listening to a nostalgic old fisherman recounting tales from his time on the high seas. Eventually, Sir Wally's recent tirade came up in conversation. "Oh, I wouldn't pay much attention to him. We're old friends, but you must remember that Wally has got an axe to grind. He wants to be credited as the first man to reach the North Pole on foot, simple as that, and your expedition has put a great big fly in the ointment."

It's one of the great injustices in exploration history that Sir Wally Herbert's extraordinary polar achievements are not widely known, and that he had been reduced to fighting an increasingly bitter battle to gain some late recognition for all he had done. It's also particularly sad that Robert Peary, a man whom Herbert had once deeply revered, should have borne the full force of his hostility. But for sheer bad luck, it could have been a very different story.

Even though Sir Wally had also directed his fire at me and my team, I couldn't help but sympathize with him. When I subsequently learned that his health had deteriorated markedly and that he had only been given a short time to live, I decided that the decent thing would be to leave the whole debate alone and delay writing this book for another time.

Before he died, the Royal Geographical Society held a gala evening of lectures and presentations in October 2006 in Sir Wally's honour to commemorate his life's work. Not wanting our presence there to spoil his enjoyment of the occasion, George, Andrew, and I kept a very low profile at the back of the lecture hall, listening intently to the explorers, scientists, and others who took turns lavishing praise on Sir Wally's fifty years as an explorer.

Herbert had led a truly remarkable life. He had spent a combined total of more than fifteen years in the polar regions, during which time he had dogsledded the equivalent distance of the full circumference of the Earth, mapped more than 45,000 square miles of previously unexplored terrain, and completed the first traverse of the Arctic Ocean – a journey which has never been repeated or is ever likely to be.

It was a wonderful and incredibly moving tribute, and a real privilege to have been there. There was hardly a dry eye left in the house when, as the night drew to a close, Sir Wally rose from his wheelchair to salute the rapturous applause from the galleries. I hope that the richly deserved eulogies and great affection bestowed on him that night more than made up for all the years of hurt and that he died a contented man. Sir Wally Herbert passed away on 12 June 2007. He was seventy-two.

THE TWIN OTTER FLIGHT THAT COLLECTED US FROM THE POLE marked the first leg of the long journey back to civilization. Looking down on the endless expanse of snow, ice, and sea beneath us was the first time that the true scale of what we and Peary had achieved began to sink in. It would be another four hours' flying before we eventually touched down at the Eureka weather station to refuel the planes and to give the pilots a night's rest before continuing on to Resolute Bay in the morning. Eating fresh food again and sleeping in a proper bed with clean sheets for the first time in six weeks was pure heaven. The date was 27 April 2005 – ninety-six years to the day since Peary collapsed into his bunk onboard the *Roosevelt* after returning from the Pole.

Overpowered by the stench of five unwashed explorers in his base, the station manager hastily dispatched us to the shower rooms with enough soap and shampoo to disinfect a dozen rugby teams. Standing alongside my teammates in front of the mirror in our underwear was an unforgettable sight. Our tanned, leathery faces and sun-bleached blond stubble stood out in stark contrast to our alabaster-white torsos. It was as if weeks concealed in the same set of clothes had drained all life out of our bodies. Noses, lips, and cheeks were weatherbeaten and peeling and eyes had retreated into their sockets.

What really horrified me was just how emaciated our bodies looked.

Ribs were exposed, and there was barely an inch of fat left on anyone. The scales revealed we had each lost some thirty pounds in weight since the start of the journey. It was a sign of just how far we had stretched ourselves in the pursuit of our goal.

THE SIXTEEN DOGS, FOUR MEN, AND ONE WOMAN OF THE Barclays Capital Ultimate North Expedition are now spread far and wide around the world, each getting on with their own lives. Throughout our time on the Arctic Ocean, Denali had pulled just as hard as any of her canine companions, but to our great surprise, just days after we returned to Iqaluit, she gave birth to a single male puppy. Despite her romantic liaison with Ootah all those weeks before, it had never even crossed our minds that she might be pregnant. With a dark coat and white face markings, the little puppy looked just like his father. We christened him Henson. There can't be many dog sledging expeditions in polar history that actually ended up with more dogs that they started with.

Despite keeping George and me entertained throughout the expedition, Baffin had proved himself to be a useless sled dog, so it was hardly a surprise to hear that Matty had given him his marching orders and packed him off to his original owners in Yellowknife. A new home was also found for Axel, and Gloria returned to Thunder Bay with Hugh.

Much sadder news came in early 2006 when Matty e-mailed me to say that Ootah had died of a twisted stomach. I was devastated. He had been my favourite and had given his all in helping us reach our goal. Ootah was the king of sled dogs, and the Arctic would be a poorer place without him.

Three years later, most of the dogs have now hung up their harnesses. Raven and Zorro have gone to stud in Yellowknife while Kimmik, Apu, Bert, Ernie, Seegloo, and Odin have all found retirement homes on Baffin Island. Just before going to print, I learned that Denali had tragically passed away after a short illness. It means that Ikki, Marvin, and K2 are the only members of the original North Pole team still left in the dog yard.

There's no doubt that the expedition gave us a new perspective on life and helped us reevaluate our priorities, because within a year of returning from the Arctic, George, Andrew, and I had all got engaged to our girl-friends. Within two years, we were all married and within three years George and Andrew had become fathers for the first time.

George quickly tired of London life and it wasn't long before he, Annie, and their daughter Lara moved to the Suffolk countryside where George's fledgling construction business continues to go from strength to strength. Andrew has switched employers and now works for one of the Scottish banks, living in Edinburgh with Rowena and baby Nicholas.

In April 2006, the three of us returned to the Swiss Alps to exorcise the demons from two years before and try to complete the Patrouille des Glaciers ski mountaineering race, which had eluded us during our polar preparations. This time, our three months' intensive training paid off, and there was a huge collective sigh of relief when after sixteen of the most grueling hours of our lives, we made it across the finish line. We were the only one of seven British teams (including two from the Royal Marines) who managed to complete the course, and the first British team in history to do so.

Shortly after returning home from the Pole, Hugh became a father again when his wife Amy gave birth to their second child, a son called Noam. Hugh soon returned to Lakehead University in Thunder Bay to complete a masters degree in Education. His teaching has since taken him all over Canada, including three months in Igloolik in Nunavut, where he hunted and fished with the local Inuit on dog-sledging expeditions across the sea ice.

Matty continues to live in Iqaluit. Although much of her time is still spent taking people out on day trips with the dogs around Frobisher Bay, she's gradually handing over Northwinds, the family outdoor adventure business, to her children, Eric and Sarah. Matty and I joined forces again in early 2007 to work on the BBC's *Top Gear* TV show, which was trying to race a 4×4 Toyota Hilux against a team of our North Pole dogs. It was great to be reunited with Matty and the dogs again, although much to our chagrin, when the show was broadcast later in the year, the impression was given that they had raced all the way to the North Pole. In fact, they had gone no farther than the 1996 position of the Magnetic

North Pole, some nine hundred miles farther south amongst the Queen Elizabeth Islands, where the ice is almost uniformly flat. Oh well, it made for entertaining TV.

Mary and I were married on a cold, frosty day in December 2006 at her parents' home in Lancashire. With George as my best man, Andrew as one of my ushers, and Mary's spectacular wedding dress trimmed with Arctic fur, it was the happiest day of my life. To top things off, we left the reception on a wheel-based dog-sled, Mary and I clinging onto the handlebars for dear life as the four Siberian husky dogs sped away up the road.

As well as researching and writing this book, I've spent much of the time since the Pole travelling around the U.K. and Europe, speaking to audiences about Peary and our expedition to the North Pole, and when time has allowed, I have managed to escape to snowier climes. In the last couple of years I've climbed and ski-toured extensively in the Alps, driven dog teams across Lapland and climbed in the Himalayas. My attempt to try to become the first Briton to ski down an eight thousand-meter mountain ended prematurely when a blood vessel in my right eye burst at six thousand five hundred meters on Cho Oyu in Tibet, causing temporary blindness. Thankfully, my vision is now back to over ninety per cent, but it has definitely made me think twice about going to extreme altitudes in the future, where hemorrhages are much more common.

So what next? Adventure will always be in my blood, and I'll never stop dreaming up expedition ideas. Everest is a mountain I'm often asked about, but it just doesn't appeal. Everest still poses a stern challenge and the failure rate (not to mention the death rate) remains very high, but the thought of sharing a mountain with hundreds of people, most of whom are trying to summit on the same day, is a real turnoff for me. I'm someone who likes to take off with a small team to get away from it all, or to do something nobody else has done before. I have a number of exciting projects lined up for the future, some snow-and-ice related, others not. Exactly what they are is a matter for future books.

Ever since I first ventured into the great outdoors, part of my drive came from a deep fascination with the polar explorers and mountaineers of the past. I had always dreamed of making my own contribution to the long history of polar exploration, however small or unimportant. I think we have managed to do that, although when looking back on those extraordinary weeks floating precariously on the surface of the Arctic Ocean, we often find ourselves asking one other, "How on earth did we manage to pull that off?"

At times, sticking up for the claims of an explorer from the other side of the Pond over those of my fellow countryman has been a lonely and contentious business. Yet, it's been an important thing to have done. The admiration and respect I hold for Robert Peary, Matthew Henson, and their four Inuit companions has grown enormously since we set out from Cape Columbia. Having followed their footsteps and seen just how they could have done it, I am more convinced than ever that they were the first men in history to reach the North Pole, just as they had always claimed. Driving dogs is the most efficient way to travel across the frozen sea, and whether you are resupplied by air drops or by support parties on the ice, the travel speeds that Peary claimed seem highly reasonable. If our relatively inexperienced party could make the Pole in thirty-seven days, then Peary's team of experts could have done it, no problem at all.

The question of permissible errors when locating the Pole by sextant and dead reckoning alone is a matter of subjective opinion. When talking about his own struggles to pinpoint the exact position of the Pole in 1969, Herbert felt that "one ought to be at least within two miles of the Pole before saying that by dead reckoning one has reached it," and I would agree with him. Peary spent thirty hours in the vicinity of the Pole, heading off in all sorts of different directions in order to box in his target. He wrote, "In traversing the ice in these various directions . . . I had allowed approximately ten miles for possible errors in my observations." I believe that at some point during these marches he would have passed within a mile or two of the North Pole, possibly even closer, and that is close enough for me.

I hope that our journey and this book help restore these pioneering and courageous men to their rightful place in the annals of polar history. We salute them.

EXPEDITION LOG

Camp	Date (2005)	Latitude	Longitude	Hours travelled	Estimated mileage	Actual mileage	Miles made good	Miles to go
	March 19	83.06.163	69.39.027					414
1	March 20	83.09.815	69.23.381	7.75	5.5	4.10	**3.64**	410
2	March 21	83.16.995	69.16.808	7.75	8.5	7.23	**7.17**	403
3	March 22	83.23.769	69.57.806	8	9.0	8.29	**6.77**	396
4	March 23	83.30.838	69.49.961	8	8.0	7.10	**7.06**	389
5	March 24	83.40.377	69.38.827	8	10.0	9.64	**9.54**	380
6	March 25	83.45.379	69.38.816	7	5.5	5.03	**5.02**	375
7	March 26	83.48.289	69.45.755	6	5.0	3.01	**2.91**	372
8	March 27	83.58.294	69.02.350	8.75	11.5	11.1	**10.0**	362
9	March 28	84.09.571	69.26.653	9	10.0	11.6	**11.3**	350
10	March 29	84.18.066	69.55.272	7	11.0	8.99	**8.48**	342
11	March 30	84.23.574	70.17.612	4.25	6.0	6.12	**5.51**	336
12	March 31	84.34.937	70.10.695	9	11.0	11.4	**11.3**	325
13	April 1	84.48.429	69.48.281	8.75	12.5	13.7	**13.5**	312
14	April 2	85.03. 114	70.08.771	9	13.5	14.9	**14.7**	297
15	April 3	85.16.575	70.12.072	8	14.0	13.5	**13.4**	284
16	April 4	85.22.359	70.10.866	3.75	6.0	5.80	**5.78**	278
17	April 5	85.39.818	70.14.869	9	18.0	17.6	**17.5**	260
18	April 6	85.56.335	69.45.354	8.5	18.5	16.7	**16.5**	244
19	April 7	86.12.403	70.05.816	9	12.0	16.2	**16.1**	228
20	April 8	86.20.040	70.59.961	9	5.5	8.40	**7.64**	220
21	April 9	86.28.579	71.43.858	9	9.0	8.99	**8.54**	211
22	April 10	86.31.026	72.26.954	5.25	5.5	3.60	**2.44**	209
23	April 11	86.27.347	73.35.204	0	0.0	5.58	**−3.70**	213
24	April 12	86.40.040	73.31.680	8.75	13.0	12.9	**12.7**	200
25	April 13	86.54.442	74.27.586	9	14.5	14.8	**14.4**	186
26	April 14	87.12.757	74.23.643	9.5	19.5	18.4	**18.3**	167
27	April 15	87.26.626	75.22.248	9	14.0	14.2	**13.7**	154
28	April 16	87.30.384	76.55.473	4.5	4.5	5.54	**3.75**	150
29	April 17	87.49.354	77.38.813	11	20.0	19.2	**19.0**	131
30	April 18	88.07.271	75.18.473	9.75	16.0	18.6	**18.0**	113
31	April 19/20	88.29.045	69.50.875	9.75	19.0	24.0	**21.8**	91
32	April 20/21	88.48.496	67.07.467	9.75	21.0	20.0	**19.5**	72
33	April 21/22	88.59.759	68.44.095	6	11.0	11.5	**11.2**	60
34	April 22	89.06.917	67.59.225	6	7.5	7.30	**7.16**	53
35	April 23	89.25.472	57.14.062	12	18.5	20.3	**18.6**	35
36	April 24	89.44.044	51.42.595	12	21.5	18.8	**18.6**	16
37	April 25/26	90 00.000	00 00.000	13.75	16.0	16.0	**16.0**	0
			Total	300.5	431.5	440.12	**413.81**	

Miles ahead/behind Peary	Average speed north (knots)	Wind Direction	Wind (knots)	Temp °C	Windchill °C	Weather
		NW	4	−43	−45	Sun/cloud
−7.2	0.47	WNW	14	−32	−56	Sun/cloud
−10.0	0.93	W	10	−35	−54	Sun
−14.2	0.85	W	8	−38	−53	Cloud
−19.2	0.88	WNW	2	−39	−31	Sun
−9.6	1.19	NW	1	−37	−21	Sun
−4.6	0.72	NW	4	−40	−42	Sun
−1.7	0.49	W	18	−33	−63	Snow
9.3	1.14	W	14	−33	−57	Sun
20.6	1.26	W	5	−35	−41	Sun/cloud
29.1	1.21	NW	3	−32	−30	Cloud/sun
34.6	1.30	W	4	−35	−37	Sun/cloud
29.9	1.26	W	10	−33	−52	Cloud/sun
31.4	1.54	NW	7	−36	−50	Sun
34.1	1.63	SW	3	−35	−33	Sun
47.6	1.68	SW	6	−37	−46	Sun
43.4	1.54	W	3	−33	−31	Sun
52.8	1.94	N	3	−33	−31	Sun
60.3	1.94	N	1	−35	−20	Sun
61.4	1.79	NE	8	−33	−47	Sun
57.0	0.85	NE	10	−29	−45	Cloud/sun
65.6	0.95	NE	12	−31	−52	Sun
58.0	0.46	NE	28	−26	−56	Sun/cloud
39.3	0.00	NE	20	−22	−48	Cloud/snow
37.0	1.45	ENE	12	−23	−41	Sun
36.4	1.60	N	1	−17	−6	Cloud/snow
34.8	1.93	NE	14	−17	−36	Cloud/sun
33.6	1.52	NE	20	−20	−44	Sun
25.4	0.83	NE	30	−24	−55	Cloud/snow
37.4	1.73	SE	7	−24	−34	Sun
55.3	1.85	S	5	−26	−31	Sun
62.0	2.24	S	15	−24	−46	Sun
61.4	2.00	S	8	−20	−31	Sun
72.8	1.87	E	8	−20	−31	Cloud
49.9	1.19	W	8	−20	−31	Cloud
25.5	1.55	WSW	12	−21	−38	Cloud/sun
19.0	1.55	N	12	−19	−36	Sun
7.0	1.16	N	5	−21	−27	Sun/cloud
	1.38					

—— Resupply point